Managing Knowledge-Based Initiatives

T0271843

Managing Knowledge-Based Initiatives: Strategies for Successful Deployment

Stacy E. Land, BA

AMSTERDAM • BOSTON • HEIDELBERG • LONDON
NEW YORK • OXFORD • PARIS • SAN DIEGO
SAN FRANCISCO • SINGAPORE • SYDNEY • TOKYO
Butterworth-Heinemann is an imprint of Elsevier

ELSEVIER

Butterworth-Heinemann is an imprint of Elsevier
Linacre House, Jordan Hill, Oxford OX2 8DP, UK
30 Corporate Drive, Suite 400, Burlington, MA 01803, USA

First edition 2008

Notice
No responsibility is assumed by the publisher for any injury and/or damage to persons
or property as a matter of products liability, negligence or otherwise, or from any use
or operation of any methods, products, instructions or ideas contained in the material
herein. Because of rapid advances in the medical sciences, in particular, independent
verification of diagnoses and drug dosages should be made

British Library Cataloguing-in-Publication Data
A catalogue record for this book is available from the British Library.

Library of Congress Cataloging-in-Publication Data
Application submitted

ISBN: 978-0-7506-8339-5

For information on all Butterworth-Heinemann publications
visit our Web site at www.books.elsevier.com

Printed and bound in USA

08 09 10 11 12   10 9 8 7 6 5 4 3 2 1

Working together to grow
libraries in developing countries

www.elsevier.com | www.bookaid.org | www.sabre.org

ELSEVIER   BOOK AID International   Sabre Foundation

Contents

Author Biography   xv
Acknowledgements   xvii
Preface   xix
   Meet Our Panel of Experts   xxi

SECTION I   LAYING THE GROUNDWORK   1

1   BASELINE POINTS of UNDERSTANDING   3
     Gates and Paths   3
        Framing Your Work   4
           Overlaying a Technology and Support Context   4
           Framing: Easier or More Difficult for Knowledge
              Practitioners?   5
        Engaging First is Key   7
           How You will Benefit from Engaging First   7
        Knowledge, Organizational, or Project Management?   9
           Funding Factors   9
           The PMO Factor   10
           The Organizational Design/Alignment Factor   10
        **Terms and Definitions in Managing Knowledge-Based
           Initiatives   11**
           Committees   11
           Firm, Corporation, Organization, Company   12
           Friendly Faces   12
           Knowledge Management   12
        How This Book is Organized   13
        Seize the Day   14

SECTION II   READY, SET, GO   15

2   BEFORE YOU GET STARTED   17
     Common Misconceptions   17
     Understanding Your Momentum   19

Isolating Change Factors   19
Participation   20
Standards   20
Scope   21
Shared Responsibility   21
Evaluating Your Company from the Outside   22
Expert Q&A: Joe McGhee   22
Questions You Should be Able to Answer   24
Broad Strokes: Where to Find What You Need   25
Financial Performance   25
Evaluating the State of KM Inside Your Company   26
Where do You Live?   27
What is Your Work Considered?   27
How Mature is Knowledge Management in
Your Firm?   27
Perception of Knowledge-Based Work in Your Firm   28

SECTION III   ORGANIZATIONAL ALIGNMENT   31

3   UNDERSTANDING AND MAPPING ORGANIZATIONAL
ALIGNMENT   33
Do You See the Big Picture?   34
What an Aligned Organization Looks Like   34
Why Firms Care About Organizational Alignment   34
Alignment Artifacts   35
Demonstrable Alignment Increases Buy In   36
The Mission Statement   36
The Vision Statement   37
The Values and Beliefs Statement   37
Example: Ten Things Google has Found to be True   37
Operating Imperatives, Goals, and Activities   41
Mapping from Top-Down or Bottom-Up   41
Example: Acme Medical Supplies   42
Why it Pays to Map Backwards   44
Likely Candidates for Alignment with Knowledge-Based
Initiatives   45
Collaboration and Knowledge Sharing   45
Reduced Administrative Expense   46
Efficiency   46
Protection of Firm Assets   47
Disaster Recovery   47
Increased Project Governance   47
Merging of Cultures   47
Enhancing the Customer Experience   48
Competitive Intelligence   48

When Organizational Alignment is a Challenge   48
How Aligned is Your Organization?   48
  Seeking Alignment in the Unaligned Organization   49
  Do You Need Alternative Alignment?   49
    Identifying Centers of Power at Your Firm   50
If Your Alignment is not Clear   51
  When Non-Alignment May Be Acceptable   51
  Executive Point of View: Michael Jackman   51

SECTION IV   SUPPORT: WHO IS ON YOUR SIDE?   53

4   EXECUTIVE SPONSORSHIP AND NETWORK BUILDING   55
Cooperative Executive or Executive Sponsor?   55
  Telling the Difference   56
Degrees of Sponsorship   57
  Reaching Up and Out to a Remote Executive
    Sponsor   57
What do You Know About Your Executive Sponsor?   58
  Why Your Sponsor Fills that Role   58
  Resources and Influence   59
  The Buzz   60
Negotiating Executive Give and Take   60
  Which Areas Will Your Executive Sponsor Help
    With?   61
    Concept Development   61
    Funding   61
    Politics   61
    Referrals   62
    Mentorship   63
What Does Your Executive Sponsor Expect of You?   63
  Just Ask   63
  What Success Means   63
  Administrative Minutia   65
  Metrics   65
  Your Turn to Support   66
Five Questions to Ask Your Executive Sponsor   66
Other Supporters   67
  Executive Advice on Building a Network   67
  Your Own Network Survey   68

5   EXECUTIVE SPONSORSHIP FROM THE EXECUTIVE POINT
    OF VIEW   69
Approaching an Executive Sponsor   69
  The Value of Channels   70
  Making the First Move   70

What Sponsorship Means   71
  The Sponsorship World According to McGhee   71
  The Nuts and Bolts of Sponsorship from Michael Jackman   72
  Jane Niederberger's Rules of the Road   72
The Question of Money   73
Sponsorship Tips   74
Thoughts from the Top   75
  Entrepreneurship, Big Champions, and Small Victories   75
  Communication   76
    Style and Choice are Key   76
    Corporate Code, No. Acronyms, Yes.   77
  Cultures and Subcultures   77
  Thoughts on Resistance   78
    When People Want to Shut You Down   78
    It is Not Personal   79
  Relationships and Behavior Count   80

SECTION V   THE VALUE OF A VALUE PROP   83

6 VALUE PROP 101   85
Value Proposition Interdependencies   85
What is a Value Proposition?   86
  Executive Points of View: Jane Niederberger and
    Santi Kumar   87
  General and Targeted Value Props   88
  Matchmaker, Matchmaker   89
Looking at the Value in Value Proposition   89
Value Prop: Public or Private?   90
Before You Begin   91
  Conducting a Cultural Landscape Analysis   92
Moving from Generic Value to Targeted Value   93
  Planning and Tracking Your Activities: How Value Props
    Can Help   95
Developing a Targeted Value Proposition   95
  Step 1: Know Your Constituents   96
    Direct Constituents   96
    Indirect Constituents   96
    Identify Friendly Faces   97
  Step 2: Identify Your Constituents' Value Hot Buttons   97
    The Formal Route: Alignment Artifacts   97
    The Informal Route: What is Really Going on   98
  Step 3: Engage Your Executive Sponsor   98
  Step 4: Assemble Additional PMO Artifacts   99
  Step 5: Synthesize Value Prop Components into Value Docs   100
    Understanding Value Docs   100

Step 6: Engage Constituents   101
Timing is Everything   101
**Example: Customer Intimacy at Acme
Corporation   102**
Mapping Bidirectional Streams   103

7   USING YOUR VALUE PROPS   107
**Sharing Value Propositions   107
Nurturing a Value Proposition   109
Leveraging Value Propositions   109
Protecting Value Propositions   110**
An Incorrect Value Prop   111
Finding the Source   111
A Rebalanced Value Prop   112
A Diluted Value Prop   112
A Minimized Value Prop   113
An Appropriated Value Prop   114
Knowledge-Based Work Needs to Remain
Autonomous   115
Not Today, Buddy   116
My Executive Sponsor is Bigger . . .   116
I am Not Sure I Understand   116
A Repositioned Value Prop   117
A Rebuked Value Prop   117
Honoring a Value Proposition   118

SECTION VI   EXECUTING ON THE GROUNDWORK   121

8   COMMITTEES, COMMITTEES, COMMITTEES   123
Committee Tips   123
Committees are Just Human, After All   123
Search Proactively   124
What are You Looking for?   124
Help is (Hopefully) Nearby   125
Engaging Your Legal Department   125
Your Committee Scavenger Hunt   126
Follow the Headcount and the Money   126
Sign-Off in Your Work Area   126
Committees that Govern the Activities of Your Prime
Customers   127
Supporting Resources   127
Technology-Related Committees   128
Non-IT Compliance   130
Funding Escalation Committees   131
Ongoing Initiatives   132

Making Sense of the Committees   133
Grouping Committees   133
Independent or Defined by Process   133
Crucial, Procedural, Optional,
Irrelevant   134
The Working Mechanics   134
Administrative Details   135
Fishing for Details   136
Who is Who?   137
The Importance of Timing   137
Post-Committee Engagement   138

9   WORKING WITH PMOs   139
More Knowledge, Less Paperwork   140
Accountability, Sarbanes-Oxley, and PMOs   140
What is the History of Your PMO?   141
Natural Affinities Between PMOs and Knowledge-Based
Work   142
Making It to Your Corporate Project Roadmap   142
A Strong Business Case Increases Odds of Longevity   143
The Importance of a Comprehensive Cost-Benefit
Analysis   144
ROI Figures in Prioritization   144
Juggling Multiple PMOs   145
What to Think About First   146
Can You Just Ignore the PMO?   146
Barter, Trade, Delay   147
Funding Creativity: Not a Bad Thing   147
The Early Bird   148
Relationships as Key   148
How Much About Project Management Do You Need
to Know?   149
Triple Constraint: The Questions You Should Always be Able
to Answer   150
Get on Board: The Customer Experience   150

10   MAKING SENSE OF DOLLARS AND CENTS   153
Finance, Procurement, and ROI   153
Before You Begin   154
Locate Support in Your Network   154
Locate Pre-Existing Staff   154
Get Organized   155
Finance and Budgets: How Do You Get Money?   155
High Level Guiding Principles   155
Questions You Must Be Able to Answer   156

Unwritten Rules   156
   Use of Surplus Funds   156
   Surplus Consequences   157
   Intentional Overestimation   157
   Intentional Underestimation   157
Procurement: How Do You Spend Money?   158
What Procurement Does   158
Typical Procurement Areas of Influence   158
   Preferred Vendors   159
   Subcontracting Relationships   159
   RFP/RFQ Process and Timelines   159
   Single Sourcing   160
   Supporting Documentation   160
   Procurement as a Supporter   161
   Vendor Relations   161
Purchase Order Process Details   162
ROI: What was the Return on the Money You Spent?   163
Executive Point of View: Jane Niederberger and ROI   164
ROI Standards   165
   Creativity in ROI?   165
   What ROI Means at Your Firm   166
   Who Cares About ROI at Your Firm   166
   When and What is Actually Used?   167
   Playing Both Ends   168
Get Help from the Outside   169
   The KM Community at Large   169
   Vendor Assistance   169
   What the Joneses are Up To   170

11   **IT – FRIEND OR FOE?**   171
But My Solution is Not About Technology   171
Why You Need IT in Your Court   173
Learning to Speak IT's Language   177
Your Company Standards   177
   Discovering Standards   178
Commonly Confused Terms and Definitions   178
Key Areas to Investigate   182
Perception of Your Work   182
Consultants – Can They Help?   185
Operations   187
   How Much Do You Have to Understand?   187

Methodologies   189
Service Level Agreements   189
   Your Role in SLAs   190
   Violated SLAs May Trigger Other Inquiries   190
   SLAs as a Compensation Factor   190
   Typical Relevant SLAs   191
Change Control   191
   Change Control as a Committee   192
   Change Control as an Activity or Artifact   192
   When Change Control is Violated   193
   Typical Change Control Areas   193
   Your Role in Change Control   193
Archiving: A Compliance and IT Interdependency   195
The Offsite Component   196
Determining the Cost of Archiving   196
Outputs: What Could be Archived?   196
How Do Things Get Archived?   197
How Do Things Get Restored?   198
How Do Things Stay Safe?   198
Mediums and Associated Costs   198
Understanding Offsite Storage Costs   199

12   EXPERT Q&A WITH BRANDON GOLDFEDDER   201
Dealing with IT Staff   201
Personality Traits, Strengths, and Weaknesses   203
Management Tips for the Non-IT Person   204
Changes in the World of IT that May Affect You   206
Communications Basics   207
Organizational Knowledge   208
What to Avoid   209
In Conclusion   209

13   ENGAGING THE HELP DESK   211
Would You Want Their Job?   211
Defining Support   212
   What Type of Support Will Your Work Require?   213
The Organizational Landscape of Your Help Desk   213
   Who Does the Help Desk Work For?   214
   Blended Modes of Support   214
Keeping a Strong Relationship with the Help Desk   214
   Why the Help Desk Must be a Fan   215
   What You Can Learn from the Help Desk   216
Help Desk and Knowledge Synergies   217
Engaging Help Desk Leadership   217

Who, Exactly, is Leadership?   218
High Level Leadership' Must-Knows   218
   Hidden Activities   219
Planning Support   219
Communicating: Who, Why, When, and How?   219
Training: Yours, Mine, and Ours   220
   Is There Help Available?   221
   General Use Training Compared to Troubleshooting
      Training   221
   How Much Do You Need to Know?   222
   General Use Training Compared to Help Desk Process
      Issues   223
   Understanding Tiers   223
   Training Details   224
Your Role in Support   225
Process   226
Tips for Ensuring a Helpful Help Desk Relationship   227

**SECTION VII   COMMUNICATIONS, SALESMANSHIP
AND PUBLICITY   229**

14 THE CORPORATE RED CARPET   231
Communications and Selling – the Same or Different?   232
What Does the Red Carpet Mean?   232
Focus on Communications   233
Why More Structure is Necessary Now   233
Why Communicate?   234
Communications Guidelines   235
Before You Begin   235
Resources at Your Fingertips   235
Beg or Borrow   236
Your Sponsor's Resources   236
The Source Matters   236
Understanding Communications Vehicles Available
   to You   237
Building a Communications Plan   238
Who Do You Need to Reach?   238
Messages and Themes   239
Details   240
One or Many?   241
Sample Communication Plans Elements   241
   Mapping Audiences by Value Prop Elements   241
   Mapping Audience as Primary   242
   Dividing by Responsibility   244
   A Phase-Based Approach   244

Selling Events   245
Why Publicity Should Start Early   245
    Ways to Generate Pre-Publicity   246
The Executive Factor   247
    What are You Asking For?   247
    Preparing for an Executive Meeting   247
        Before the Meeting   247
        During the Meeting   248
        After the Meeting   249
Your Selling and Communication Content Toolkit   249
    Baseline Ingredients   250
    The Elevator Pitch   250
    The Power of Multimedia   251
Charting the Red Carpet at Your Firm   252
    Speaking Opportunities   252
    Road Shows   253
        What Road Show Participation Means   253
        Road Show Expenses   254
Ensuring Your Continued Success   254
    Communicate Constantly   255
    Get Organized   255
    Develop Your Own Scorecard   256
    Network Extensively   256
    Keep a Clipping Folder   257
    Let Your Story Evolve – and Then Publicize It   257

15   SELLING KNOWLEDGE-BASED WORK IN REAL LIFE   259
    Everyone Sells – and That Means You   259
        The Executive Point of View   260
    Dave Snowden's Guiding Sales Principles   261
        Do You Understand and Believe What You are Selling?   261
        The One True Path   262
        Language Matters   262
        Engage Interpreters to Enhance Credibility   263
        Sell the Journey, Not the Destination   263
        Fail-Safe or Safe-Fail?   263
        Basic Sales Skills are Key   264
        Do Not Expect Credit (Even if It is Due)   264
    Selling Knowledge-Based Work in Australia   264
        Public Sector: Pressing on a Pain Point for Results   266
        Private Sector: Enlisting Superiors at Strategic Junctures   267
        Show and Tell in High Tech Defense   267
        Starting Small Can Increase Sales Leverage   269

Index   271

Author Biography

Raised between the Florida Gulf Coast and the Amazon rainforest, Stacy Land's interest in Knowledge Management began early – although she didn't call it that. Growing up among multiple languages and cultures gave her an early marker for understanding context, a lesson that served her well during her studies in comparative literature, graduate work in Linguistics, and early career as a stand-up trainer.

Although she began on the technical side of solutions designed to empower and enable knowledge workers, she quickly moved into investigating the question of how to account for the most difficult to quantify variable: the human being in the equation. For the last 18 years, Stacy has maintained that knowledge-based focus, coupled with and around technology, moving between academia and business.

In the mid 90s, while working for Indiana's largest property and casualty insurance company, she led the effort to bring in the Internet, including Internet e-mail, and established the first ever web site for the Indiana-based firm. She also represented Indiana Farm Bureau as a Communications Expert in Central Asia for three weeks in conjunction with the Citizens Network for Foreign Affairs and USAID. Later, at Braun Consulting, she co-founded the firm's first Knowledge Management department, which was developed to help integrate a newly acquired practice into the existing infrastructure.

In 2002, at the nation's largest healthcare provider, Stacy led the first Enterprise Knowledge Management effort, gaining C-level consensus and rolling nearly half of the firm's teams onto the new collaboration and content platform in less than a year. After spending a few years at a multimillion-dollar management consultancy based out of Atlanta, Georgia, heading their Knowledge Management activities, Land is currently Director of Process and Quality, Senior Medical Management at USA-based WellPoint, Inc., where she holds responsibility around process, knowledge management, and communications.

Acknowledgements

I owe gratitude and acknowledgements to many people, including:

- Every boss I ever had to encouraged me to speak my mind and explore what I saw, even if it meant learning the emperor had no clothing . . . and he or she was the emperor.
- My publishers, Karen Maloney and Ailsa Marks, for believing in my idea, and their feedback and support.
- My cheerleaders, including Jane Pozek, Sheri Isgrigg, Barbara Martin, Lyuda Land, Dahris Clair, Ben Cagle, Katie Young, Reginald Anderson, Club 33, Shelley Cannady, Zoher Karu, Ron Williams, Joby Jerrells, Jeff Herbert, Michael Weis, and Janet Klochko.
- My technical gurus, including Robert Bouchard, J. Coleman, and Blane Land and subject matter experts Kevin Sheridan and Kristi Beyer.
- My experts, who gave generously of their time and expertise, including John Collier, Brandon Goldfedder, Michael Jackman, Joseph King, Santi Kumar, Joe McGhee, Kate Muir, Jane Niederberger, and Dave Snowden.
- The Knowledge Management community at large, in particular Dr. Cindy Gordon.
- All those who believed in and are beloved to me, including H.C. and Bobby Land, and Scott Faerchild.

Preface

Managing Knowledge-Based Initiatives is intended for the brave souls who are facing what can be a daunting task: implementing a knowledge-based initiative in a large entity, whether that is a privately held business, corporation, or large government or academic institution.

You may be a junior member of a Knowledge Management team, a team lead, or a Director who has just had a knowledge-based initiative dropped in your lap. Perhaps you are experienced in leading initiatives, but this is your first experience with implementing a knowledge-based, rather than technology or process-based, solution. You might be consulting in an organization and while you are clear about the goals of the knowledge-based initiative, are not sure how to help your client make the leap from an idea/pilot to actual implementation.

In *Managing Knowledge-Based Initiatives*, we don't debate whether your initiative qualifies as "knowledge-based" or "Knowledge Management," or offer guidelines to help you slot your work into a methodology, although we briefly explore the pragmatic definition of Knowledge Management that we advocate. Instead, we focus on the unique challenges that a knowledge-based initiative – as you define it – may face when it moves from a small scale, perhaps a pilot, to a large scale, whether that be regional, state, national, or global.

We review the common pitfalls that can slow – or even halt – the implementation of knowledge-based initiatives particularly in large entities. Although these same challenges may be found in smaller entities, in general the complex structures that this book addresses will be found in larger firms with huge operating budgets.

Because each firm is different, this book is not a "cookbook" of steps that ensure success. Rather, *Managing Knowledge-Based Initiatives* identifies areas you need to be concerned with, details where those areas are, why it is likely to matter, and suggests the activities you should undertake.

For example, consider the issue of compliance. In a corporation, compliance will likely be found in multiple areas: legal, IT, departmental, and if you are in a regulated industry such as healthcare, perhaps other areas. *Managing Knowledge-Based Initiatives* will help you frame an implementation element, such as compliance, in multiple contexts so that you can uncover each path the implementation element might lead to (such as IT and Legal) and well as new gates that hide other paths (such as IT security compliance compared to standards compliance compared to change control compliance).

To help you see how things work in different companies so that you can identify potential challenges inside your own, we spoke with executives and practitioners who have experience in large, complex firms. For example, we harvested real-life success stories from a knowledge practitioner who teaches how to sell knowledge-based initiatives at an Australian university. If you are new to dealing with executives, we asked five executives spread across the nation operating in multiple industries to describe the best ways to approach, engage, and negotiate with them. Their insight about how to navigate in large organizations, particularly coming from a knowledge focus, is invaluable – and sometimes surprising.

If you are stumped by how to engage technical staff at your firm, we have an IT executive who offers tips about how to recognize the type of IT person you are working with, so that you can motivate and communicate more effectively with technical staff. We have also included advice from people who are "in the trenches," including a technology expert who translates terms that crop up frequently around knowledge-based initiatives, and a PMO (Project Management Office) leader who manages a more than $60 million budget who describes what really happens at the project negotiating table.

At the heart of *Managing Knowledge-Based Initiatives* is that you are passionate about your work, believe in what you are doing, and are ready to take the steps to make it succeed in your organization.

This book will assist you if:

- This is your first major implementation in any large company.
- You have been pushing for a new knowledge-based tool or process and leadership has given you the green light – but you are not sure where to start.
- You are plowing ahead with a knowledge-based initiative and have not interacted yet with other parts of your company.
- Your solution has an element of technology, but you have not formed a partnership with the technology experts in your firm.
- Your solution will necessitate equipment purchases, new head count, or consulting.

- You are managing a budget for the first time, and do not know how things work.
- Although people who have seen your knowledge-based initiative think it is great, you need to spread the word throughout your organization.
- You will be meeting and negotiating with senior people in your organization for the first time.
- You know politics exists in your company, but do not see how it impacts your work.
- Other groups in your company will be expected to support your work.
- You have an executive sponsor, but are not sure what that means or why it matters.
- You have not set up any measurements or benchmarking around your work.
- Your work has been mandated from the top – and the people it is going to affect do not know it is coming.
- Your company has one or more PMOs (Project Management Offices) that you have not engaged with.

Meet Our Panel of Experts

Because each firm is different, we called on a number of seasoned veterans in the corporate world to share their experiences. These experts are referenced throughout *Managing Knowledge-Based Initiatives* and offer practical advice and guidelines based on their real-life observations and learnings.

John Collier has a degree in architecture – but quickly moved into the world of technology after graduation. After consulting as a Project Manager for a number of years, he now manages a segment of the IT PMO for one of the world's largest manufacturers. John shared his challenges in managing a PMO, how to interact with PMOs, the reality of getting your project on the table, ensuring that you have the resources and support necessary to execute it, and the benefits of forming strong relationships.

Brandon Goldfedder is currently a Vice President at IET, a services firm that specializes in research, development, and implementation of knowledge-based expert systems for decision support, information fusion, and modeling of complex phenomena. Brandon has nearly two decades of IT experience and has filled the roles of Enterprise Architect, Architect Designer, Software Engineer and CRM Package Architect for dozens of Fortune 1000 clients.

Before IET, Brandon held the positions of Vice President of Braun Consulting in its Enterprise Application Solution Group, and CTO of Emerging Technologies Consultants, Inc. Prior to his career in consulting, Brandon served as an officer in the US Air Force.

A published author, Brandon is also recognized for having developed several commercial programs under Windows and Unix. He has been involved in architectural approaches for coding in embedded system and enterprise applications, as well as the proper application of the J2EE and .NET frameworks. He earned his B.S.E., Electrical and Computer Science Engineering, and his M.S.E., Computer Science Engineering from Johns Hopkins University.

Michael Jackman serves as a Vice President for Eastman Kodak Company and is the General Manager of Healthcare Information Solutions. Before moving to General Manager, Michael headed global research and development operations for Kodak's Health Group. Prior to joining Kodak, he was founder and CEO of a consulting firm, which specialized in technology development and strategy for companies in the wireless, IP telephony, security and software infrastructure areas. Jackman has held top marketing, sales, and development positions at various technology companies. During a successful 18-year career at IBM, he held several senior management positions, including Vice President, Systems and Technology. In this capacity, he was responsible for integrated product solutions, technology strategy, strategic alliances, engineering services, and licensing activity. He also led worldwide business operations and product management for IBM's ThinkPad line and served as Technology Advisor to IBM's Chairman and CEO.

Joseph King qualifies as a geek – but this Atlanta-based technology expert speaks the language of Knowledge Management, as well. Through the years, Joseph has worked as a programmer/analyst and architect for companies that represent the consumer packaged goods, pharmaceutical, real estate, insurance, and financial services markets across the nation. In *Managing Knowledge-Based Initiatives*, Joseph serves as our translator around technical terminology and offers us a different point of view of change control.

Santi Kumar is Vice President at Fidelity Employer Services Company (FESCo), a division of Fidelity Investments. FESCo provides defined contribution and defined benefit retirement services, employer benefits and human resources, administration, and payroll services to approximately 20 million employees in the United States. Within FESCo IT, Santi has accountability for the execution of Large Complex Programs within FESCo – externally and internally facing.

In a previous role at WellPoint, Inc., Kumar managed Integration projects as part of Mergers & Acquisitions, and earlier had responsibility for business planning, business process excellence, metrics and reporting, operating model, and research and competitive analysis to drive overall organizational effectiveness and cultural change initiatives.

Ms. Kumar has also served as Lead Architect and Strategist and Manager of Business Development and Services for Agilent Technologies, a Hewlett Packard spin off company, IT Manager at Hewlett Packard's Healthcare Solutions Group, and other roles in Procter and Gamble, MCI Telecommunications and Digital Equipment Corporation.

A founder of J. Devien Capital, **Joe McGhee** was formerly a Division President at Asurion Insurance Services. His previous work experience includes various senior executive level positions with Cisco Systems, Avaya, IBM, LOTUS software, and Siemens. Mr. McGhee has extensive global operations experience and has conducted business in over 20 countries including leading Cisco Systems' $400M+ Operations in Korea as Executive Vice President and COO. In addition to his experiences throughout Asia, he has also conducted business in Latin America and the Caribbean, as well as various European countries while working for Siemens. From 2001 to 2003, Mr. McGhee was responsible for driving over $2 billion in total revenue and leading all associated business and strategic initiatives as Vice President of Sales, Americas East, for Avaya Communications.

Kate Muir was the first person in the Australian Federal Government to have the word "knowledge" in her title as the National Manager of the Knowledge Team of Centrelink, the Australian federal government services provider. In a position that required a unique combination of theory, domain, and technical expertise, Kate was responsible for the strategic development of the agency's overall knowledge framework as well as the delivery of the technical systems needed to support Centrelink's knowledge workers. Systems included Documents and Records Management, and an online reference guide and thesaurus that supported all text and content management systems on the web. Kate also folded in MIS rigor around the uptake of policy, policy modeling data, policy evaluation data, and demographic information used by other tiers of government, academia, executive government and the Australian Parliament into a holistic solution.

Kate is also expert at building and nurturing collaborative teams. Muir is a co-founder of actKM, a community of practice founded to support government initiatives around KM, which has become a leading community of practice in the world around KM. She has lectured in Knowledge Management Systems at University of Canberra and teaches Knowledge and Information Management at the Canberra Institute of Technology.

Jane Niederberger already had a solid career in healthcare behind her when she stepped into the role of the Vice President of Business Transformation at Anthem Insurance (now Wellpoint). Two years later, Jane moved to Senior Vice President and Chief Information Office at the Indiana-based firm. In addition to leading major systems consolidations that resulted in significantly lower costs, Jane signed on as the executive sponsor for the first Enterprise Knowledge Management effort at the firm. Anthem moved from 444 in 2000 to 45 in 2004 on the InformationWeek 500 listing and was awarded the CIO 100 Agile Award from the CIO Magazine in 2004. In 2005, Anthem and Wellpoint merged, transforming it into the nation's largest healthcare provider, with an estimated customer base of over 34 million people. Jane's tenure at Wellpoint was rounded out with a stint as Vice President of Operations and she is currently Chairman of Medical Animatics LLC based out of Indianapolis, Indiana.

Dave Snowden is the Founder and Chief Scientific Officer of Cognitive Edge, which focuses on the development of the theory and practice of sensemaking. Cognitive Edge exists to integrate academic thinking with practice in organizations throughout the world and operates on a network model working with people in academia, government, commercial organizations, NGOs, and those who consult independently. A native of Wales, Dave was formerly a Director in the IBM Institute for Knowledge Management and founder of the Cynefin Centre for organizational complexity. He is a leading keynote speaker at major conferences around the world and is known for his iconoclastic style, pragmatic cynicism, and extensive use of stories. Tom Stewart, editor of the Harvard Business Review, stated in the context of tacit knowledge that, "Dave Snowden, (is) the best thinker I've found on the subject," although by way of counter he also comments that, "He is Welsh and a bit mad."

Deep personal thanks go to each of our experts for their time, expertise, and wisdom.

Section I

Laying the Groundwork

1

Baseline Points of Understanding

Not all knowledge-based initiatives succeed. At the most granular level, the reasons they fail are perhaps as numerous as the initiatives themselves. You, as the implementer, have an individual day-to-day experience that is like no one else's day-to-day experience. Because every corporation has unique procedures, political environments, and cultures, there is no foolproof, always-true set of steps that, when followed, ensure that a knowledge-based implementation will succeed.

However, when examined from a distance, the factors that contribute to the failure of knowledge-based implementations tend to be concentrated in a few areas. Where we see knowledge practitioners fail is not a lack of awareness of the challenges inherent in the solution itself, but rather a lack of understanding of how elements of the knowledge solution need to interact and fit in with the business as a whole.

Gates and Paths

One way to conceptualize how the elements of a knowledge-based solution need to interact with other parts of a corporation is to view the planning and implementation of your work as a series of gates, and associated paths. When certain criterion is met – for example, when an idea is approved for pilot or implementation – a gate opens, revealing a path. Other gates with their own paths may open or spring into existence, simply because the first gate opened. As the implementer of a knowledge-based solution, you must be aware of and explore every path behind each gate. Some will be of negligible importance and others will be critical.

Here is the challenge: in a complex environment, it is easy to miss those additional gates when they appear, never mind the paths behind them, if you do not already know they exist.

Framing Your Work

The trick to understanding the gates, their paths, and impacts lies in how you frame the activities associated with your project. An implementation element can be framed through multiple viewpoints: technology, politics, compliance, support, and others. As you frame your activities through multiple viewpoints, the relationships that emerge between the gates and paths that open will often resemble a spider web. You will rarely encounter an easy-to-follow linear path that will pull you along the activities you need to execute.

The best way to ensure that you are aware of the gates and their associated paths is to force yourself deliberately to frame events and activities through multiple viewpoints. Time and time again, in speaking to successful implementers, common themes arise. The involvement of your Project Management Office (PMO), the level of executive support and funding are common challenges that won't surprise veterans of any large organization. As an implementer, you need to frame your activities by each of these elements. The importance of networking firm wide may be new to you, and the fact that much of your success or failure will depend on how you communicate and work with people. Knowing who to communicate with, when, and which elements are at play is, again, largely a question of framing.

In *Managing Knowledge-Based Initiatives*, we explore not only the gates and their associated paths, but also how to frame your activities in multiple contexts as dictated by the paths and gates. As you follow the activities we outline in *Managing Knowledge-Based Initiatives*, you will gain a much larger appreciation for how the moving parts of your organization fit together, and where you need to plug in to succeed.

Overlaying a Technology and Support Context

We know that framing can be tricky in dynamic environments. Knowledge Management itself is new and constantly evolving. Companies change not only because of external pressures such as legislation, world events, and social concerns, but also because of internal pressures. Knowledge practitioners should be comfortable with the idea of remaining flexible, and changing how they frame their own paths and activities.

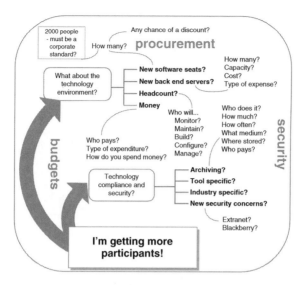

Figure 1-1 Viewing increased participants through a technology lens.

For example, consider this event: You receive an email from your executive sponsor that says, "Buckle up! We just got buy in from several C-level executives. I'll call you later with details." To you this means: *I'm getting more participants in my knowledge-based initiative!*

That single event can be viewed in multiple ways. You can view the increase in participants through a technology lens, as shown in Figure 1-1. Two potential areas within technology – there are certainly many more – are the impact on the environment itself, and standards and security. Note that technology topics also have procurement, budget, and security implications.

Not surprisingly, how you are going to support those additional participants is also a consideration, as shown in Figure 1-2. Notice that again, the support question, viewed within a context of technology, has bled into multiple areas.

Here's the point: if you examine both figures, you will see the elements contained in both overlap each other in increasingly greater detail the deeper you drill into activities. A single event or concern spins into areas that may have significant dependencies on other events and areas. That is why being able to frame your work is so important.

Framing: Easier or More Difficult for Knowledge Practitioners?

The very nature of knowledge practitioners and the roles they play in organizations makes some portions of the framing exercise easier – and some more

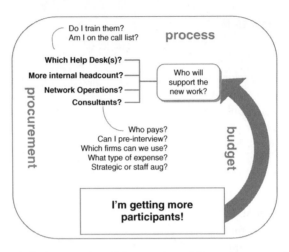

Figure 1-2 Increased participants viewed through a support lens.

complex. The importance of continually ensuring context should be simpler. The necessary wading through bureaucracy and paperwork may be more frustrating. Assuming you have a high degree of passion for your work, influencing others to see the benefits of your work might be easier – but if you are a zealot, your credibility may be impacted. Likewise, you may operate from the assumption that knowledge sharing is the right thing to do, not only for business success, but from an ethical/behavioral point of view. Recognizing and dealing with individuals who do not share that belief may be frustrating. Because you are passionate, you likely have a sense of urgency about implementing your solution; the steps, timelines, and bureaucracy may frustrate you on that level, as well.

As a knowledge practitioner in a large business, you may be better at managing some of the activities associated with framing your work than others. However, you will have to become minimally proficient in all of them to succeed.

That idea, and the recognition that some of the elements make knowledge practitioners unique – and highly effective in their roles – is the reason we created *Managing Knowledge-Based Initiatives*. In the following pages, we explore the typical gates, and associated paths, that dictate how work often happens in large organizations. Some of the paths are fairly linear and easy to follow. Others rely heavily on difficult-to-quantify elements like politics or relationships.

As we explore each path, we frame it in multiple contexts to help you determine which are most important in your organization. All these elements together will help ensure not only the successful implementation of your knowledge-based initiative, but its longevity in the organization.

Engaging First is Key

The challenge that lies ahead of you is many-fold. First, you must stay true to the goals of your knowledge-based initiative itself. However, in order to get the chance to execute that initiative, you have to navigate within your organization.

That may mean a multitude of committees, approvals, metrics reviews, compliance hearings, new procedures, and many other things. Your challenge is to find out what these things are and proactively engage the entities who have control over your work.

The primary reason that it is up to you to engage first is simple: if you wait for committees and the people who comprise them to come to you, they may not. And stop or slow your work anyway. One practitioner we interviewed routinely appeared on agendas for committees she had never even heard of while taking her knowledge-based initiative through the approvals process – and was not notified that she was scheduled to appear. Perhaps the situation is not as dire in your company, but the larger the firm, the greater the need for you to take a proactive stance.

The genuine reason that you should engage first is that it is the right thing to do, both for your personal success and that of your project.

How You will Benefit from Engaging First

If you are the type of person who shies away from initiating cold contacts, even within your own organization, the idea of proactively engaging the entities who have a voice in your work may be distasteful to you.

Perhaps you feel silly phoning or emailing people you have never spoken to before. Perhaps you are hesitant to reach out to your organization's leaders because of their professional stature or reputation. In this process, you will contact individuals who do not have to sign off on or support your work, and you might feel foolish for calling the wrong person. However, the benefits of proactively engaging all concerned parties – even if you inadvertently knock on some incorrect doors – far outweigh any risk on your side.

You establish yourself as proactive. When you engage others, whether they are juniors, peers, or seniors, you are forming a business-based relationship. Establishing yourself as proactive is a good thing and shows people that you are thinking ahead and playing out multiple scenarios.

You get an early indicator of progress and success indicators different entities may require. If you engage people up front – for example, a PMO representative who is an expert in how your corporation measures return on investment (ROI) – you will be able to build in measures at the beginning of your work, rather than try to measure indicators on the fly, or retro-quantify activities after they are over. You will also begin to gather the information you will need to build your own corporate calendar with critical dates.

You gain a degree of control in the interaction. There is a subtle difference between being summoned to justify your work in front of a committee compared to your asking for an invitation. Your level of excitement and the proactive nature of engaging people first won't be lost – and you will get early exposure.

Every contact grows your network. Even if you contact people who do not need to sign off on your work, you have just grown your network. Engage each person you speak with. Find out what they do, the role they play in your organization, and their pain points. Share your story and explain how your work is going to benefit the organization.

You tell your story, your way. Two things may happen when someone else tells your story: critical elements may be left out or significantly changed.

For example, imagine that your knowledge-based initiative is designed to support the integration of several recently merged work groups. Not only do the groups have a history of conflict, but they feel their importance is diminished by being lumped in with the other groups. Leadership knows that the two groups are duplicating work and failing to cooperate – or even connect on a social level – resulting in a waste of money and a morale-killer.

After extensive requirements gathering, you design a unique program that involves face-to-face knowledge sharing, expertise location, a six-week exchange program, strong leadership communication, and a centralized knowledge repository. You have pinpointed the formal and informal leaders of all groups and found people who are willing to give your program a chance. You successfully developed and sold a comprehensive value prop to all involved groups and identified a number of tangible ways they will benefit from embracing the new relationship.

Someone else telling your story may translate it as, "Yeah, they're building a database because all these groups work for the same Director now."

Big difference.

You can spot early warning signs. Just as important as finding supporters of your work is finding people who may not support it. We isolate people, and not committees, because committees are made up of people that shape its actions. Identifying the power players in key groups is crucial to resolving difficulties you may encounter. Locating non-supportive parties early on helps you avoid being blindsided when it is potentially too late to do anything about it.

You locate "hidden" influencers and committees. In the course of your organizational exploration, you will probably stumble on key players and committees that you never knew existed. Particularly if you are in a regulated industry, for example, the Legal Department may play a huge role in your work. Even if these "hidden" influencers do not have direct sign-off on your work, take the opportunity to tell your story your way. They can be valuable allies, both in navigating organizationally and formulating strategies to address problems.

Knowledge, Organizational, or Project Management?

If you are thinking, "Wait a minute! My work isn't about organizational design or project management. Why do I have to deal with benchmarks, executives, or committees?" then it is time to swallow a tough pill: your project is one of many that will be competing for dollars, resources, and recognition in your firm.

To the people who make judgment calls around funding and priority, your project is no more special than any other. In fact, because knowledge-based initiatives often struggle with demonstrating ROI, your project may appear to be a less desirable choice than another project with numerically bounded objectives and projected paybacks. Accept the inevitability of your need to successfully navigate – and negotiate with – whatever structures may be in place at your organization.

In the course of your work, you will find yourself in the center of a swirl of activities where the lines become blurred. Is it project management, organizational design, or Knowledge Management? It will likely be some of all of these elements. In today's corporate environment, that is the reality, and does not dilute the focus of your knowledge-based initiative if you recognize and manage the dichotomy appropriately.

Funding Factors

Even if you have the funding to begin your knowledge-based initiative, continued funding may be another question entirely. Just because a business partner found money for your work in their budget, or an executive freed up seed money to launch your initiative does not guarantee that funds will be available from year to year. To gain that sort of support, you will have to demonstrate continued success and draw direct lines between your work and your company's goals to show how your knowledge-based initiative contributes to your company's success. And, you will need to demonstrate that success within the framework that your company recognizes as valid.

In addition, do not make the mistake of assuming that because your project is funded, you have a blanket green light. There is a tacit nod that goes along with those funds that says, "And of course, as the project owner, you'll ensure that everyone approves, compliance is intact, technical standards are met, and your activities will conform to our company's project standards." If you missed that nod, read on – there are plenty of hidden landmines that it is your job to find before you accidentally step on them.

The PMO Factor

Because *Managing Knowledge-Based Initiatives* is intended for people who work in large organizations, we assume that your firm has some form of PMO in place. Your firm may have a central PMO, or multiple PMOs. If there are multiple PMOs, they may be umbrella-ed beneath a central organization, which will help you navigate them.

PMOs, their level of control over activities, and the degree to which they can help or hinder your efforts vary greatly from organization to organization. In some corporations, a PMO may simply consist of representatives from different areas who get together to find out what other areas are doing. In other corporations, all projects must be initiated, or approved, by the appropriate PMO.

Some companies take it a step further, and projects are prioritized, funded, and scheduled by the PMO. This means that if your project does not "cut the mustard" by PMO standards, even if you have a funding commitment, your work may not be allowed to proceed. If your company embraces a project management methodology that perhaps includes a software system designed to track and report on projects, then you will most likely have to conform to those standards when approaching your knowledge-based initiative. That may mean altering project plans, following predetermined phases and activities, and establishing milestones and goals at the junctures your firm's methodology dictates – not the ones you think are logical.

The bottom line is this: the implementation of your knowledge-based initiative will likely be considered a project. Assuming you are in a large organization, the dollar figures and participant numbers involved will probably qualify your work as a project by your PMOs standards. If it falls beneath the purview of the PMO, they have a voice in how your work progresses. At points in your project planning and implementation, you will probably begin to feel like your responsibilities are more project or process-centered than knowledge-centered. It is inevitable. Our point of view is that starting the relationship with a strong handshake benefits not just your work, but the PMO as well.

The Organizational Design/Alignment Factor

You may be wondering why we include organizational design/organizational development in this section. In the final analysis, a large percentage of knowledge-based work revolves around helping resources work more effectively together. For example, you may be investigating vehicles to help your firm pool and share historical or current resources, team more effectively, or uncover expertise. Part of the exercise that usually remains unspoken is figuring out why teams are not working together the way they should. Sometimes, that answer may simply be a tools or process gap that can easily be filled. Other times, however, it may come down to the "sticky stuff" that makes us all human.

As we explore in Section III, groups of people who work at cross-purposes are often organizationally misaligned. A knowledge-based initiative can inadvertently shine a spotlight on organizational misalignment.

For example, perhaps your project involves helping two sales teams collaborate and share information about prospects and clients. During discovery, you uncover that the teams are compensated on a comparative basis – bonuses go up, or down, depending on how well one team does compared to other sales teams. Naturally, they have no compelling reason to share information, albeit to the organization's detriment. It is "Pandora's serendipity": while seeking an answer to one question, you may discover a myriad of other dilemmas that do not have easy solutions, and you may not be in a position to influence.

In addition to sometimes addressing problems that can be traced to organizational misalignment, you will have to demonstrate the organizational alignment of your initiative on an ongoing basis. Understanding how your organization works as a whole will help you identify the moving parts you need to interact with, and perhaps most importantly, align with.

Terms and Definitions in Managing Knowledge-Based Initiatives

Key to working in any organization is speaking the organization's language. That includes expressions, buzzwords, and acronyms. In *Managing Knowledge-Based Initiatives*, we use a number of terms in the broadest sense possible, knowing that the same word may have a slightly different meaning in your company.

Committees

We loosely define a committee as a group of people who come together for a common purpose or mandate. In your organization, they may be called workgroups, advisory boards, boards, teams, or any number of other names. Remember to translate what we refer to as "committees," "entities," "areas," or "divisions" into your own corporate language.

Firm, Corporation, Organization, Company

Managing Knowledge-Based Initiatives is targeted to knowledge practitioners who are implementing a solution in a large firm. We do not differentiate between whether your firm is privately or publicly held, or whether it is a commercial or government/not-for profit entity. The terms firm, corporation, organization, or company may be used interchangeably throughout *Managing Knowledge-Based Initiatives*.

Friendly Faces

We frequently refer to "friendly faces" throughout *Managing Knowledge-Based Initiatives*. Friendly faces mean people who are at a minimum open to your knowledge-based initiative. At a maximum, they are avid supporters of your work. They are valuable to you for many reasons, including their ability to influence others.

Knowledge Management

The field of Knowledge Management is young; we are evolving at a rapid pace. Constant debate rages around the validity and relevance of some of the very elements that five years ago were considered foundational to understanding Knowledge Management. This debate and the shifting views of Knowledge Management are necessary to its growth – and it is fascinating to jump in and get your feet wet.

Whatever your views on Knowledge Management, understand that the corporate environment is not necessarily the place to expect spirited debate or appreciation for the nuances of what makes our field special. Express your passion – yes. But do not expect a potential executive sponsor of your work, or a committee reviewing the technical specs of your solution to get excited about how your knowledge-based initiative empowers knowledge workers (or whatever your linkage to the larger work of Knowledge Management maybe) or how your work contextualizes information so that it can be considered knowledge. We speak later in this book about aligning your work with your organization's goals and speaking your organization's language, and this is the tactic we encourage you to pursue.

As a practitioner of any field, you should remain aware of, and be challenged by, new developments. Many Knowledge Management practitioners hold new and exciting views about our field that are theoretical or academic in nature. However, remaining focused on the *direct impact that your knowledge-based solution will have on your organization* will help ensure your success.

In *Managing Knowledge-Based Initiatives*, we adhere to a very pragmatic view of Knowledge Management, best expressed by Dr. Melissie Rumizen. Dr. Rumizen is perhaps best known for her groundbreaking knowledge-based work at Buckman Laboratories, and authorship of *The Complete Idiot's Guide to Knowledge Management*. During her lifetime, she was a visible, welcoming, and cohesive force in the Knowledge Management field and is sorely missed.

In a discussion with the Association of KnowledgeWork (http://www. kwork.org), Dr. Rumizen emphasized remaining focused on the business of your organization, and keeping Knowledge Management theory and jargon to a minimum. "*We are not as interesting as we think we are*," Dr. Rumizen cautioned. "People respond to action. It's concrete; it's real. Folks who sleep through your dazzling explanation of theory will come to life once you talk about how you plan to do something and the potential ROI. Much fascinates us as knowledge geeks but it often bores others to tears. Likewise, ditch the jargon. We don't talk about KM (at our organization). We do things that make sense for our business."[1]

In *Managing Knowledge-Based Initiatives*, we do not debate whether your solution qualifies as "Knowledge Management" or "knowledge-based." In fact, depending on the climate and history of your workplace, you may need to consider de-branding your work as Knowledge Management, because there is so much confusion about what it is. In some organizations, the phrase "Knowledge Management" evokes heavy skepticism.

How This Book is Organized

In the next section, we will look at a number of "factors of understanding" that you should do your best to fully own before launching your knowledge-based initiative, such as understanding how you arrived at the point of building out your work, how your company is performing, and evaluating the state of Knowledge Management inside your firm. In Section II, you will also meet the first of our executive informants when Joe McGhee shares his executive point of view on how to evaluate your company from the outside in.

Section III focuses on organizational alignment, what it is, and how leveraging it can benefit you with funding and cooperation. Section IV explores the question of support, focusing on the relationship between you and your executive sponsor. The nature of a value proposition, why you need one, and how to build one

---

[1] Used with permission from the Association of Knowledgework.

is explored in Section V. In a perfect world, most of the items addressed in Sections II through V would be integrated into the project planning process, well before actual implementation. Even if you are already implementing your solution, the content in this sections will help you identify gaps and familiarize you with the framing exercises that will support the growth of your work.

Section VI focuses on a number of tactical activities that you should undertake around building relationships, establishing credibility, and demonstrating the value your work brings to the organization, again through multiple contexts. Topics covered include how to locate and engage the committees you will need to deal with, working with PMOs, handling money matters like budgets, procurement and ROI, and working with technical staff and the help desk.

The final section, Section VII, covers communications, salesmanship, and publicity. We explore how to build a communications plan, some general rules about generating publicity, and tried-and-true real life examples of selling knowledge-based work.

Seize the Day

One final word before we move forward. Because of the youth of our field, our thought leaders are largely not only still around, but active in the field. Therefore, they are accessible to you. Consider what a rare chance this is and do not be afraid to reach out to others on discussion boards, via email, or at conferences. It is a unique moment in time; take advantage of it.

Section II

Ready, Set, Go

2

Before You Get Started

In this section, we outline some of the legwork that should factor into the planning and launch of your knowledge-based initiative. If your work has already moved beyond those stages, these exercises will still be useful in spotting gaps that need to be addressed when you, for example, want to expand your work later or form new alignments.

Key to fulfilling these pre-launch activities is your recognition that understanding how you got where you are, what is about to change, and the overall state of your firm is necessary for your success. You will also evaluate the current state and perception of Knowledge Management inside your firm.

Common Misconceptions

Newcomers to large implementations do not always recognize that the world as they know it, organizationally, may change significantly when they are no longer in pilot/idea mode but implementation mode. For examples see Table 2-1.

Some common misconceptions include:

I already had to appear at committee and PMO meetings to get approval for my pilot, so I don't have to get approval for implementation. You probably do. What is true at one level may not be true at others. If your work started, for example, at a state level and it is now moving to regional or national, there may be additional entities you need approval from. If you have already engaged with committees and your PMO, you have a head start and at least know who to ask.

I did something similar a year ago, so things will work the same way now. How things worked in previous projects, other jobs, or the same organization six months ago may not matter anymore. Rules in corporations can change quickly

TABLE 2-1 Analyzing your momentum, implications, and action items

Momentum Factor	Implications and Action Items
An executive bought into your initiative, and suddenly doors started to open	Is this executive your executive sponsor? Have you approached them? If so, what support do they provide you? Did the doors that opened do so willingly, or did you encounter resistance?
This initiative was thoroughly planned; you followed process, and funding and approvals came through as expected	You probably have a strong PMO or procedural presence in your organization. Make sure you know all the ins and outs so that you continue to navigate effectively
One or more business partners recognized the value of your solution and is eager to participate	You have ready-made fodder to tie your solution into current business needs since you are partnering with business people. More than likely, the number of participants and scope of your work is increasing. Is the business partner fully, or partially, funding your work? What organizational alignment will this allow you to demonstrate?
A new internal business imperative has focused attention on a problem your solution helps address	For example, if the new business imperative is to reduce travel cost, and your solution helps teams collaborate remotely, you will need to put the structure in early to harvest results that can translate into ROI
An external force, such a new legislation or an industry scandal, has focused attention on a problem your solution helps address	Educate yourself on the external pressure and investigate what other companies in similar situations have done to address it. You may uncover hidden opportunities, best practices, or landmines

and with little notice. Has your company, division, Information Technology (IT), or PMO reorganized? Has there been significant merger activity, a leadership turnover, or legislation that affects your industry lately?

I got dozens of approvals just to pilot my work – that means I'm clear to implement if the pilot succeeds, right? The sign-off you had to pilot your solution may not carry weight – and least not all the weight you need – in actual implementation. In some corporations, the rules around what you can pilot are significantly looser than the rules around what you can implement.

No one felt my pilot violated compliance, so there are not concerns about implementing it later. Compliance rules may be different from pilot to implementation, as well. A solution that was allowed to pilot – for example, perhaps a form of knowledge sharing using wireless technology – may raise new compliance concerns once you try to implement it. Make sure you know how it works in your firm.

Understanding Your Momentum

If you are on the verge of launching your knowledge-based initiative, somewhere along the way you gained momentum. Understanding that momentum – how you got where you are now – is key to your continued success.

The allies you made, the hot buttons you touched, and the synergy between your initiative and your company's current challenges need to remain foremost in your mind as you prepare to build, then deploy, your initiative.

Take a moment, and jot down the elements that changed in the course of your work and brought you to this point. Some likely candidates are:

- An executive bought into your initiative, and suddenly doors started to open.
- This initiative was thoroughly planned; you followed process, and funding and approvals came through as expected.
- One or more business partners recognized the value of your solution and want to participate.
- A new internal business imperative has focused attention on a problem your solution helps address.
- An external force, such a new legislation or an industry scandal, has focused attention on a problem your solution helps address.

Why does this matter?

As you start to plot out the who, how, and when of your initiative, all these factors come into play. You not only need to understand the momentum factor, but the implications, and resulting actions items.

By building this list, you will identify many momentum factors and associated implication items. Isolating and understanding the momentum your initiative has gained is the key to being able to isolate the change factors that are in play. Fully understanding the change factors that will result from moving your knowledge-based initiative forward will help you conquer your prime challenge as we have defined it: engaging all concerned entities proactively to ensure your success.

Isolating Change Factors

When momentum changes, boundaries do too. They have most likely expanded. Which boundaries are changing around your work? We explore likely candidates below, but remember to think through how your own organization works for the most comprehensive list.

Participation

Is the number of people using your solution increasing? Is the number of business units, regions, or divisions that will use your solution increasing as well?

What this means to you. In some organizations, once participant numbers reach a certain threshold, the rules can change, particularly around compliance and standards. For example, in one organization we know of, if more than 3,000 people are using a certain technology, by corporate governance it must become a standard.

In addition, different business units, regions, or divisions may have numbers-driven triggers. The Atlantic Region review board that did not care about your knowledge-based initiative when 40 people were participating may need to review it when 400 people are.

Do you have any numbers-driven thresholds in your organization? Look at all levels: location, regional, business unit, national, and global.

Standards

Has any element of your work been declared a standard, or will it need to be? For example, if there is a technology component involved in your knowledge-based initiative, is that technology new to the company? If your work is partially defined by streamlining or instituting a new process, will that become a standard?

What this means to you. Your work may have gained a degree of stability in the organization if it is become a corporate standard; this is a check mark in the longevity column of your initiative. As mentioned earlier, the standards question may be number/participant driven, and it is something to be aware of.

You also need to understand which components of your work have been or will likely be declared a standard. Is it the entire activity (this is now how we share information) or a specific portion of it (we will use this technology to provide collaborative workspaces for all sales people)? This makes a difference because if the entire work, as opposed to the technology component of it, is standardized, you may find yourself dealing with different owners of the standards. Perhaps your PMO owns the new way of working with project teams, while IT owns the specific technology.

From a political aspect, be aware of competitors. If you are competing with a similar initiative, you may be engaged in a standards approval race without even knowing it. To win, your work will need to be declared a standard before the other initiative's work is. If your work triumphs and becomes a standard, it is in your best interest to involve the stakeholders in any initiatives you may have inadvertently stalled, and try to build an alliance with them.

Scope

Has your initiative expanded boundaries significantly? This question may be answered by examining the participation change factor closely. However, even if the number of participants remains relatively low, when your initiative crosses divisional, business unit, state, region, or country lines, new degrees of sign-off may be required.

What this means to you. Look for scope-based (which are frequently geography-based) entities that may have a stake in your work. Moreover, you will need to look in more than one place.

For example, if you are working with the Marketing Department on a knowledge-based initiative that has a technology component in it, first you will need to map out any marketing-specific review cycles that your corporation mandates. You will then need to also trace the review chain for the technology component. If you are in a regulated industry, you may have additional approval streams to track down.

Shared Responsibility

When any new project or initiative begins, the leader tends to serve as the hostess, waiter, cook, and bartender all in one. This is particularly the case with knowledge practitioners. We wear many hats and are comfortable cycling in and out of different roles.

When your knowledge-based initiative moves from small to large, you will have to leverage other resources for support. It may not even be your choice. As we mentioned earlier, growth in participants or scope can trigger, for example, elements of your initiative being declared a corporate standard. Once that happens, you may have an entirely new support structure that you are expected to embrace. For example, levels of support in terms of your corporate help desk or IT support may need to be instituted or increased.

What this means to you. If your solution has any element of technology in it, you will need to become well versed in how your organization's technology support is structured. By technology support, we do not necessarily mean the help desk; there are multitudes of levels of support inside large firms. For example, there are people who monitor server operations, often called the NOC, Network Operations Center.

Your help desk may or may not be affiliated with IT and may have a separate reporting structure. You may have education responsibilities or might be expected to participate within their structure as upper tier support. We examine the question of support in detail in Section IV.

Evaluating Your Company from the Outside

When you are one of thousands – or tens or hundreds of thousands – of employees, it is easy to become "niched" in your part of the corporate world. Even if you fulfill your job responsibilities fully, you may not see a clear line between your everyday activities, your company's bottom line, and the paycheck you take home every month. In other words, you may not see the big picture of your firm, its performance, and its current concerns.

Part of the big picture has to do with your organizational alignment, which we explore in detail in Section III. The other part contributes to your overall understanding of your firm's current position and challenges. Combining both viewpoints will help you uncover key opportunities to create that linkage.

In addition, as you interact with new levels of leadership, being aware of your company's position in the outside world will benefit you. It may not affect your day-to-day activities – but it certainly affects those of executives.

Expert Q&A: Joe McGhee

Joe McGhee is a veteran of driving multi-billion dollar shifts in international firms. He spoke to us about the importance of understanding your firm from the outside-in, the facts and figures that are important, and offered tips on where to find that information.

Q: *As an executive, when employees approach you, will you take them more seriously if they seem to be well-informed about the business from the outside-in?*

A: "Of course I will, no question. If you approach me with something that's not aligned with the business, at a minimum I'm subconsciously not going to be interested because my boss is saying we have to, for example, get revenue numbers up. If you approach me with something that is just a small percentage of my business, it's not that important.

"On the other hand, imagine that you position it like this: you tell me that you have a program that will help 2% of my accounts and if it works out well, we can roll it out to the rest of my accounts. That will tell me that you understand the big picture and I'll support you in your trial or pilot. It's this understanding the big picture that will differentiate how you think from your counterparts. It doesn't take a genius to know that your largest customers will always be important to the company. Anything you can do to help that, improve that relationship, maintain it, or increase revenue is something I'll take seriously. If you're smart, you'll tie all those factors into your work."

Q: *What signposts can tell a non-executive what is happening inside a company?*

A: "Pay attention to the movement of people inside any problem areas. Not only could that be a place that your solution could help – but look for job movements that are not clear promotions. Experienced executives can tell you in a minute whether a job movement is genuine, or a way of 'helping someone out.' Often, when a special position is created? It's not a real job. That hasn't changed in all the years I've been in business. Unless you know this special position or special project is critical to the organization, it can be a red flag.

"Although it may seem overwhelming, you learn this through experience, observation and listening. You learn so much more listening and observing than speaking. If you have any kind of intuition, street sense, gut feel about a situation, trust it – that's much more important than book sense. It's critical to your success."

Q: *There is so much information out there. How can a person be sure that they are looking at and listening to the right sources?*

A: "You should check the external news, check the financials, know how the last quarter went. The easiest way to do that is to look for any communication from the CEO. It will give you a very good idea of what's going on, and whether what you're trying to do is in alignment.

"The overall performance of the business will tell you a lot. Stay in tune with how the business is performing, which groups are performing well and which groups aren't. I can look at the financials and in 30 minutes, tell you how the company is performing and where the problem areas are. Use the data that is available to you, whether that's internal or external. For example, I recently saw a press release about the CEO stepping down from a company I used to work for. If you go back and read the press releases from Q1, you'll see the company's performance was down 77%. It doesn't take a Harvard MBA to understand why he's stepping down – there were many quarters of bad performance.

One source of information is your "internal news channel.' Every firm has one. Although you don't want to get caught up in the latest gossip, you should keep your ear in tune to it. Know who the gossipers are, but keep them at arm's length.

"Keep your eyes and ears attuned to the decision-making of executives and the results of those decisions. Look at the movement of executives. That will give you clear indications; you don't need gossip. Stay on the bigger picture and keep up with the financial results and press releases."

Q: *Which metrics should a person concentrate on when evaluating their company from the outside-in?*

A: "When we do financial performance reviews, executives may spend multiple hours going through 30 pages of numbers. When we issue a press release, those 30 pages will be boiled down to a couple of paragraphs. Those are the numbers you need to understand.

"You don't have to understand everything about finance, but understand the metrics your CEO or CFO constantly talks about, because those are the key metrics in your organization. Realize that even within a single organization, there are different metrics you may need to be aware of.

"Once you have a handle on what those metrics are, the next step is understanding what drives them. That's when you can make yourself a superstar."

Questions You Should be Able to Answer

You should have your finger on your company's performance pulse to the extent that, throughout the lifecycle of your initiative, you can speak knowledgeably about your firm's activities and challenges. Can you answer these questions?

Performance. How is your company doing financially? If you are publicly traded, how is your stock doing? Are you meeting goals? What do Wall Street analysts have to say about your firm? How quickly have you grown – or not grown – over recent years?

Leadership. What leadership changes have happened in the last year? Do you have new C-suite players? What, specifically, were they brought in to shore up, change, or implement? Was there a shake up, or a smooth handoff?

Rank. Where does your company rank among its competitors? Although you may find varying evaluations, are you in the top three? Bottom 50?

Goals. What are your company's publicized goals? For example, if you work in the automotive industry, is your firm's stated goal to build the safest car? The greenest car? Have the highest degree of customer service?

M&A. Has there been recent M&A (Merger and Acquisition) activity? Has your company bought other companies, or have you been bought?

Regulatory. What is happening in your company from a regulatory point of view? Are there new or existing government regulations to which your company has to conform? Are there "looming clouds" that car manufacturers, pharmaceutical firms, or insurance companies, for example, are struggling with?

Public perception. What is the public perception of your company? Are you fighting to regain consumer goodwill after a scandal, or is your firm well regarded by the public? Do your leaders intentionally keep a low corporate profile?

Broad Strokes: Where to Find What You Need

There is a multitude of public resources where you can find information on your company.

The Internet. Using your favorite search engine, key in your company and see what turns up. This seems simplistic, but may show you news articles or places your company's name appears that you are not aware of. In particular, if you work for a firm that shares good news with its employees, and little else, this exercise can be eye opening.

Pay special attention to recent mentions of your firm in online news sites. Increasingly, detailed views of such information is on a pay basis, but you should be able to view article headlines and perhaps a synopsis free of cost.

Your company's web site. Often, leadership biographies, annual reports, and press releases are published on your company's web site. If you have a dynamic, useful intranet, you may rarely visit your company's external-facing website. Incorporate regular visits into your normal routines; you may gain a new perspective. Browse through press releases and see if you can spot trends.

Corporate Communications. Check with your Corporate Communications department (be aware that there may be more than one) and request to see external-facing publications they have put together for the last 12 to 18 months. Your Corporate Communications department may also keep a "clipping file" that contains mentions of your firm. Ask if you can examine it.

Internal research personnel. Your firm may have a group that specializes in research. If so, that group probably has access to popular news aggregators, such as Factiva, and may be able to provide you with media clippings.

Financial Performance

How is your company doing financially? If you are publicly traded, company performance is public record. If you are not a financial type, you may learn best by skimming analysts' reports that you find online. Map mentions of figures back to the metrics your leadership frequently mentions. You will find financial information on the Internet, inside your company, and contained in your company's annual report.

Town meetings. Large corporations frequently hold "town meetings," although they may be called something different in your company, where leadership speaks to employees in a casual forum. Often, meetings like this address financials. Pay attention and see if you can get a copy of the presentation. Don't be afraid to ask questions.

Your manager. Particularly if you work in a well-aligned firm, your manager may be able to provide you with a thumbnail sketch of your company's financial performance and explain how all the figures work together to support your company's goals.

Your annual report. Your company also publishes an annual report. If you are a stockholder in your firm, you may receive a copy automatically. Otherwise, you may have access to an electronic company buried somewhere in your intranet. If you cannot locate your firm's annual report, stop by the executive offices and ask an administrative assistant if there is a spare copy that you can have. Do not ask to discuss it with the CFO – simply request a copy.

The Internet. There are a multitude of resources on the web that provide snapshots of firm performance and links to analyses. You will need to know the symbol that your company trades under; you can find that information using any major search engine. Then, start clicking. You may be surprised at what you find.

Evaluating the State of KM Inside Your Company

After you have critically examined your firm from the outside-in, it is time to turn your scrutiny to the perception of Knowledge Management inside your firm. You should explore the perception of these areas:

- The Knowledge Management field in general;
- The performance of past knowledge-based initiatives;
- The effectiveness of your work group;
- Your personal effectiveness.

Getting the answers to these sometimes hard-to-ask questions will help you identify potential allies, and detractors. You will also begin to spot gaps that you may need to concentrate on in your implementation.

Where do You Live?

In many firms, knowledge-based work is not centralized beneath a Knowledge Management department. Where do you fit into the organizational scheme of your company?

If you, for example, report through technology services, you may have an easier time dealing with any technology components of your solution. If you are in a business unit, you might have access to additional funds, and are probably an expert in the business problem your solution will address. Take a moment and frame "where you live" in the context of what you know intimately, and what you do not know.

If you belong to a centralized Knowledge Management department – whatever it may be named in your firm – where do you ultimately report? Is your group aligned with a particular business unit, multiple business units, or technology?

In addition, where do other knowledge practitioners in your firm report? Do you have a matrix-ed relationship with them, or no formal relationship at all? You may have knowledge practitioners in your firm who do not have that responsibility in actual job descriptions – they just do it because it is how they work. How do other knowledge practitioners fit in with your solution? If they play no formal role, should they? Are they influencers who can help you?

What is Your Work Considered?

Is the term "Knowledge Management" used inside your company? For example, in some firms, Knowledge Management is functionally equated with information management. Whatever your point of view on the terminology usage, it is beneficial to have a clear understanding of what your work is considered. An offshoot of information management? An element of organizational development or change management? An HR function? Or, an autonomous group or activity?

Does your firm have a universally agreed upon and commonly held definition of Knowledge Management? If there is a formal definition, is there an informal one as well?

How Mature is Knowledge Management in Your Firm?

Knowledge-based work was around long before the term "Knowledge Management" came into being. The question here is whether your firm explicitly recognizes knowledge-based work as a valid field in and of itself.

Is knowledge-based work stand-alone in your firm? Is your work umbrella-ed beneath other initiatives? Who owns those initiatives, and how do they fit into the larger picture of your firm? Can you plot a timeline of how Knowledge Management has evolved in your organization?

Perception of Knowledge-Based Work in Your Firm

What is the perception of knowledge-based work in your firm, even if it is not called "Knowledge Management"? Particularly, if you are in a large company, it is probable that you will find multiple perceptions. The ones you should be most concerned with are the perceptions held by people who may help – or hinder – your implementation efforts. This includes, at a minimum, PMO representatives, executives who will support your work, business units who will be your customers, support staff who will keep your initiative working behind the scenes, and technology support. If you have additional stakeholders in your company, be sure to investigate their perceptions of Knowledge Management, as well.

Take a moment and think about how your workgroup and you as an individual are regarded in the firm. Do you have a high degree of credibility and a track record of success? Or, are you a relative newcomer? Is this your first major project? Does your group have exposure throughout the firm, or do you routinely encounter people who have never heard of your group or its work?

As you answer these questions, you will begin to develop a set of action items and isolate potential areas of resistance. For example, if your work group is not well known throughout your firm, what can you do to change that? In Section VII, we offer practical guidelines to publicizing your work. If your group is regarded as, for example, a glorified training group and you need to shift that perception to help drive your initiative, how did that perception evolve, and who among your key stakeholders holds that view?

Even if this is an uncomfortable exercise, in order to counter negative or incorrect perceptions, you must uncover and confront what those perceptions are, and who holds them. The list below outlines common perceptions that can hinder your work. You may uncover additional perceptions in your firm.

Nice to have – but not a must have. People who hold this perception view knowledge-based work as a luxury, not an essential. For them, knowledge-based work is an "if we have time and resources" type of activity. Your challenge in engaging them will be to demonstrate that your work is critical, not optional.

Nothing more than a fad. Individuals who were exposed to, or perhaps bought into, the early excitement surrounding Knowledge Management may now view it as nothing more than a passing fad. To sway people with this viewpoint, explain that knowledge-based work has been around a long time; it is no fad. Point out that it is the work itself – not the label – that really matters, and be willing to relinquish the term Knowledge Management in favor of a label that may be more palatable to decision makers with this point of view.

Be aware that even if you do not have a history of failed knowledge-based initiatives at your firm, a key stakeholder may have developed this point of view at another firm. Discreetly probe to discover the roots of a perception like this. You may find that the holder is generally suspicious of all new business trends and buzzwords. Or, you may learn that the holder has previous experience with a knowledge-based project that did not succeed.

A soft discipline that does not offer quantifiable results. At the heart of dealing with people who hold this viewpoint is understanding what quantifiable means to them. You may encounter people who see business in a balance-sheet fashion, and need numbers, rather than anecdotes, to assign a value to an activity. You will also likely find individuals who will readily accept anecdotal or effectiveness-based results as valid. Tailor how you communicate to decision makers with this point of view, based on what they consider quantifiable.

An idea that has not worked here before. Does your firm have a history of failed knowledge-based initiatives? If so, you need to learn what the initiatives were, why they failed, who the key executors and stakeholders were, and be ready to demonstrate that your initiative is different.

Joe McGhee shared a story with us about how he overcame this sort of resistance at a past employer, and the importance of knowing the background of any failed initiatives. "Understand the history or your organization, your business, and your group," Joe advises. "Particularly when you encounter resistance, understand *who was involved* with that history. One area of resistance where history really matters is when you hear, 'We've already tried that, and it didn't work.' My answer to that line is that it may be the same game – but with different players."

A note of caution: as you differentiate yourself and your work from earlier unsuccessful attempts, avoid placing blame or denigrating the work of those involved in the failed project. If you are countering resistance because of a failed initiative in which you had no personal stake, you do not know first-hand what really happened. Even if you know that the initiative failed because of mismanagement or incompetence, avoid making personal comments that could be spread or misinterpreted.

Joe explained how he once overcame this type of resistance. "At a previous company, I bumped into this at a distribution center that receives broken phones and ships out replacement phones. Instead of repairing phones, which was the least expensive replacement method, the distribution center was primarily shipping out new ones – and had a negative bottom line impact of about $4 million a month. When I investigated why they were sending out so many new phones rather than more repaired phones, the answer I got was simple: we tried to increase repair production before and it didn't work."

Joe continued. "We restructured how things got done in the repair center, and within 60 days had doubled production. Instead of a negative $4 million a month impact, we quickly began having a positive $4 million a month impact. Essentially an $8 million a month swing.

Am I a genius? No. It's just that different people can make a difference. We focused our efforts. We motivated people differently. And with the existing team, we doubled production."

Joe summed up how to position yourself when you encounter decision makers who have been disappointed with past results. "The bottom line is this," Joe said. "You have to do a better job of explaining why it didn't work before, and *why it can now.*"

Section III

Organizational Alignment

3

Understanding and Mapping Organizational Alignment

No matter what type of organization you are part of, your job, ultimately, is to enhance that organization. Truly enhancing your organization – and perhaps most importantly, convincing the decision makers in your firm that your work will add value – lies largely in your ability to deliver what the organization needs at a particular moment in time.

One way to ensure that what you contribute is relevant – and that it is viewed as relevant – is to present and position your work in a way that demonstrates you are organizationally aligned with your company's vision and goals. That alignment demonstrates that your knowledge-based initiative not only meets a company need, but also is consistent with the company's timeline for action.

Depending on the size, scope, and duration of your project, finding and demonstrating alignment may be an iterative activity. A relatively small, limited project may be able to establish alignment during planning, and never need to revisit it. A large, ongoing program will need to have its alignment tweaked over the lifecycle of planning, initiation, and execution. Your company and its needs will change over time. Your project's alignment may need to shift, too.

There are dozens of popular methodologies for aligning an organization, managing and measuring alignment, and more. For example, some firms use balanced scorecards to measure and refine organizational alignment. Others do not. Even within the balanced scorecard family of methodologies, there are dozens of scorecarding frameworks. How do you know which methodologies and practices matter to you?

What is key is that you learn how alignment is regarded, instituted, and measured in your firm. You can then ensure that your work is in alignment and be ready to demonstrate that alignment.

In this section, we explore aspects of alignment that are commonly found in most large firms. As you investigate your workplace, remember to factor in alignment elements that may be unique to your firm or industry.

Do You See the Big Picture?

Take a moment and think about the goal or goals behind the implementation of your knowledge-based initiative. For example, imagine that you are leading a project designed to help two newly merged departments function more effectively. Is your entire goal to help the departments share knowledge more effectively? Is that the beginning and end of what your work supports?

If you believe it is, you are probably missing the larger picture of organizational alignment.

What an Aligned Organization Looks Like

In an aligned organization, everyone is familiar with the firm's mission, vision, goals, and beliefs and strives to support them. Regardless of seniority or position, all employees can identify how their daily activities support, for example, their firm's Mission Statement. Employee behaviors and attitudes reinforce the corporate culture, and employees embrace the methods of interacting internally and externally that are acceptable and rewarded in the organization.

Employees also prioritize work appropriately in a well-aligned organization. Organizational alignment is as much about how work gets done – and not done – as it is the goals that completing a piece of work may fulfill. Everyone speaks the same language, too.

An aligned organization offers everyone a linked and causal view of activities, both from the top-down and the bottom-up. Executives see their strategies translated and activated by the activities of their workforce. Employees understand how their work contributes to their firm's success. In addition, the softer side of culture is taken into account; everyone is playing from the same rulebook and has the same, or at least complementary, values.

Why Firms Care About Organizational Alignment

Most executives believe that organizational alignment offers their firms a competitive advantage. They gain that advantage from the effective translation of their business strategies into day-to-day activities. Effective translation means they can deliver on the promises executives have made both internally and externally.

In addition, employees flourish in an aligned organization. Knowing how one's activities add to a business' value engenders a sense of teamwork and contribution and may lead to job satisfaction. As a knowledge practitioner, you probably recognize that the importance of job satisfaction and how it is derived are part of the characteristics of knowledge workers overall.

Jane Niederberger, former CIO and VP of Operations at Wellpoint, explains. "In general, organizational alignment matters to executives because of the line of sight it offers us. If you're going to do something, you need to know how it's contributing to the overall vision of the company, because it's usually not apparent at first flush. You need to connect the dots. That means up the hierarchy, down the hierarchy, across – who knows?"

Niederberger agrees with the idea that good alignment contributes to the workplace, too. "If people understand how what they're doing ties into the vision of the business," she said, "they're more energized – and they also make better decisions. Your company's mission statement should be your 'mantra' over everything you're doing, and why you're doing it. If push comes to shove, you go back to that mission statement. It provides the guiding principle."

Alignment is not only for people on the lower rungs of the organizational hierarchy, either. It is important to remember that your alignment helps support your boss' alignment. "Executives have to align, too." Jane said. "We're accountable to the Board of Directors, or the CEO – to someone – to talk about how our work supports the business. We have to demonstrate how we're moving the strategy forward. If an activity comes out of left field with no alignment, it's hard to rally any support for it. In fact, an executive who supports an activity like that looks irresponsible – like they're supporting a hobby, rather than a real organizational initiative that will move the company, its vision, or strategy forward."

Alignment Artifacts

Behind organizational alignment are a number of "alignment artifacts" that you need to collect in your own firm. They may include the following:

- A mission statement.
- A vision statement.
- A values and beliefs statement.

The second chunk of alignment artifacts are derived from the first:

- Operating/strategic imperatives/initiatives.
- Objectives.
- Goals.

You may not find every element on the list above in your firm, and you may uncover additional artifacts depending on how your organization views and has institutionalized its own alignment. When you set out to locate the alignment artifacts in your own firm, you must look in multiple places:

- Your firm as a whole undoubtedly has its own mission statement, values and beliefs, and other alignment artifacts.
- Other areas inside your firm may also have developed their own alignment artifacts, which ideally support those of the firm overall.
- Even if, for example, your work group has not developed its own mission statement, it most likely owns or is involved in supporting one or more derivative artifacts.
- Also, look for the alignment artifacts of your internal customers' work-groups or divisions, and those of any concerned entities such as IT or your PMO.

The key is to look for a cascading relationship between the highest level vision, and the derivative goals and objectives. Then, identify the artifacts that your solution can support the fulfillment of, or fulfill in a freestanding fashion.

Demonstrable Alignment Increases Buy In

So, why does calling out how your solution supports alignment matter? Santi Kumar, Vice President at Fidelity Employer Services Company, explained. "Part of getting buy in is pitching and selling, yes," she said. "But a large part of it, if you go deeper, is in partnership, collaboration and alignment. Alignment is very key. Even if you don't collaborate every day with other areas in your firm, at some point or another, all the work you do does in fact converge. Understanding that point of convergence is paramount as there is an absolute need for the entities in a given company to align in both strategy and execution."

Demonstrating your alignment does more than prove you are a good corporate citizen. It is also a form of selling your work because it increases the chance that others will buy into it since they will be able to see more clearly how efforts/initiatives impact them.

The Mission Statement

The mission statement is the highest level, broadest statement of what your firm does and may include elements of why, for whom, and the value your firm and its activities generate. Mission statements are sometimes merged with vision statements and may have elements of values and beliefs scattered throughout. Some firms prefer short and pithy mission statements, while others may be paragraphs in length.

The company Google has a simple, yet visionary mission statement: "Google's mission is to organize the world's information and make it universally accessible and useful."[1] Note that Google's mission statement says what they do (organize information and make it accessible), who they do it for (the world), and why they do it (universal access and usefulness).

The Vision Statement

The vision statement offers the crafters' view of what things will be like when their goals are fulfilled. It is your firm's vision. Vision statements tend to be aspirational and represent how the world will be, not as it is today. Often, the vision statement or elements of it are rolled into the mission statement.

The Values and Beliefs Statement

In the values and beliefs statement, the organization spells out the values that (hopefully) permeate its members' work, including interactions with customers, suppliers, other firm members, and the public at large. Values and beliefs may be viewed as the "softer" side of organizational alignment, but are fully as important as other elements.

Elements of the values and beliefs statement may be rolled up into other alignment artifacts. In general, organizational alignment models offer two paths: strategic and management, and values and beliefs, so look for both in your organization.

Example: Ten Things Google has Found to be True

Google's values and beliefs are contained in a document named "Ten Things Google Has Found to be True." Each value and belief is described in detail, and Google offers examples of how they have, and continue to, exhibit the quality. "Ten Things Google Has Found to be True" is publicly available on the company's website.

---

[1] Used with permission of Google Inc.

Values and beliefs do more than just describe, for example, how employees of the firm will work together. Values and beliefs set the tone, both public and private, for the entire firm. Google has a unique public image that includes elements of youth, innovation, fun, customer focus, and uncompromising quality. Those themes, along with others, can be found in their values and beliefs.

Let us examine a few of Google's values and beliefs and analyze how those values and beliefs might impact project selection and activities.

1. Focus on the user and all else will follow.

From its inception, Google has focused on providing the best user experience possible. While many companies claim to put their customers first, few are able to resist the temptation to make small sacrifices to increase shareholder value. Google has steadfastly refused to make any change that does not offer a benefit to the users who come to the site:

- *The interface is clear and simple.*
- *Pages load instantly.*
- *Placement in search results is never sold to anyone.*
- *Advertising on the site must offer relevant content and not be a distraction.*

By always placing the interests of the user first, Google has built the most loyal audience on the web. And that growth has come not through TV ad campaigns, but through word of mouth from one satisfied user to another.

In this first value and belief, Google clearly states its allegiance to the customer, even at the possible expense of revenue generation. What implications might this have for someone trying to gain support for a new initiative?

- Even a potentially-profitable initiative most likely won't find support unless it offers users a clear benefit. If it negatively impacts users, if definitely would be out of alignment.
- Any sort of redesign that would muddy Google's simple, clean interface or increase page-loading time would be unlikely to gain support.

3. Fast is better than slow.

Google believes in instant gratification. You want answers and you want them right now. Who are we to argue? Google may be the only company in the world whose stated goal is to have users leave its website as quickly as possible. By fanatically obsessing on shaving every excess bit and byte from our pages and increasing the efficiency of our serving environment, Google has broken its own speed records time and again. Others assumed large servers were the fastest way to handle massive amounts of data. Google found networked PCs to be faster. Where others accepted apparent speed limits imposed by search algorithms, Google wrote new algorithms that proved there were no limits. And Google continues to work on making it all go even faster.

One reason for Google's success is, simply, how well their toolset works. Speed is a huge part of that success, and Google knows it. In this value and belief, Google isolates speed as a top priority. This compliments the first value and belief because again, the user's desire for instant answers is put first. Note how Google offers concrete examples of how it has acted on this belief compared to other companies.

It is easy to see that a project that slowed the performance of Google's solution set would be out of alignment with this value and belief.

6. You can make money without doing evil.

Google is a business. The revenue the company generates is derived from offering its search technology to companies and from the sale of advertising displayed on Google and on other sites across the web. However, you may have never seen an ad on Google. That's because Google does not allow ads to be displayed on our results pages unless they're relevant to the results page on which they're shown. So, only certain searches produce sponsored links above or to the right of the results. Google firmly believes that ads can provide useful information if, and only if, they are relevant to what you wish to find.

Google has also proven that advertising can be effective without being flashy. Google does not accept pop-up advertising, which interferes with your ability to see the content you've requested. We've found that text ads ("AdWords") that are relevant to the person reading them draw much higher clickthrough rates than ads appearing randomly. Google's maximization group works with advertisers to improve clickthrough rates over the life of a campaign, because high clickthrough rates are an indication that ads are relevant to a user's interests. Any advertiser, no matter how small or how large, can take advantage of this highly targeted medium, whether through our self-service advertising program that puts ads online within minutes, or with the assistance of a Google advertising representative.

Advertising on Google is always clearly identified as a "Sponsored Link." It is a core value for Google that there be no compromising of the integrity of our results. We never manipulate rankings to put our partners higher in our search results. No one can buy better PageRank. Our users trust Google's objectivity and no short-term gain could ever justify breaching that trust.

Here, Google fully discloses that it is a business and as such generates revenue. One way that Google creates profit is by advertising. Google has a clear point of view about what types of advertising are permissible within the framework of their beliefs. The firm describes in detail advertising tactics it will not use – popups, irrelevant links, advertisements disguised as search results, or advertiser promotion in search results – and essentially make a promise to users that it will not breach the agreement contained in its values and beliefs statement. Taking this and other nuances that can be gleaned from the statement above into account, it is logical to believe that a proposed project or initiative that impinged on any of these promises would not be welcomed.

In fact, any initiative that would nudge Google away from its current advertising stance and closer to "evil" would be grossly out of the firm's alignment. Likewise, anything that would negatively impact the end user's ability to clearly view search results would probably not make it past the idea stage.

9. You can be serious without a suit.

Google's founders have often stated that the company is not serious about anything but search. They built a company around the idea that work should be challenging and the challenge should be fun. To that end, Google's culture is unlike any in corporate America, and it's not because of the ubiquitous lava lamps and large rubber balls, or the fact that the company's chef used to cook for the Grateful Dead. In the same way Google puts users first when it comes to our online service, Google Inc. puts employees first when it comes to daily life in our Googleplex headquarters. There is an emphasis on team achievements and pride in individual accomplishments that contribute to the company's overall success. Ideas are traded, tested and put into practice with an alacrity that can be dizzying. Meetings that would take hours elsewhere are frequently little more than a conversation in line for lunch and few walls separate those who write the code from those who write the checks. This highly communicative environment fosters a productivity and camaraderie fueled by the realization that millions of people rely on Google results. Give the proper tools to a group of people who like to make a difference, and they will.

In this value and belief, Google positions itself as unconventional in many ways. While the statement does not belittle corporate America, it is clear that Google's culture does not include an emphasis on hierarchy, process for the sake of process, meeting for the sake of meetings, a corporate dress code, or any other corporate trapping that could slow the speed at which they like to move.

One takeaway of this value and belief is that Google may not be the best fit for people or initiatives that are overly hierarchically or process oriented. The statement also makes it clear that Google leadership expects hard work and lots of it from their employees – but they also believe that work can be fun and have built their teams around people who share that belief. Taken a step further, one could surmise that their unconventional culture has added to their success.

This statement also sets anyone straight who might confuse unconventional with unprofessional, unproductive, or unprofitable. It is also clear that Google values diversity among its employees and recognizes both team and individual accomplishments.

Operating Imperatives, Goals, and Activities

As you move from the boardroom to management levels, operating imperatives, goals, and activities are established. You may have some or all of these elements in your firm; much depends on how your firm institutionalizes organizational alignment. The thing to remember is that everything cascades down from the highest levels and that in an aligned organization, lower levels must support one or more of the alignment artifacts in the higher levels.

Goals describe the "how and who" of an activity that will support the firm's overall mission, its vision, and/or its values and beliefs. Goals may include a numerical measure that will allow them to be evaluated for success. For example, a goal might be to increase customer satisfaction by 20% in the new fiscal year. Assuming that baseline figures for customer satisfaction are available, and a vehicle to monitor customer satisfaction exists and has been recognized as valid by your leadership, the success of this goal would be fairly simple to evaluate. The success of other goals may be harder to quantify, such as a goal to become the employer of choice or the leader in breakthrough technology.

Goals, in turn, spawn activities. Activities may be called action plans, projects, or initiatives, but they are simply a more granular view, through an implementation lens, of a goal. If a goal is to increase customer satisfaction by 20%, the action plan that supports that goal would include activities designed to accomplish that. Perhaps customer satisfaction would increase if response time to support requests decreased. Alternatively, perhaps customer satisfaction would increase if the amount of free support offered by a company increased.

Mapping from Top-Down or Bottom-Up

You should be able to draw a clear line, from the bottom-up (from your initiative all the way up to the mission statement) or from top-down (from the mission statement to your everyday activities) that shows how both are linked and your work supports your organization's missions and goals. To illustrate, we will use a fictitious medical supplies firm, Acme Medical Supplies, as an example.

Example: *Acme Medical Supplies*

First, examine Acme's alignment artifacts.

Acme Medical Supplies' mission statement: To become the preeminent source of medical supplies and equipment to doctors and hospitals in the Midwest, known for superior customer service and the best pricing.

Acme's vision statement: By 2015, Acme Medical Supplies will triple our distribution base and double current sales, thereby increasing shareholder value and decreasing costs to our customers, and ultimately, consumers.

Acme's values and beliefs: We demand honesty and integrity in all customer dealings, pricing and support. We honor our commitments and believe that serving our customers is everyone's job. Cooperation, respect, and diversity shape our workplace.

Let us focus on Acme's vision statement. Acme plans to expand in the near future, including doubling sales to existing customers, and tripling its distribution footprint. From the vision of doubling sales to existing companies, a number of operating imperatives/strategic initiatives may be established. Among them, for example, might be:

- Retain and grow current customers.
- Achieve and maintain superlative levels of customer service.

However, Acme has a problem: customer retention. Until it can keep its customers, it will be unable to fulfill its mission or vision statement. Acme leadership has identified multiple root causes of their poor customer retention, including the following:

- Some customers follow price; levels of customer service do not matter.
- Most customers that leave do so because of poor customer service, including the following:
  - ☐ Call center representatives (CSRs) give incorrect or incomplete answers, necessitating multiple calls and involvement of Account Representatives. Doing business with Acme is not easy.
  - ☐ Excessive hold times cause customers to hang up.
  - ☐ Navigating the automated customer service menu is tricky and frustrating; there is no opt-out to get to a live person.
- Callbacks by promised dates frequently slip.
- Fulfillment and contract terms are not coordinated with what sales representatives promise when they are in the field calling on customers.

To help combat the customer retention issues, leadership forms a Customer Service Center of Excellence. A number of projects are spawned beneath the Center of Excellence, and your team is called in to evaluate the knowledge atmosphere of the call center.

You uncover the fact that four different call centers recently merged, and they are still using different software systems. Your first "big find" is that there is no common knowledge base, which partially explains why customers are receiving differing and therefore inaccurate answers. There is a larger cultural element at play, though. Little change management was taken into account when the teams merged, and roles and responsibilities were not clearly defined. Frustrated, a number of senior call center reps resigned; the remaining reps have had three different managers in the last six months. To top if off, even before all these changes, call center training was minimal.

You are asked to view these issues through a knowledge lens and investigate solutions. The creation of a shared knowledge base by cleansing and integrating the four existing ones is a planned project, but management knows that is only part of the solution. Because much institutional knowledge recently left Acme in the form of attrition, you recommend immediately engaging key players in an intensive knowledge sharing effort. You also recommend that HR be involved to put some parameters around actions they can take to halt or slow the attrition. Your well-liked and visible executive sponsor agrees to own strong, direct, and supportive communications to the CSRs. You also have this executive's pledge to follow up on all unfulfilled promises to the call center reps, such as offering training and clear career paths. Your project is named "Call Center Integration" and encompasses multiple workstreams.

So, what does your project support? Does it just support helping the Call Center reps work together more effectively? Examine Figure 3-1.

- Your knowledge-based project supports the mission statement, because it will help Acme become known for superior customer service.
- It is aligned with the vision statement because Acme wants to double current sales. To do that, Acme must improve current customer service levels.
- You support Acme values and beliefs because the people-focused aspect of your project engenders cooperation and respect and emphasizes the value that serving customers is everyone's job.
- There is an element of integrity and honesty in Acme Medical Supplies recognizing that it is responsible for the faulty answers customers sometimes receives, and taking steps to remedy that.
- Finally, you support two operating imperatives: retain and grow current customers, and achieve and maintain superlative levels of customer service.

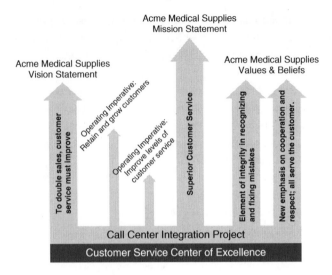

Figure 3-1 Linking a knowledge-based initiative with Acme's Alignment Artifacts.

Why it Pays to Map Backwards

You can certainly identify the goal of your project or initiative and its immediate scope. Why bother mapping your activities back to the highest level?

- You will likely be engaging with executives who are not aware of your initiative or project. As part of telling your story, creating an alignment linkage in their minds not only demonstrates your awareness of the firm's larger challenges and vision, thereby adding to your credibility, but helps them place your work in the context of their challenges.
- There are probably executive owners or champions of the strategic imperatives – as well as other items – from whom you may be able to get support.
- You will identify multiple candidates for alignment, which is valuable even if at the beginning of your initiative, you may not need, or be able to support every potential constituent with your solution. If you plan to later expand your work, mapping backwards will help you identify new potential customers.
- If you map out all the other initiatives and projects that support the same alignment artifacts that your work supports, you may find synergies – or competitors. As you identify other projects similar to your own, find out implementation timelines. In Chapter 9, we discuss project negotiations

that may happen behind the scenes; it pays to map out potential partners early on.

- As part of your organizational processes to secure funding or support, you may be required to explicitly identify your organizational alignment.

At the beginning of this section, we stated that if you viewed your project as the beginning and end – a completely self-contained activity – you were probably missing the larger picture of organizational alignment. If you follow the processes outlined here, you should now be able to link your work to a much larger vision than just your own.

Likely Candidates for Alignment with Knowledge-Based Initiatives

After this exercise, you can hopefully demonstrate a degree of alignment from your project all the way up to your firm's mission statement, and back down again. When you examine alignment artifacts from the derivative levels down, you may be able to identify more potential customers or constituents than you can possibly support in your current state. Even so, it is to your benefit to investigate areas you can potentially align with.

Budgets change; challenges change; leadership changes. With each change, your customers' alignment may change too, necessitating a shift in their activities. That shift may result in a reprioritization of their participation in your knowledge-based solution. In addition, over time, you may want to expand your work. Returning to this exercise will help you locate likely candidates to replace a former customer, or become a new one.

As you know, the breadth of knowledge-based solutions is wide, and in *Managing Knowledge-Based Initiatives*, we do not argue what qualifies as knowledge-based or not. With that in mind, here are some places you should look when scouting for potential alignment partners.

Collaboration and Knowledge Sharing

If your tool has a collaborative focus, whether that be bringing together disparate groups or helping already-related workgroups collaborate over geographic distances, you may find a fit around a value and belief that espouses the importance of collaboration and/or knowledge sharing.

Reduced Administrative Expense

Many firms have key metrics that include administrative expense. Typically, firms want to reduce administrative expense to increase profit. The exact formulas will vary, but some focus on reduction of administrative expense is desirable in every firm. It make take the form of reduced travel – which can arguably support a focus on collaboration – or, a reduction in any sort of activity that is coded, for example, in time cards as "administrative expense." Think about what sort of activities count as "administrative" in your firm.

For example, in one firm that we investigated, a group of sales leaders spread across the United States spent four hours on the phone every Monday morning approving change requests that came in from field representatives. In this firm, internal meetings are considered an administrative activity.

Approximately 90% of the requests that were discussed on the weekly call could be "rubber-stamped"; they did not require in-depth discussion. The remaining 10% of requests were complex. Using an existing collaboration tool that was built and deployed beneath the umbrella of the Knowledge Management team, a simple workflow was instituted that allowed routine requests to be approved or denied on-line in an asynchronous fashion. The 10% of complex requests were the only things discussed at the Monday morning meetings, which were reduced from four hours to 90 minutes. Eventually, the change control meetings began occurring every other week, rather than every week. Aggregated across all attendees, most of whom held management positions, the amount of time spent on this administrative activity decreased by more than half.

In this case, the use of the knowledge-based tool offered the Sales group a quantifiable reduction in administrative expense, which was in alignment with their organization's goals. In addition, a clear ROI opportunity presented itself not only to the Knowledge Management team, but also to the Sales leaders who backed the institution of the new tool.

Efficiency

If you find an alignment artifact that emphasizes the need for increased efficiency – which may be intended to reduce administrative expense, or potentially increase value to shareholders or improve customer service – see if you have a tool or methodology that enhances efficiency within your knowledge-based solution set.

Protection of Firm Assets

Frequently after an asset "scare," whether in your firm, a related company or your industry, businesses place an increased importance on protecting firm assets. If your knowledge-based solution helps your firm protect its intellectual assets in any way, you may have uncovered a new alignment.

For example, if you are developing a mentoring program designed to connect soon-to-be-retired leaders with junior staff with the goal of passing on learnings, you are protecting firm assets. Likewise, if you are focused on the data side and establishing any sort of repository, you are arguably helping to protect firm assets as well.

Disaster Recovery

Knowledge-based solutions can find strong alignment with disaster recovery initiatives. There is a large difference between being able to recover all the data a company has archived compared to being able to recover the critical data a company needs in order to operate. Is your solution suited to an alignment with a disaster recovery initiative?

Increased Project Governance

A common business imperative in today's market is the need for increased governance to ensure that businesses are tackling the right issues and allocating funds and resources in the most judicious way. One way that firms do this is through the institution of PMOs. Although we will explore the world of PMOs in depth later in *Managing Knowledge-Based Initiatives*, does your knowledge-based solution have any element that would lend itself to a consistent project experience?

Merging of Cultures

Has your firm recently undergone any merger and acquisition (M&A) activity, or a significant reorganization that is forcing disparate groups to fold into one? If so, there may be an opportunity to find new alignment if your knowledge-based initiative includes elements of culture sharing, knowledge pooling or recognition. Sometimes, cultural issues can be addressed by something as simple as an exercise to ensure that everyone speaks the same language. Perhaps there are process gaps that could be filled by creative storytelling, formal knowledge-sharing sessions, or a flavor of a technology solution.

Enhancing the Customer Experience

Price is not the only thing that drives consumer purchases or loyalty; the entire customer experience matters. Chances are good that your knowledge-based solution is not outwards facing, but could it support the people who in turn support your customers? Think about Call Center staff, sales people, and the marketing department for possibilities.

Competitive Intelligence

Some believe that Competitive Intelligence (CI), as a field, has little to do with Knowledge Management; others believe that CI is a subset of KM. Still others believe the reverse is true. Without quibbling over definitions, nearly everyone can agree that CI relies on gathering, synthesizing, and then putting information into an actionable vehicle or form. Sounds a lot like Knowledge Management, doesn't it?

If you do not have an area in your firm that you can easily identify as CI, look for groups that are concerned with strategy. In addition, many marketing or sales functions have CI embedded in their processes.

When Organizational Alignment is a Challenge

In our make-believe organization, Acme Medical Supplies, it was easy to see how elements of a project designed to enhance customer service mapped back to every level, demonstrating our fictitious knowledge-based solution's alignment. In a real company, things may not be that simple.

Common challenges around organizational alignment include firms that are poorly aligned as a whole, divisions that are not clearly aligned with a larger firm alignment schema, and how to position your work if it does not seem to be aligned with your firm's stated alignment artifacts.

How Aligned is Your Organization?

Your success at demonstrating the organizational alignment of your knowledge-based initiative depends partially on how aligned your own firm is. Instituting or driving alignment probably is not in your purview, unless you manage a group of people and can help them see how their daily activities support your organization as a whole. Even then, the linkage that you need to create for your team must be cascaded to you from higher levels. If executives are not cascading that alignment or ensuring that it is institutionalized, it will be a challenge for you to align your team.

The larger challenge will be how to align your knowledge-based initiative with an unaligned organization.

Seeking Alignment in the Unaligned Organization

If you work for a large organization that is in poor alignment, the first thing to keep in mind is that the lack of alignment is likely a temporary state. As a business fundamental, it is probable that alignment is not going to be ignored forever.

Questions to ask include the following:

- Has the firm historically paid little attention to alignment?
- Are there abundant alignment artifacts in place – which everyone ignores?
- Have significant changes recently caused alignment to drop in priority?
- Do portions of your organization seem to have strong, clear alignment, while others do not?
- Have you heard rumblings about alignment or organizational restructuring lately? Keep in mind that it may not be referred to as alignment in your organization and organizations sometimes restructure in an attempt to drive alignment.
- Is there an assigned person or team that is in charge of alignment?

If you determine that your organization is in a period of flux, then you can anticipate that formal alignment is going to occur in the future. In the interim, determine whether you need to pursue other avenues of alignment. Depending on your situation, your executive sponsor should play a leading role in this exercise.

Do You Need Alternative Alignment?

The factors that determine whether you need to pursue additional or alternative alignment include the following:

- Will additional alignment help you secure funding?
- Will additional alignment help your knowledge-based initiative receive the priority it needs to be executed?

- Will additional alignment ensure that your work has the degree of visibility it needs?
- Will additional alignment ensure that your knowledge-based solution will actually be used?

If you answered "yes" to any of these items, then you will need to seek alignment with centers of power at your firm.

Identifying Centers of Power at Your Firm

Because you have already evaluated your company from the inside-out and the outside-in, you have a good idea of your firm's financial state, know about recent leadership shifts, and have an idea who is – and is not – in favor right now.

The aspects of power that you need to be concerned about fall loosely into two categories: funding and influence. Which alignments can help you get the funding you need? Are there additional alignments that will help your work actually happen?

Behind every powerful group are individuals who drive that group. Identifying first the groups, and then the individuals who control, manage, or influence them, will point you in the right direction.

Some likely candidates are:

- Individual executives.
- High level committees.
- Business units, which will ultimately be driven by a smaller group of people.
- Segments of a PMO.

Once you identify a center of power that you need to align with, you must evaluate that center of power to determine whether it has generated alignment artifacts outside of the larger organization. For example, does it have its own mission statement, vision statement, or publicized goals and initiatives?

If not, demonstrating alignment with a center of power will essentially be a sales exercise, consisting of demonstrating how your tool with benefit that group. This is slightly different than demonstrating your knowledge-based initiative's value to an entity that has sign-off on the implementation of your tool but is not directly impacted in other ways. In this case, you will be offering your solution set for consideration and directly asking for their support in the form of funding or influence.

We discuss developing your value proposition in Section V, and offer guidelines around interacting with executives and publicizing your work throughout *Managing Knowledge-Based Initiatives*.

If Your Alignment is not Clear

If you work at a well-aligned firm, have followed the activities outlined here, and still cannot determine how your knowledge-based project aligns within your firm, there are two possibilities:

- Your initiative truly is out of alignment – depending on the state of your firm, this could be acceptable.
- You are missing a part of the picture, most likely somewhere around the strategic initiative part of the hierarchy.

The first place you should go for clarification is your immediate supervisor, or executive sponsor. If he or she cannot clarify how you align, go a level or two higher. Locate a peer who has executed similar initiatives that may be able to guide you. If you have a good relationship with members of one or more of your firm's PMOs, engage them as well.

When Non-Alignment May Be Acceptable

Earlier, we discussed the importance of knowing your firm from the inside-out and outside-in. If your firm, or its industry, is in the midst of significant change – and you work or are sponsored by a champion of that change – your initiative may appear to be out of alignment, while it is actually designed to nudge the firm in a direction leadership supports.

Executive Point of View: Michael Jackman

Michael Jackman, General Manager of Healthcare Information Systems and a Corporate Officer for Eastman Kodak Companies, explained his point of view on how a non-aligned initiative may work in a firm and as an executive, why he might support it.

"I *would* consider an initiative that's not clearly aligned," Jackman said. "It's better when everything is aligned; that would be the perfect world. But there are organizations, depending on the stage they are in, that are stuck in the mud; have something wrapped around the axle. They might be very resistant to change and change requires breaking through and completely rethinking things. Even if a portion of the organization isn't aligned, it might be the thing to drive. As part of effective change management, you have to pick the *right* thing."

Jackman continued. "For example, look at manufacturing. Imagine that man-ufacturing positions are moving from the US to China. Factories in the US cer-tainly are not aligned. But perhaps that decision is necessary. The move means the company can compete, or survive. Things like that are 'breakthrough' and some times you have to try things that aren't in alignment throughout the organization."

If your executive sponsor is a visible change-agent throughout your organi-zation, your non-alignment could be part of a larger plan. Do not be afraid to engage him or her and ask for clarification. We dive into how to work with executive sponsors in Section IV.

Section IV

Support: Who is on Your Side?

4

Executive Sponsorship and Network Building

Having a strong executive sponsor, like many of the other elements that we identify in *Managing Knowledge-Based Initiatives*, is key to getting your knowledge-based work off the ground, and once launched, being able to continue it from year to year. The right sponsor can help your knowledge-based initiative in the following ways:

- Getting or keep funding.
- Gaining buy in from other executives.
- Guiding you through tricky political waters.
- Ensuring your work achieves and maintains a level of priority.
- Strategizing about positioning and growth.
- Generating publicity and other visibility.
- Identifying and win new clients.
- Negotiating with stakeholders for concessions when needed.

Of course, you are involved with your executive sponsor to some degree in most of these activities. Don't expect your sponsor to do it alone.

Cooperative Executive or Executive Sponsor?

No matter what path your knowledge-based initiative has taken to reach the point of execution, executive cooperation, if not overt sponsorship, factors in somehow. Even if your work is entirely grassroots, someone is paying your salary. In fact, if your work is grassroots in nature, the chances are greater that you haven't actually negotiated with an executive to be your sponsor. You might be aligned beneath a cooperative boss who happens to be an executive. The problem is that a cooperative executive is significantly different from a true executive sponsor.

Even if executive cooperation as opposed to executive sponsorship got you this far, you should:

- Actively harvest other executive support; you can never have too much.
- Transform your current cooperative executive into an enthusiastic supporter, or seek out a true executive sponsor.

Telling the Difference

Answer the following questions to help determine whether you are positioned with a cooperative executive, or a true executive sponsor.

- Have you had a "Will you be my executive sponsor?" conversation?
- Does the executive understand what you are trying to do, and believe it is the right thing for the company?
- Has the executive helped you with funding, resources, or priority?
- Is the executive available to you within reasonable timelines?
- Does the executive follow up on his or her commitments to you?
- Is your knowledge-based initiative a priority – perhaps not the highest priority, but at least on the list – with the executive?
- Does the executive speak of your work publicly?
- Does the executive publicly acknowledge your involvement in the work?
- Does the executive publicly acknowledge his or her involvement in your work?
- Does the executive coach you on how to approach delicate situations?
- Does the executive speak candidly with you about situations such as politics or funding?
- Does the executive listen to your point of view and suggestions?
- Is the executive senior enough, or well-aligned enough, to make things happen?

If you answered no to a significant number of the items above, you may be dealing with a cooperative executive or reluctant executive sponsor rather than a true executive sponsor. To learn more about approaching an executive to serve as your sponsor, read on.

Degrees of Sponsorship

You may also be in a situation where your "day to day operational sponsor" is not your executive sponsor at all, but is fulfilling the day-to-day obligations on behalf of your genuine executive sponsor. Particularly in large corporations, this is not unusual, so do not feel completely defeated if you do not even know your "on paper" executive sponsor. It is up to you to turn a situation like this into a positive.

Reaching Up and Out to a Remote Executive Sponsor

Even if the sponsor relationship continues to be largely executed by someone else, your ultimate executive sponsor should know who you are, the problem or issue that your knowledge-based initiative will address, and understand the leadership that you are contributing to the initiative.

Get over your reluctance to reach up and out. If you do not let the executive know about your involvement, how will he or she be able to support you or your work later? This includes both personal support and support for knowledge-based work in general. Even if your daily sponsor is passing on key tidbits of information about your work, they are probably positioned as one item among many.

Involve the appropriate people in the reporting chain. Do not reach up and out by stepping on your daily sponsor's shoulders – or toes. Ask for an introduction and opportunity to debrief with the executive sponsor. If it does not happen the first time you ask, keep asking; there is every possibility the executive is the scheduling problem, not your daily sponsor. Ask if you can begin copying the executive on relevant reports, which should be high level metrics of your progress. Make your daily sponsor feel confident that you will make him or her look good in front of the executive.

Remember, no one cares about your knowledge-based work as much as you do. Through no ill intentions, your story may not be passed on to your executive sponsor correctly or in its totality if it comes second or third hand from someone else. Forming a direct relationship with your executive sponsor ensures that he or she knows the whole story.

Reach up and out through as many channels as you can. Strike up a conversation with your executive sponsor's assistant. Contact other people who work directly for the executive, or have done project work for him or her in the past. Let them know you would welcome an opportunity to debrief the executive on your work and ask their advice. See if you can find "accidental" meeting opportunities. For more information on selling your work, including real life success stories that include examples of how an executive's curiosity was piqued, see Section VII.

As you publicize your work, publicize the sponsorship too. Your mentions of the executive's sponsorship will get back to the executive.

What do You Know About Your Executive Sponsor?

Just as we advise that you conduct landscape surveys about the perception of knowledge-based work, your reputation, and the firm overall, you should also survey your executive sponsor. What you discover may encourage you to seek additional executive support, help you work more effectively with a current sponsor, or persuade you to look for a completely different sponsor.

Why Your Sponsor Fills that Role

Why is your current executive sponsor your sponsor? The answer to this question may well form the unpinning of your relationship with your executive sponsor. There are several possibilities.

By default. In a case like this, a person is serving as your executive sponsor because he or she sits somewhere in the reporting chain above you. This is not necessarily a bad thing, as long as you form or cultivate a genuine sponsorship relationship.

You initiated the relationship. This is one of the strongest of all executive sponsor relationships, because you actively reached out to an executive who in turn accepted the responsibility of sponsorship and everything associated with it. A relationship like this generally implies that the executive has a level of understanding and excitement about your work and your ability to execute it.

The executive initiated the relationship. Although rare, this happens particularly when an initiative falls in line with an area an executive has a degree of passion about. We have also seen it occur when a relatively young executive spots a project that has large potential to positively impact the organization and wants to be associated with it. This relationship is positive for all the reasons mentioned above. The key is for you to try to understand why they approached you. If it is simply for visibility and association with a successful project, you need to be aware of that. It is not a bad thing, but you should know if they do not hold a genuine passion for knowledge-based work. This type of relationship is vulnerable if the initiative results do not pan out exactly as the executive anticipated, so be sure and nail down the details.

They were assigned. This is the weakest of all executive sponsorship relationships because it implies that neither party had a choice. We have seen this happen multiple times when a high level executive, such as someone in the C-suite, chooses to pursue a project or initiative, but does not have the capacity to be a hands-on executive sponsor. There are multitudes of reasons a relationship like this may be difficult. For example:

- Funding that you need from your sponsor's reserves may bump another project he or she wants to pursue off the table.
- He or she may genuinely have no interest in what you are trying to do.
- He or she may not have the capacity to really get involved in your work.
- He or she may feel bullied into taking on your project.

An assigned relationship can work, but it is probably founded on shaky ground. If you find yourself in a relationship like this, look for signs of reluctance and actively seek opportunities to get your sponsor involved in positive ways. As always, keep an eye open for other executives you can involve at any level. Over time, one of them may grow into the ideal executive sponsor.

Take a moment and think through the history of your relationship with your executive sponsor.

Resources and Influence

Does your executive sponsor bring resources or special areas of influence to the table? For example:

Headcount. How large is your executive sponsor's staff? At some point, you may need to borrow or barter headcount. It is also a good idea to know about any specialized skills that could be useful which reside in your executive sponsor's reporting structure. For example, if your knowledge-based initiative will require significant training, do any instructional designers report up through your sponsor?

Sign-off limits. What is your executive sponsor's sign-off limits? You should be aware of this because it tells you how far up the food chain you must go to get approval to spend money. It is possible, too, that your executive sponsor may not actually be the person to sign off on any expenditures you make; get the answer to this question early on.

Committees. Does your executive sponsor lead or participate in influential committees? For example, if your executive sponsor chairs the prioritization committee that determines which work happens when, this could be a very good thing for you.

Connections. Who does your executive sponsor report to, and how far removed is your executive sponsor from C-suite influence? Does he or she have well-known affiliations with people in positions of power in your firm?

The Buzz

What is the "grapevine" buzz about your executive sponsor? Even if you disregard or disbelieve everything the rumor mill has to say about your executive sponsor, it is valuable to understand how he or she may be perceived in your firm.

Some common perceptions to look out for include the following:

- **Heir apparent.** The heir apparent is the person that everyone believes is next in line for leadership. Heir apparents often work for someone who is approaching retirement, or is about to be promoted. They may work below or parallel to someone who is on the way out for other reasons.
- **Rising star.** Rising stars have a solid, if young, record of accomplishment behind them.
- **Key player.** A key player is solid in his or her position and has been regarded as a go-to person for some period of time. Key players might not have as much flash or popularity as a rising star, but may be more reliable.
- **Short timer.** A short timer is a person who is leaving the firm soon, whether voluntarily or involuntarily.
- **Teacher's pet.** A teacher's pet in the corporate world is not much different than in the classroom. The teacher's pet is clearly a favorite, and people may whisper (correctly or incorrectly) that the pet's promotions or plum assignments are solely because of favoritism.

There are dozens of other categories into which your executive sponsor may fall. One of our executives, Joe McGhee, advised, "Ask questions. Ask them about people. You want to know who is not in a solid position – not being seen in a good light – right now. They could be on their way out and you probably don't want to align with them."

Negotiating Executive Give and Take

As you approach building a relationship with your executive sponsor, it is important to remember that you are forming a business-based association. It may become a relationship characterized by personal good will, but business is at its core. Therefore, you need to negotiate exactly what your executive sponsor will do for you, and what you are expected to do for your executive sponsor.

If you do not think that executive sponsorship is a negotiation process, but rather one where you should just "take what is offered" then be sure to read the interviews from multiple executives at the end of this section. You will see that each person has a slightly different point of view about what executive sponsorship means. You will also see that they value strong communication and leadership skills. Although there is a tone and method for communicating appropriately with executives – and what is right for one person is not necessarily right for all – do not be afraid to ask direct questions.

Which Areas Will Your Executive Sponsor Help With?

There are many areas where your executive sponsor may potentially assist – but every relationship is different. Not only will your needs vary according to your personality, skills, seniority, and project requirements, but your company may have its own culture around sponsorship that is different from models you have encountered before, or we describe here.

Concept Development

You may have a great idea – but as multiple executives interviewed in *Managing Knowledge-Based Initiatives* point out, they expect to help refine and expand initiatives that they sponsor. Not only will your ideas take on new life when coupled with input from your executive sponsor, but they will also become increasingly bulletproof to skepticism, criticism, or pushback.

Funding

What role does your executive sponsor play in funding your work? Does he or she provide the money to get started, assume all costs, or partner with you in raising the funds you will need? Does your executive sponsor have any funding approval rights over your work?

Politics

Throughout *Managing Knowledge-Based Initiatives*, we encourage you to seek out and identify the entities that have influence over your work. Your executive sponsor can help as you locate, engage, and perhaps struggle with various boards, committees, and individuals. Sometimes, that support may be overt; other times, it may be as simple as explaining the behind the scenes maneuvers that you are not aware of.

As the former CIO of Anthem (now Wellpoint), Jane Niederberger believes that the political savvy your executive sponsor can provide is crucial, particularly if you are new to the arena. "The reality is that companies are very political, and you're naïve if you don't take that into account," Niederberger said. "You could be stepping on toes and not even know it, or walk on a landmine and have no clue it's even there. Your executive sponsor can play a role here. For example, I might say, 'You know, that is a good idea – but the people who head up that area have a lot on their plate right now. Instead, we'll approach another team for now, because that's where you can make real headway.'" In other words, Jane will steer a protégée away from a group that she knows cannot participate or a situation that she suspects might turn into a disaster. She may not explain the reasons in depth – but she will offer the advice that in turn protects both the work and the person she's supporting.

Your executive sponsor's vantage point is invaluable. Remember that they not only have greater knowledge about what is happening today in your firm, but also understand what activities are slated for the future. As Jane continued, "You may know that you have something really good, but not know how good it is! I may be able to connect an entirely different set of dots than you can."

You should understand whether your executive sponsor sees the following activities as part of his or her role:

- Protecting your work from funding cuts.
- Protecting your work from prioritization shifts.
- Supporting your work through compliance concerns.
- Backing you up in the face of conflicts, or attempted appropriations.
- Alerting you when activities or judgments are based on the tip of the iceberg you can see – and need to be reconsidered because of the invisible mass below the surface.

Referrals

Your executive sponsor is a prime source for friendly faces. As you navigate your firm organizationally, he or she should be able to refer you to the resources you need.

When your executive sponsor introduces you to key people in other areas, it is much more than an introduction; it is an unspoken validation that your work is important to him or her and warrants the time you need from other people.

As John Collier, our PMO expert, mentioned, "It's very easy to look you in the face and say, 'No.' It's a whole different enchilada if you're an executive. An email can change everything."

Is your executive sponsor willing and able to give you warm introductions when needed?

Mentorship

Do not forget that while you work with your executive sponsor, you have the opportunity to learn about more than just your firm. Even if you do not aspire to join the executive ranks in the future, learn what you can about how your sponsor deals with people, wields influence, navigates politically, and handles dissent.

What Does Your Executive Sponsor Expect of You?

Different executives have correspondingly different expectations of people who lead the work that they sponsor. Be sure that you understand what your executive sponsor expects of you.

Just Ask

The easiest way to find out what you executive sponsor expects of you is to ask. Chances are good that your sponsor has a particular way that he or she prefers things be done. Before you can adhere to those ways, you need to know what they are. Consider asking administrative assistants or other people who have worked with or for your sponsor in the past.

What Success Means

One key issue you must understand is what, exactly, constitutes success in your executive sponsor's mind. Keep in mind that your sponsor may see your work as characterized by distinct phases, and not necessarily envision serving as sponsor throughout the entire lifecycle of your initiative. Earlier, we mentioned that even if you have funding to begin your work, it does not guarantee that you will have funding for subsequent years. The same principle holds true for an executive sponsor's involvement. Because of this, you may be expected to work towards multiple definitions of success spread over time.

For example, imagine that you approach an executive for sponsorship who has a strong reputation for backing innovations. The executive reviews, and is excited about, your knowledge-based initiative and agrees to serve as your executive sponsor. This does not mean that the same executive will sponsor you year in and year out throughout the lifecycle of your initiative. However, the executive's involvement can help you reach that stage.

To understand what success means to your executive sponsor, you will need to ask several questions:

- What does success mean to you today? What needs to happen in order for you, at the end of the project, to call our work a success?
- What needs to happen in order for you to continue supporting us after this first phase? What form might that support take?

Understand that if an executive opts out of formally sponsoring your work after a phase has been successfully completed, it does not necessarily mean the executive no longer supports your work or is not interested – or that your sponsor secretly views your work as a failure. It may be that organizationally you will be better served by institutionalizing your work to the point where no project executive sponsor is needed. The executive can continue to support you and your activities. For example, once your work is institutionalized, a former executive sponsor would be a perfect candidate to serve on a steering committee or advisory board. Your relationship may also shift into one of mentorship.

Santi Kumar offered us her thoughts on how she, as an executive, might quantify success for a knowledge-based initiative. As you will see, she does not expect bottom line impact. Instead, she expects to see differences in behavior and thinking. "There's a lot of power in bringing together people from different perspectives," Kumar said. "If I think about Knowledge Management initiatives I've been involved with in the past, what they did, and what they tried to do, that's the shift: bringing together people with different perspectives. It's about thinking differently, *not about the bottom line*. In my mind, nothing epitomizes a journey more than Knowledge Management and the user experience it can provide or enable."

Santi continued. "To me, that's the power of any idea. What did you strike in terms of a flame (or seed planted) to get people to start thinking differently? For any great idea, that's the success area. Did you change how people think from the current state? If your answer is yes, right then and there I believe your idea qualifies as a success, however else it might be measured. Remember to look at how things were before your idea, how they were the day you launched, and how they were afterwards. Look for changes after you opened up new possibilities."

Administrative Minutia

Make sure you understand the small details, including the following:

- Will you have regular meetings with your executive sponsor? We strongly encourage this, particularly at the onset of your relationship.
- What 1-1 time will you have? The regular meetings mentioned above may qualify, but if you share those meetings with 20 other people, carve out some time to meet solo with your executive sponsor, even if those meetings occur virtually.
- What type of status updates will your executive sponsor find helpful, in what format and how often? Can he or she provide you with a sample to follow?
- What is the preferred method to contact your executive sponsor? Email, phone, or is it OK to drop in?

Note that you can probably get much of this information from the executive's administrative support.

Metrics

What metrics does your executive sponsor want to see from your work, and do those metrics figure into your sponsor's definition of success? This can be a tricky question because as knowledge practitioners, we know that metrics that can be gathered in a knowledge-based initiative are not necessarily true indicators of whether the work is succeeding. For example, the amount of content posted in a centralized knowledge repository does not mean anything in and of itself. Rapid content growth can even be a negative indicator of success if un-cleansed, un-contextualized data are dumped into a repository without careful forethought or human intervention.

Keep in mind that your executive sponsor, while he or she cares whether the "knowledge mission" succeeds, cares just as much whether the project is executed successfully. This means on time, and on budget. You may be asked to provide metrics around your project's progress.

As you work with your executive sponsor on useful metrics, look for opportunities around the following:

- Any scorecards or dashboards your executive sponsor feeds.
- Any reports he or she provides to the next level up.
- How many people your work touches.
- Any time windows your work can shorten or eliminate.

- Any measurable thresholds your work affects.
- Any organizational goals that you support, with associated figures.

Your Turn to Support

Do not forget or underestimate the extent to which you can support your executive sponsor. How? You will have to ask to be sure.

A good way to begin the conversation is to ask about your sponsor's goals for the year. Preface your question by explaining that you are interested in locating opportunities that you may have to assist him or her in reaching those goals. Ask about other general opportunities to offer your support and make sure to project an open, helpful attitude.

Perhaps most importantly, you are expected to support your executive sponsor through your actions. Later, Jane Niederberger shares her viewpoint on this topic.

Five Questions to Ask Your Executive Sponsor

Be sure to ask your executive sponsor the following questions.

What does your boss consider to be success? Related to the item above, you may be able to help your executive sponsor shine if you find out the definition of success from your sponsor's superiors.

What roadblocks do you foresee? Ask your executive sponsor, candidly, about the roadblocks that he or she predicts you may encounter. Ask who-what-where-why-when for each potential roadblock.

Who should I pursue as early strategic partners? Particularly if you are in the process of building a participant roster, your executive sponsor may be able to match you with ideal candidates for your knowledge-based initiative. This assumes that your work is not a solution in search of a problem; hopefully, a genuine business need spurred your early work. Your sponsor is far more in tune with the challenges of other executives than you are. If you engage the parties your sponsor identifies as strategic, you have the added bonus of a warm introduction from your executive sponsor. If your project has high visibility and is in high demand, early inclusion may be a "favor" for strategic partners.

What can I to do to ensure continued funding? Earlier, we mentioned that your executive sponsor may not necessarily be your sponsor throughout the lifecycle of our project, and that this should not be viewed as a negative. If your executive sponsor is funding your work, this question contains multiple layers:

- Does any activity, project result, or level of support ever guarantee funding?
- Organizationally, what processes do you need to follow around funding?

- Politically, what should you be aware of around funding?
- What percentage of funding in the next funding period is coming from your executive sponsor (if any)?
- What other sources does he or she believe will or should provide funding?

How will expansion happen? Some knowledge-based projects are truly project-based and have a distinct beginning and end; turning them into permanent programs inside a corporation is not appropriate based on what they are designed to do. Other knowledge-based initiatives, however, may be destined to become a part of your firm's organizational landscape if they succeed.

You will need your executive sponsor's insight on how your work is most likely to become institutionalized in your firm, assuming it should be. You need to know typical timelines (is one year enough of a "show me" period?), related organizational changes (would you head up the work? Do you get a promotion and headcount? Would you get a new boss?) and likely candidates for expansion. For example, your executive sponsor may know that your firm is planning to grow quickly in one geographic area. That rapid growth could make that region a strong candidate for your work in the future.

Other Supporters

In every firm, there is a cast of characters that can offer your initiative support in a multitude of ways. They can warn you when delicate situations or key power structures change; they might alert you to the latest feedback about your work inside the firm. Senior and more experienced supporters might be able to help you work through a sticking point with a particularly difficult committee. Perhaps your junior supporters believe passionately in what you are trying to accomplish and are willing to lead the charge in their own work areas.

You should retain and cultivate all corporate supporters. It does not matter whether a supporter is a fan of you personally or has a natural synergy with your knowledge-based initiative. Even if there is no immediate place that their support will assist you, valuing people, what they know, and what they care about should always remain a priority in your mind.

Executive Advice on Building a Network

Joe McGhee offered us advice on how he views building a network of supporters. "You have to understand who your constituents are," he said, "and who you have to rely on to get the project completed. First: build your alliances. Build them

across the board. Why? You may not need a certain group's support at this time –
but later, you will. You'll need that support when you get to an approval stage."

"A lot of people lose sight of that," he said. "Although functional skills are
important, knowing how to read financial statements, how to do whatever you
do – the first thing is to understand who the players are. Build a good working
relationship with everyone that you can."

As you build your network, do not forget to look for the sometimes "unseen"
power players. "I always try to understand who the *real* influencers are. That's
very different than identifying the decision makers," Joe explained. "You might
assume that an executive is the person you need to go to – but you also need
to figure out who that executive's influencers are. In fact, if you don't, and go
directly to the executive, you could offend the influencer by bypassing them."

McGhee continued. "Understand who the decisions makers are, who has
go/no-go decision-making power, and understand the level that it's appropriate
for you to approach. Recognize that there's an informal and a formal process.
I learned that if you get people's support informally first, it's a lot easier to get
formal buy in later."

Your Own Network Survey

With that in mind, conduct a quick survey of your own network. Does your
network include the following?

- People with inside information about crucial committees, such as approval,
  compliance, change control or PMO-related.
- Direct reports of each executive that you need to remain visible with.
- Representatives of your current and probable customers.
- A wide variety of administrative informants who can help you understand
  executives, their availability, and finesse time for you on executive calendars.
- Technology experts.
- Other administrative experts, who can tell you how key things get done at
  your firm in areas like Procurement, Finance, and HR.
- At least one person each from Legal, Marketing/Sales, and Corporate
  Communications.

In addition, if you know that you will be competing for items, cultivate a
supporter in each area that you will be up for competition.

5

Executive Sponsorship from the Executive Point of View

No one can better explain what executives look for, how to interact with them, and their general expectations than actual executives. In this section, a cross-section of executives offers their perspectives on not only executive sponsorship, but other important topics such as the importance of communication, interacting with people, reacting to resistance, and the importance of corporate culture.

Our participants are Joe McGhee, Jane Niederberger, Michael Jackman, and Santi Kumar. Each of them has unique viewpoints and valuable advice for knowledge practitioners seeking an executive sponsor. One piece of advice from us before you hear from them: remember to treat each situation – and person – as unique. As Joe McGhee explained, "Recognize that there are different approaches to getting things done from organization to organization – and *within* organizations."

Approaching an Executive Sponsor

Securing the right executive sponsor may be the single biggest factor which determines whether your knowledge-based initiative will succeed or fail. Surely, an activity that important deserves some planning.

With that in mind, should approaching an executive armed with a really good idea be your first step? Probably not. There are plenty of things, from figuring out how to deal with the executive on the human side to running up early estimates around project costs, size, and implications, you need to do first.

The Value of Channels

How will you reach out to the executive you would like to have serve as your executive sponsor? One approach that has proven successful for many is the use of channels. You deliberately employ multiple channels to reach your target and to ensure that your target has heard about your work before you approach him or her. In Knowledge Management terms, this is not dissimilar to enriching context around an interaction.

For example, consider asking one or two of the executive's direct reports to mention that you are leading an exciting knowledge-based initiative in their next staff meeting. Encourage them to point out the multiple synergies that your project has with the executive's own work. Understand that when you make this request from the executive's direct reports, you are providing them with the language and tone around your work that they will then pass on to the executive. Always count on providing the information you want passed upwards; do not ask people to synthesize it on their own.

As a next step, you might ask your immediate boss to chat informally with the executive about your project. When you later secure an appointment with the executive (with your boss' full blessing), he or she has heard about the project a few times, even if you as an individual are an unknown.

Joe McGhee advises that you be sure to work appropriately through channels. "First," he counseled, "be realistic about the level you occupy within the company. You should get support and buy in from your immediate boss and at least one level above. If you go around someone – even inadvertently, and even if you have a great idea – it can make the person you left out look, or feel, bad. There is a human element you cannot discount and typically, missing that element can cause you problems."

Another channel you cannot miss is the support personnel that surrounds executives. Michael Jackman advised, "One important channel is my administrative staff. They control my office, and can help or hurt you."

Making the First Move

There is no single best way to engage an executive in the hopes of persuading him or her to become your executive sponsor. As Jackman mentioned earlier, it is wise to develop channels to reach and then work with executives. But do reach out, even if you are nervous about it.

"The first thing people who want my support can do wrong is *not* come up to me," Jackman said. "A lot of people are afraid. They think somehow executives aren't 'normal employees' or we're not accessible. I think as an executive you have to be positive about being flexible and listening to new ideas and let the organization know it's a good thing to speak up in a good way. I believe in showing examples of how someone, regardless of level or position, can have an impact in the organization by publicly and visibly supporting them."

Earlier, we mentioned this quality when evaluating whether you have a true executive sponsor: does your sponsor publicly acknowledge you?

Jackman continued. "For example, I hold town meetings. Town meetings are the perfect opportunity to bring up how such-and-such came up with an idea. I give them public credit, and that creates the feeling that new ideas *are* welcome, and recognized. Executives have to work to *not* cultivate a perception that they are inaccessible."

Joe McGhee also encourages people to contact him directly. "Approaching me is easy," McGhee said. "I believe in the open door policy and don't worry about titles or levels. After all, we're all on the same team. Other executives may follow a more traditional path."

What Sponsorship Means

Executive sponsorship may mean something very different from person to person and organization to organization. At a minimum, when you go seeking a sponsor, be prepared to address the following:

- How will your idea impact the organization?
- What problem does it solve?
- What support will you need?
- What roadblocks do you envision?

The Sponsorship World According to McGhee

Joe McGhee is pragmatic about what it takes to enlist him as an executive sponsor. First, be prepared to explain exactly how your knowledge-based solution solves a problem that is causing pain to the firm or a customer. Next, assemble all the details – and be able to express them succinctly – around what it will take to launch your solution, including timelines, cost, benefits, people involved, and potential roadblocks.

Joe elaborated. "If you approach me with an idea, the first thing I'm going to ask you is: does it solve a business problem that my group, my company, my customer, or I am facing? Typically, those problems are how to increase profits, increase revenue, reduce expenses, or solve a customer issue. Make sure that your idea is going to help us, help me, or help the company in some way."

McGhee is a good example of an executive who knows exactly how he likes to see information presented. "I won't sign up to be a project's executive sponsor until everything is fully laid out: what the initiative is, its benefits, the investment, the potential return, the timeframe – everything. And, you need to do it in *ten slides or less*," he said. "If you come to me with an undefined idea, I'll send you back to flesh out the details. I'm adamant about timelines – never leave those out. If you come back and your story is tight? I'll say, let's run with it."

The Nuts and Bolts of Sponsorship from Michael Jackman

"My view of executive sponsorship is that it's a basic business transaction. If I sponsor an initiative," Jackman said, "I'm making a contract with the person who is asking for my support. It'll typically start with a, 'Here's what I agree to do, you have a great idea, let's explore it,' conversation. Count on my trying to expand your idea, too."

Jackman does not unilaterally dictate what happens next, though, even if he is impressed with an idea's potential. "After the initial conversation," he said, "I'll next approach the direct manager of the person who needs my support, express my support, and set up a review. Everyone will attend the review meeting, and the person who needs my support will present the idea. At this meeting, we'll try to develop the idea and see if we can blow it out into a plan." A persistent theme in *Managing Knowledge-Based Initiatives* is that it is wise to always involve those a level above you in your plans. Meetings like this are one reason why.

Jackman continued. "Based on that meeting, if it's something I want to pursue, I'm going to look for ownership, accountability, and complete involvement from that person, assuming I can free up their time. They might be working on something their immediate manager can't cut them loose from. In order to move the effort forward, it has to be aligned with all associated lifecycles, and the managers in between the requestor and me."

Jane Niederberger's Rules of the Road

Earlier, we discussed the importance of determining what you can do for your executive sponsor. Related to that idea is understanding that sponsorship is, in fact, a relationship even if it is grounded in business. "I have a number of 'high level rules of the road,'" Niederberger said. "Don't take me by surprise. Don't embarrass me. Keep me informed so that I can cover my back – and yours. If someone comes and tells me that you're doing something, I can nicely say that yes, you are. And you're doing it with my full support."

The Question of Money

So, who will pay for your work? Several consistent themes arose when speaking to our executives about funding.

- Do not assume that your executive sponsor will pay for your initiative out of their budget.
- If they are contributing funds, do not expect them to pick up the entire cost.
- Do not expect your executive sponsor to single handedly find funding in other parts of the firm; you have a role to play too.
- Do expect your executive sponsor to block and tackle at the executive level.
- Do expect a level of negotiation around how finances are handled.
- Do not expect to discuss finances first thing; the idea, its value and impacts matter far more.

McGhee offers a high level of support to the people he sponsors and expects them to proactively identify potential problem areas. "Once I agree to sponsor you," McGhee said, "I'll know if there are budget, funding, or other obstacles – and I'll remove those barriers to execution. I also expect you to anticipate hurdles or barriers early on. Know what groups will likely be involved in your project, and let me know if you anticipate problems."

Joe recognizes that he has an executive vantage point that you do not and expects to help you shape the project. He also believes it is his job to sell his fellow executives on an initiative that he is sponsoring. "As an executive, I'll know if your project's scope includes other functional areas, like IT, Financial, or Services," he said. "At my level, I'll start getting the support and buy in that's needed. I'll talk to my peers informally first and in that conversation I'll stress how this project *will benefit them*."

As you can see, McGhee uses the WIIFM (what is in it for me) tactic with his colleagues; everyone, including and perhaps especially executives, is interested in how they will benefit from supporting or participating in an activity.

Michael Jackman's viewpoint is much the same. He cautions those seeking executive support to understand that funding is not the first issue to be addressed; plenty of other things take higher immediate priority. "Funding is something to be negotiated," Jackman said. "Obviously, this is a typical concern for anyone attempting to launch a new product or idea but funding is the *second* stage. First, you come up with the idea, define the problem and solution, and get everybody aligned. As part of alignment, you size the effort."

Specifically, Jackman wants to know about everything that will change or be impacted by projects he considers for sponsorship. He steps in and helps with funding – after the project leader has comprehensively laid out everything. "For example, what changes to existing systems would happen?" Jackman said. "Would we have to hire staff? What would we need to pay new staff or consultants? Once these questions are answered, you create a budget and fund the budget. From the executive point of view, I expect the person who leads the initiative to work out the elements of what has to happen. I'll help with finance or budgets."

Although she might provide the funding and sponsorship to help get a new initiative launched, Jane Niederberger does not believe that the executive sponsor holds complete responsibility for funding a project indefinitely. The person she sponsors must be able to sell – and persuade – others of the value of the work, although she will help. "As executive sponsor, I provide the seed money – what you need to get started. But, you need to be able to sell it to the CFO or my financial person. How much is needed is key; that determines whether it's a hallway conversation or a formal sit-down," Niederberger said.

Sponsorship Tips

Consider these sponsorship approach tips:

- Approach executives yourself. Do not wait for them to come to you, and do not count on word of your work "bubbling up" to reach them. Use channels, but count on building and cultivating the channel yourself.
- Include your immediate boss in attempts to secure an executive sponsor, including the "reaching out" activities.
- Establish more than one way, or channel, to reach your executive sponsor. Find out what you can about the executive before you actually engage him or her.
- Develop an irresistible story. Michael Jackman counseled, "As you're approaching executives, make people perceive that you have something important to say."
- Clarify expectations in your own mind. What do you want from the meeting? An indication of interest? Firm commitment to serve as your sponsor?
- Seek, and practice, clarity. How clearly can you express your idea or initiative? Does it make sense to someone unfamiliar with Knowledge Management? Are your thoughts well ordered? Can you logically and succinctly describe it in less than two minutes? For more details, see Section VII.
- Understand that your sweat is expected, too – lots of work goes into being sponsored.
- Accept that different executives like things done differently.
- Know as many details as possible around things like cost, headcount, timelines, and implications of your work.

Have you already landed an executive sponsor? Keep these details in mind as you build the relationship.

- Even executive sponsorship does not mean that every problem goes away. An early nod may mean, "I want to hear more," not, "Great! Here's your blank check."
- Executives care how you treat others. Make sure that your actions cannot be perceived as intimidating or heavy handed. Your actions reflect on your executive sponsor.
- Protecting your sponsor is part of the bargain.

Thoughts from the Top

In the course of discussing sponsorship, our executives kept returning to several related topics, including the importance of communication, the value of starting small, and general advice about cultivating relationships. Although each topic is related in some manner to dealing with or understanding executives, in fact they lead back to a single lesson: how to deal with people.

Entrepreneurship, Big Champions, and Small Victories

Several of our executives mentioned the importance of beginning small when you introduce knowledge-based work into a corporation for the first time. There are a myriad of reasons this is wise, from funding to scope management to risk mitigation. Santi Kumar pointed out another reason: you cannot change an entire corporate culture all at once.

"Try to remain entrepreneurial in the KM space; don't sacrifice the excitement you have around introducing new ideas," she advised. "Knowledge practitioners – or anyone with a great idea – shouldn't be constrained by the practicalities of a corporate culture. Draw parameters that you can live with around the areas that you will pursue. Don't go after the entire corporate culture." In other words, find small victories first.

And, Kumar advises, make every effort to locate a friendly workplace home while you are getting started. "Find a pocket where you can let your entrepreneurial spirit take over and blossom. There is one in every organization – you just have to find it," Kumar said. "Treat it as your haven for a while to let your ideas seed and grow. If the first thing you try survives, it survives. If it doesn't, it doesn't. Try something else."

Michael Jackman believes that although strong leadership is key to succeeding in knowledge work, grassroots momentum is critical as well. "In terms of leadership around a knowledge-based initiative, I believe everything that's successful starts with a big champion – a strong leader. Then, you need small victories," Jackman said. "As people, a community, start using the Knowledge Management system and seeing the results, they tell somebody else and they tell somebody else. It's a viral thing; everybody gets excited about it. You have much more chance of succeeding if it's natural and people actually use a Knowledge Management system to get their work done, instead of something that is force-fed."

Communication

One of McGhee's pet peeves is the lack of skill around communications in the business world today. "Don't underestimate the importance of communication," he said. "I'm amazed at how many people – senior people – don't communicate well. I'm not talking about illegible handwriting or poor grammar, either: it's knowing when, how, who, and what to communicate. As an executive, communicating and interacting with people is probably 80% of my work."

Style and Choice are Key

Grammar matters; your skill as a speaker matter too. But that is not where the problems are, according to McGhee. "Where people fail is in the choice and style of communication," he explained. "Before I go into board meetings or deal with my partners, I consider how I want a particular message to come across. If you're trying to get buy in to accomplish something, how you communicate is probably the most important part of that." For example, an essentially neutral message can be perceived as negative or positive, depending on how it is communicated. Any topic may be softened or sharpened by the choice of words, tone, and vehicle of delivery.

"There are many elements necessary for effective communication," Joe continued. "One that is very important is to keep anyone – particularly influencers – from being blindsided. Another key: learn how to make people *want* to do things for you . . . make things happen for you. This is key whether you're young, old, male, female, at any level of an organization. There's no pure way to get people to do things; they're people. You have to figure it out."

One of the assumptions about you, as a knowledge practitioner, that we made in putting together *Managing Knowledge-Based Initiatives* is that you are passionate and driven about your work. To stay in the field, knowledge practitioners have to be. At the beginning of *Managing Knowledge-Based Initiatives*, we referred to Melissie Rumizen's definition of Knowledge Management and included her caution that knowledge geeks are not as interesting as we think. She advised cutting down on the KM jargon and focusing on the business. Similarly, you will see in Chapter 15 that Dave Snowden cautions knowledge practitioners to avoid being a zealot. Joe McGhee sums it up like this: "It's one thing to be passionate and driven – and another to be confrontational or forceful. Let your passion come through," he said. "Don't alienate people along the way. And think about what will make that person *want* to help you and see you succeed."

Corporate Code, No. Acronyms, Yes.

We all know people who seem unable to communicate without relying on the buzzword of the day. Throwing around non-terms when you are trying to communicate with your executive sponsor – or any other executive – can hurt you, as McGhee discusses below.

"Don't speak in 'corporate code,'" he said. "Tell me exactly what you want; get to the point. Spell out what you're trying to accomplish. Don't expect your audience to figure it out."

Acronyms falls into a different category. Although you should avoid using acronyms that your audience does not know, you are on the hook to learn as much of your audience's language as possible. "Learn the language – learn all the acronyms," McGhee advised. "Every company has its own language. When I'm new to a company, for the first 30, 60, 90 days I make a handwritten list of key acronyms." You will see that we advise that you include constituent-specific terms and acronyms in the value document that supports each constituent's value proposition in Section V. Essentially, this is the same exercise.

"Understand your company's buzzwords," McGhee continued. "It may sound stupid, but you'll be amazed at fast you'll be accepted in different parts of your organization – and how fast you'll learn – by understanding the acronyms and terms. This simple exercise will help you get up to speed quickly. Remember, though, that an acronym in one company may mean something completely different in another one."

Cultures and Subcultures

Knowing whom you are speaking to through organizational scans and tailoring your message to your audience are constant themes throughout *Managing Knowledge-Based Initiatives*. Joe McGhee has learned through the years that moving effectively in different parts of an organization means recognizing and respecting the distinct cultures found within it.

"Learn the company culture – the entire company's culture and subcultures – not just your part of it. There are subcultures everywhere. Sales and marketing do things one way, Finance another – and they're not just functional differences. I really believe engineers are different from sales people," Joe said. "IT people are different from financial and marketing people. Some work on theory; others work on exact facts and figures. The ten slides that work for a salesperson might not take you anywhere with the CIO if the CIO demands a lot more detail." Recognizing cultural differences will help you navigate a multitude of activities in a large organization.

Thoughts on Resistance

There are many different types of resistance you may encounter in the course of your knowledge-based work. People may actively oppose your work, for example. Or, they may choose not to support it, which could be viewed as a form of passive resistance. In order to respond to resistance, you need to understand the source of the resistance, the people involved, any relevant history and then devise a strategy to counter it.

When People Want to Shut You Down

"I can't remember who it is attributed to," Jane Niederberger said, "but I once heard that when people start shutting you down, you know you have a really good idea. You're onto something. When people challenge you and say, 'Here's why it won't work,' it usually means you're on track. And you're scaring them. They're afraid of something – their own security, their own status, maybe just dealing with change."

Since you conducted multiple landscape investigations at the beginning of your knowledge-based initiative, you should already have a good idea of what will change inside your firm because of your work. What you cannot anticipate is how people will respond to those changes.

Jane continued. "The fact that someone is trying to shut you down is a warning you need to heed. It doesn't mean you should stop – but you need to figure out where your detractors might be coming from, and how to rally their support. The best thing you can do when someone tries to shut you down is to win them over as an advocate."

It is Not Personal

When you pour all your energy into furthering something you are passionate about, such as a knowledge-based initiative, it is easy to become disappointed, cynical or angry if you do not get the support you need to move forward. While our executives understand that, they caution you to remember several things:

- Do not assume that failure to support your work is personally motivated and therefore take it personally.
- It does not mean that your idea is not good – it just may not be the best at a particular point in time.
- Your work may be passed over in favor of activities that firm leadership deem more important for reasons you do not have any visibility around.
- Asking tough questions and making tough decisions is part of an executive's job.

McGhee explained. "First, understand that when you don't get the support you need, it's not always because a person doesn't *want* to support you. It's because executives better understand what is strategically important, or a firm priority, than you do. You have to understand outside looking in what's going on in the company as best as you can." Unless, that is, you have an involved executive sponsor to help guide you.

Santi Kumar believes that your business case is more likely to fall apart beneath executive scrutiny if you do not have a strong executive supporter. Executives who challenge your work are not being deliberately obstructive, though. In most cases, they are just doing their job. "If you don't have strong executive support, you don't have a lot of control over the situation. So, you bear the burden of doing a lot more of the hard work and analysis around the substance, around the idea," she said. In such a case, you may be forced to build a business case or value proposition without the benefit of an executive viewpoint.

Kumar continued. "That's often where your business case or value prop may fall short. People who resist it, perhaps those who don't want to buy into the idea, or aren't aware of it – aren't necessarily coming from a negative place. Often, they're asking the right question – but the hard question. The person on the receiving end of those questions, the person selling it, really has to package the idea. Make the idea totally defensible so that it doesn't fall apart. That's the hard part: often, it *will* fall apart."

Relationships and Behavior Count

We have spent a lot of time in *Managing Knowledge-Based Initiatives* discussing how you should investigate everything in your organization from people to politics to external perceptions of your firm. Do not forget that a similar investigative exercise may, at some point, be turned on you. Your past performance, employment history, or education may be scrutinized. In addition to hard facts, your command of softer skills matter too.

We asked our executives that if when selecting whom to support and perhaps sponsor, a candidate's people skills factored into their selection criteria. Is it possible that an employee who is polished and effective with executives but boorish and inconsiderate with peers and subordinates might be turned away when seeking sponsorship or support? The answer was a resounding yes.

Some reasons are easy to understand. If an executive publicly supports you and your work, your behavior in turn reflects upon that executive. As a rule, executives will avoid probable embarrassment. In addition, executives want to support people and projects that are likely to succeed. As you interact with executives to gain support for your knowledge-based initiative, you are essentially asking them to believe in your potential to be a leader.

As Santi Kumar explains, treating people well is a strong leadership trait. It is one indication that shows executives you have genuine leadership potential. "Treating people well is paramount," Santi said. "It's table stakes. I absolutely *do* care how you treat people on your way 'up' to see me. Of course, you should be organizationally aware of whom you're dealing with, but people's role or title is of no consequence at all when it comes to how you treat them."

It should not matter – but is that possible? Santi pointed out that those who operate by status or rank may struggle with this. "It's hard to be egalitarian if you're overly position conscious. Certainly, there are egos. I get that," she said. "But how you treat an admin or the grounds crew at your firm should be no different from how you treat your CEO or a peer."

Never heard that from an executive before? Kumar is not surprised. "How you treat people is often considered part of the 'soft stuff' but I actually don't think it is. I prefer to look at it as foundational. It's a cornerstone for any framework, for any organization, for any company that aspires to be successful." She elaborated. "From an executive point of view, if you want to build a high performing team, you cannot do it unless you treat people well. The word 'well' has to be quantified: it includes respect. After all, it's not just about compensation, is it? It's a holistic sort of well. I don't mean to be overly philosophical but there's merit in looking at productivity and innovation in high performing teams that are made up of people who are committed, share values, and are focused and agile. Everyone wants teams like this, but how do you get there? The journey of treating people well."

Executives who are being asked to trust you with a team of people and financial resources need to know that you will manage them well. Part of that is treating people appropriately.

Kumar recognizes that not every executive is a role model for this type of behavior. "If you look at the many, many executives that are out there," she said, "there are fewer fantastic leaders among them. Those leaders – the common thread that you will find – is that they are fairly humble, and they are consistent in the way they treat people. It doesn't mean they are less driven, less forceful, less direct, but they are *consistent* in every engagement they have with other people, regardless of position. That consistency is a powerful thread. And I think that's leadership," she concluded.

Joe McGhee's view is equally pragmatic. "*How to Win Friends and Influence People* is the second most important book after the Bible, in my view," McGhee stated. "No matter what your level, my advice is to understand that whatever you do, you do it with *people*. I don't care what technology you use, what services you're offering – none of that matters. At the end of the day, you deal with people to get things done."

Section V

The Value of a Value Prop

6

Value Prop 101

If you are developing a knowledge-based initiative for an organization in which you have been entrenched for some time, it can be a challenge to quantify what your work is "worth" in terms of value rather than "cost," "money saved," or "problem solved." Even if your vision of the value your knowledge-based initiative is clear, it can be difficult to get others to concur with estimates of the value your knowledge-based initiative provides.

In this portion of *Managing Knowledge-Based Initiatives*, we will take you through how to think about value, how to develop a value proposition, and the relationship between your value prop and other areas in *Managing Knowledge-Based Initiatives*, such as working with your executive sponsor, selling your work, ROI, and organizational alignment. We will also explore exactly what you should do with a value prop once you have developed it.

Value Proposition Interdependencies

Your value proposition does not stand alone. Like the other elements that we explore in *Managing Knowledge-Based Initiatives*, your value prop is related to other parts of your work. In fact, your value prop defines your work to a large extent.

Your value proposition will:

- Be partially determined by alignment in your firm.
- Reflect your firm's culture; check for common usage and vehicles.
- Be selectively shared using presentations, emails, a communication plan, personal interaction, and other vehicles you may employ, such as a road show.

- Be shared by you, your leadership, your customers and your customers' leadership.
- Evolve over time, as your firm's needs and therefore the challenges of your internal customers evolve.
- Partially define what you will be evaluated against over time.
- Become an integral part of your team's alignment artifacts.
- Be easy for your customers to articulate.
- Serve as you and your team's "gold standard" concerning the issues you will tackle, the scope of your work, and the experience you will offer your customers.
- Help you identify customers inside your organization who will benefit the most from your knowledge-based initiative.
- Become the promise between you and your customers that, if broken, will be very difficult to repair.
- Be an agreement point between you and your executive sponsor.

In order to develop the strongest possible value proposition:

- You will convert your customers' challenges into a value they will recognize as valid once that challenge is addressed.
- You will include a WIIFM (what is in it for me) statement when appropriate.
- You will extract a value from accomplished goals/addressed challenges and build a "value repository" that you will use on multiple occasions.
- You will refine a generic value proposition into targeted value statements.
- You will phrase value statements in the language of your customer – no KM jargon.
- You will juggle soft and hard value, such as an activity that helps your customer meet an alignment artifact compared to an activity that generates a tangible dollar savings or return.
- You will juggle formal value – that which is echoed in your organization's formal alignment artifacts and stated goals – and less formal value.
- You will form strong relationships with your constituents because your value proposition to them will evolve over time and you must remain aware of their challenges.
- You will rely on what you learned in the alignment exercise in Section III.

What is a Value Proposition?

A value proposition describes the value that anything – goods, services, tangibles, intangibles – offers to those who use or purchase them. As a consumer, you make decisions every day, at least partially because of a value proposition. For example, why do you bank where you bank? Convenient location, or the fact you can bank online free? Why do you return to your favorite coffee shop – is it the coffee, or the atmosphere? What is it about your bank or favorite coffee bar that holds value for you?

In the corporate world, "you" is replaced by your firm's corporate identify as a whole. This is one reason that knowing your firm inside and out is critical. A level beneath that collective corporate "you" lay the individuals that comprise your corporation, and are your customers.

Do not expect your customers to figure out your knowledge initiative's value proposition. It is up to you to educate them using a neat, easy to understand vehicle; you will discover, then reinforce why your solution holds value for them. Particularly because knowledge-based solutions can be broad, you must assist your customers in understanding and describing what they will gain from participating in and supporting your knowledge-based initiative. Your solution won't have a "one size fits all" robust value proposition, because what is valuable to one customer is not necessarily valuable to another.

Executive Points of View: Jane Niederberger and Santi Kumar

Jane Niederberger, former CIO and VP of Operations for Wellpoint, the United State's largest healthcare provider, shared her thoughts about what a value proposition in a corporate environment should include. "What I look for in a value proposition is an articulation of the problem a solution will solve. If you come to me for support, I'll ask you three questions: Why should we do this? What does it do? What does that mean for our business? When you articulate the answers to those questions, your value proposition takes shape and becomes really compelling."

If you cannot answer those questions before you approach an executive for buy in, you are better off waiting. Executives like Jane expect you to be able to communicate the value that your solution will offer them. "That's how I look at it," Niederberger continued. "What problem will this solution solve? An internal function? A customer's issue? If you can't articulate that, then the next question is: Is this just a cool thing to do? A hobby?"

This is the first lesson about value propositions: have a firm idea about how your work will benefit your company overall, and then the person you are speaking with, before you try to gain support for it.

Santi Kumar, Vice President at Fidelity Employer Services Company, pointed out a few additional aspects to building your value proposition. She advises that you keep in mind that the immediacy of tangible rewards is key, and expectations must be accurately set around when an individual will realize those rewards. "In the case of KM," Kumar said, "the source of the value prop is the tools themselves, and the benefits offered by immediate communication and the associated gratification. That immediate gratification is a luxury that is offered by some types of knowledge-based work – in other types of work, users, or executive sponsors might have to wait and see the benefit."

In addition to the immediacy of gratification that some knowledge-based efforts offer, Kumar also believes in pointing out what the supporter of your work will gain by participating. "A value prop for knowledge-based work has to include WIIFM (what's in it for me) and answer the question: what do I gain? The next important question is: when will I see the return on this?"

Return, in this case, may not mean dollars. "This is related to ROI, certainly," Santi continued, "but maybe not the financial part of it. Think of it as, 'When do I get to see my *reward* for investing in this initiative?' When you answer that question, you can really whet appetites. If an executive supporter of your work doesn't see a reward for a long time, it can be a problem. Everyone has a threshold. If a supporter doesn't see the value prop and what they are seeking from within that threshold, that's when they start to say, 'By the way, why am I investing in this? What am I getting back?' "

General and Targeted Value Props

The type of value prop you need to develop to support your knowledge-based initiative is simpler to construct than building a value prop for a new consumer brand, but a great deal of thought should go into it. Some general characteristics of a value prop include:

- Your value proposition will explain the value that your knowledge-based initiative offers your customers.
- A value proposition is not a static document that, once complete, never has to be tweaked or revised.
- Over time, your value proposition will grow in richness and adjust, based on the maturity of your solution, your company's circumstances, or your customers' challenges.
- Although your value prop may be constructed on paper, it will be most effectively expressed contextually by humans.

As a first step, you will develop a generic value proposition that can apply in the broadest sense to every customer. Then, drawing from the generic value proposition, you will develop targeted value props for your customers. In general, you will work with two types of customers and the value proposition lifecycle for each will vary slightly.

- Built-in customers who will participate, by default, in your knowledge-based initiative (whether you want them as customers or not).
- Customers you need to actively "sell."

Particularly as your work matures, you may find yourself running a single Knowledge Management program that has multiple projects or initiatives beneath it. In a case like this, it is to your benefit to have a generic value proposition for the program overall and for each child activity.

We will show you an example of developing a generic value proposition and a simple process to help you develop targeted value props later in this chapter.

Matchmaker, Matchmaker

Sometimes, a value prop for a particular customer will be obvious and require little investigation. On the other hand, if you are approaching, or investigating the feasibility of approaching, areas inside your company that you do not have close ties with, determining whether you can offer them a robust, compelling value proposition may be time consuming – and it can be a tempting step to skip.

Do not skip it. The process of fleshing out a value prop with a potential customer may identify that the customers' needs are not a good match for your knowledge-based initiative. Although disappointing, it is best to avoid mismatches when you spot them. Recognizing a poor fit before you invest time into building a business relationship is a good thing for both parties. Cultivate customers you are sure you can serve well.

Looking at the Value in Value Proposition

At heart is what your firm, and the people you will be dealing with, considers "value" to be. Value can be conveyed using many different vehicles; the trick is to communicate your initiative's value appropriately to different audiences. For example, if you are engaging a numbers-driven group, be ready to pull out facts and figures. If you are addressing a group that has a historic problem, for example, with managing information, be ready to discuss how your initiative will solve their problem in the context of their challenges.

In addition to vehicles, value can be expressed in many forms:

Anecdotal. Your value prop may include stories that illustrate how your tool has helped resolve a problem or accomplish a goal. Use anecdotes from pilot as well as production experiences. Where appropriate, extrapolate from anecdotes and identify other problem areas inside your firm where your solution may be able to assist. Once your knowledge-based solution is deployed, you will continually update your repository of anecdotes.

Do not hesitate to look outside your firm for anecdotes. Look for relevant examples from your industry and companies that have faced and addressed similar problems with a similar solution. Do not underestimate the potential power of anecdotes harvested from your firm's external competitors.

You will find external anecdotes in a number of places. If you are working with a vendor on any portion of your knowledge-based initiative, ask them for relevant anecdotes. Reach out to knowledge practitioners via the web, discussion groups, contacts that you may have made at conferences – leave no potential source untapped.

Alignment. If you work for a firm where strong organizational alignment increases the chances that work will viewed as valuable, being able to demonstrate and describe your alignment at multiple levels of the organization, and at multiple levels of granularity on a functional basis, will be key.

Dollars and cents. If your initiative offers a clear financial advantage over other efforts in place, the cost of doing nothing, or will help your firm avoid future expenditures, your value proposition will include elements around the financial benefits of executing or supporting your work.

There may be other attributes that are considered valuable in your firm. Generally, they can be found embedded in your organization's alignment artifacts at some level. For example, if your solution offers a new and innovative way of looking at a business problem, and the importance of innovation is part of your company's values and beliefs, you have the opportunity to demonstrate alignment.

Value Prop: Public or Private?

The value proposition in its totality is largely internal to you and your group. When you share it with other members of your firm, you will articulate the relevant points of the value prop in a few sentences or paragraphs. Although coming up with a few sentences may seem simple, the work behind forming that value prop is appreciable. How you will share your value prop with potential customers will be governed by your communications plan, which we discuss in Section VII.

Building your generic value proposition as a team exercise is a tremendous tool to strengthen your team's internal alignment. If your entire team is involved in brainstorming your generic value proposition, they will:

- Understand the foundational elements of your work.
- Be able to articulate those elements, and how they tie together.
- Be able to generate and refine targeted value props.
- Make better decisions about adapting your work.

As the leader, you will make better decisions, too. For example, a well-crafted value prop will help as your work evolves over time and you must choose between alternative paths and activities. Evaluating new options against your knowledge-based work's value proposition will help ensure that you make wise, supportable choices. That evaluation process will also help you evolve your value proposition over time in a deliberate, rather than reactive, fashion.

Part of the art of using a value prop in a corporation effectively is becoming comfortable teasing out portions of the value prop that are appropriate for your audience. As you begin developing your own value proposition, think big: do not worry if it seems large and unwieldy at the beginning. You will trim off excess fat later. In this section, we will take you through the exercise of honing and refining your value prop depending on your audience and needs.

Before You Begin

Before you turn outwards and start looking at the value your knowledge-based initiative will provide your customers, examine these preliminary building blocks that must be in place.

Customers. Who are your customers? What are their challenges, their alignment artifacts, what ties do you have to their leadership, and what is their individual culture? We will refer to your customers as constituents for this portion of the value prop exercise.

Leverage points. Can you identify any leverage points that will make potential customers not only want to participate in your knowledge-based initiative, but make them eager to participate? How can you exceed their expectations? Can you identify a good-better-best continuum for different audiences?

Alternatives. Are you aware of, and understand, alternatives to your solution? For example, are there tools already in place in your organization that do some of what your tools do – but not everything? Are there tools or programs in use that have been perhaps poorly retrofitted or patched to solve a problem your initiative also addresses? Are there informal programs in place that your initiative may displace or subsume?

History and position. Do you understand the history and current political positioning of any alternatives to your knowledge-based solution?

Promise and delivery. Are you confident you can support what you are proposing? Even if you do not have firm commitment on funding or headcount at this stage, you should be able to estimate the number of resources that will be required to support your work, and the skill sets they need to possess.

Conducting a Cultural Landscape Analysis

Santi Kumar also advocates being aware of the cultural landscape of your company or firm. She contends that understanding cultural markers is key to building a relevant value proposition that will resonate with consumers today.

Kumar explained. "Another element that is important in the formation of your value proposition: scan your environment, and the landscape of the current marketplace. Assess what the current culture is. The reason I say that is that we live in an environment of consumerism, and will likely continue moving that way in the short term."

Santi believes that understanding what drives individual buying choices outside the office may help you market to them inside the office. "Play that idea out," she continued. "It's all about individual choice at the end of the day – empowering individuals. Today, everyone has individual choice for decisions; they aren't made for people anymore. The genesis of that was perhaps shopping online. Consider healthcare. It used to be offered through companies and now consumers are saying, 'Wait, I want my own stuff, my own healthcare products, and only what's relevant to me.' Financial services were already highly focused on the consumer because they had to be to remain competitive."

Kumar continued. "Understand that, because from a KM value proposition perspective, you should say, 'OK, that's the world I live in today. However I wrap up my value prop, it has to hit home to that feeling. It has to have elements of the end user experience of what I can control by having this KM tool or this KM policy. What does it do for me and my ability to choose and control my decisions?' IM (instant messaging) is a great example. It's not a phone call; you don't have to pick up the phone. You can set your status to do not disturb, and you won't be. You can say you're away, or just choose not to respond. The KM tool in the shape of IM does allow end users to make a choice in a very non-threatening, non-confrontational manner: do you want to engage or not? That's indicative of where culture is today."

An additional part of the cultural element is understanding what tools and skill levels are common in your organization before, during, and after the launch of your knowledge-based work and whether those skill levels and expectations are met and complimented by your firm's current landscape. There are a few facets to this.

Everything changes. Your firm is not a static pool of beings; new people, with their own experiences and expertise, are joining every day and changing what is considered the norm. Similarly, those who hold older, perhaps more traditional views on how your firm should be are retiring every day.

People do not easily relinquish what works for them. As people in your firm move about, they will be exposed to new ways of doing things and certainly develop preferences. Once users find tools that effectively meet their needs, they are generally loathe to forsake those tools. At least, not without a heck of a fight.

Dialing back expertise and savvy is impossible. We like to say that younger generations arrive in the workplace "Google-ized" with a high level of expectation about what they can find, how quickly they can find it, and how accessible information should be. Santi expanded on this idea. "The end consumer is so well informed now because of the Internet. Information is easily accessible. What they don't know, they can easily find out. They can ask questions in the privacy of their own home without paying a fee. That's the landscape of society today." Kumar sighed. "I have a 14-year old at home who found YouTube just as I was beginning to hear about it. How did she find it so quickly? And now that she has, what expectations have been formed in her mind?"

As you interact with different groups of potential customers, you will quickly begin to gain a sense of how open they are to change, and what their norms are. Do not forget to factor in those elements when you build targeted value propositions for each customer.

Moving from Generic Value to Targeted Value

You already have a sense of why your work is valuable. For this first step, create a rough draft based on your gut instincts: why is your knowledge-based initiative valuable to the people who will use it? Do a mind-dump and create a first-pass document, calling out audiences at a high level. Once you have refined this, it will be your generic value proposition.

For example, a Knowledge Management team that is focused on remote collaboration might have a generic value prop something like this:

Because our associates are spread across the United States, collaboration is a problem on several fronts. We frequently travel hours to attend a single meeting – that incurs administrative expense, and significant time away from our desks. More common is that we do not collaborate at all, and frequently reinvent the wheel. We often do not know what our peers in other states or regions are working on.

By providing virtual workspaces that will allow associates to share documents, share their desktops, and instant message, we will enable teams to collaborate more easily. This will reduce travel, associated administrative expense, and lost time. We will also provide an way for people who do not collaborate today to do so. Countless avenues for new efficiencies will open up.

Over time, and depending on your audience, you will tweak your value proposition. For example, if you were presenting this value proposition to an executive, it might sound like this:

As the Vice President of the Pacific Region, you have associates spread out across four states.In speaking with your directors, it seems that there are two challenges: people travel hours to attend meetings – which means they are away from their desk and your administrative expenses skyrocket on mileage – or people do not collaborate at all. Work is duplicated, and efficiency plummets.

The virtual workspaces we plan to deploy can help on both fronts. Your employees will be able to share documents – without emailing them back and forth – so they will always know the latest and greatest version. We will further reduce your administrative expense by in-housing desktop share – no more minute by minute charges to see what is happening on someone else's computer. Instituting secure private chat will help reduce phone tag and is a great way to get quick answers.

Note that if you reference speaking with others – such as "directors" are mentioned above – you must be ready to back it up with names.

Your value prop becomes even stronger when you plug in real numbers. For example:

Last year, over $200,000 was charged to mileage in your region, and $180,000 was spent holding virtual meetings using an outside vendor for desktop share. All of that money was processed as administrative expense. Since one of your operating imperatives for this year is to decrease administrative expense, our program is a natural fit for you. If we can eliminate just 20% of the travel, and 80% of the external charges for sharing desktops, that is over $180,000 in savings. The Atlantic Region, after participating in our program for just a quarter, has already realized over $50,000 in savings.

See how it works? Start with your general value proposition, and then refine it according to each constituent's needs. Of course, if the Pacific executive is interested enough to take the conversation to the next level, detailed discussion and more numbers would follow. None of the example value propositions here would be the end of the conversation. Often, though, you will find that a fairly general value proposition that does not attempt to encompass an entire project plan is enough to get a executive's attention. People who work for that executive will more than likely collaborate with you in hammering out the finite details.

Strategy tip: Wondering where to get figures that will catch an executive's attention? Conduct your own survey. There are multitudes of free online tools that can help, and old-fashioned pen and paper can work too. Let your executive sponsor know what you plan to do, in case your organization prefers that surveys be initiated from the Corporate Communications office.

If you are including savings or cost reductions as part of your targeted value prop, make sure your figures and projected savings are accurate, and defensible. Finance can usually help you track down past expenditures, although you should be prepared to do some data analysis yourself.

Next, we will take you through a simple process to discovery, quantify, rank, and manage constituent needs. These needs, and the priority you assign them, are key in defining your value proposition(s).

Planning and Tracking Your Activities: How Value Props Can Help

Examine the sample Pacific Region value prop above. The numbers referenced – $180,000, $50,000 – are potential savings. The value prop contained no numbers around activities, such as the number of Pacific employees that would roll onto using the solution from quarter to quarter. That is because the executives of the Pacific Region care about how their expenses will be reduced, and by how much. They care much less about the details. However, you can extrapolate goals and evaluation points for your team from this customer-focused value proposition after you break down the goals into activities.

Focusing on the desktop share portion of the goal above, for example, your team's goals may be, "Roll on 200 Pacific Region associates per month, including desktop installation and training, to the desktop share tool." Focusing on the collaborative spaces portion of the solution, your goals might be, "Identify the top 20 mileage-expense employees in the Pacific Region. Map them back to their workgroups. Prelim evaluation of their workgroups for appropriateness for the collaborative spaces. Work with management to plan their roll on," and so forth.

Once you have pulled out finite tasks, you can begin to track your progress. If you have never built a project plan before, this activity can help you identify discrete tasks.

Developing a Targeted Value Proposition

In the example above, we refined a generic value proposition for presentation to an executive who had a very specific set of challenges. For your purposes, the primary difference between a generic value proposition and a targeted value prop is legwork and discovery. Below, we offer a six-step process to help you develop the most targeted value proposition possible.

Step 1: Know Your Constituents

Take a moment and consider whom your constituents are. Cast a wide net and include every group that will (or could) contribute to your project in the form of funding or influence, or benefit from your project in the form of participation or, again, influence. Your constituents will fall into two categories: direct and indirect.

Direct Constituents

The firm as a whole. Your value proposition should elucidate how your initiative benefits the entire firm. Most frequently, this will involve demonstrating alignment at a high level.

Customers inside your firm. Your value proposition also describes how your work will benefit your direct customers. You may need to describe related benefits at multiple levels. For example, imagine that your executive sponsor leads your company's Atlantic Region. Your work might offer a blanket benefit for the entire Atlantic Region that should be called out. In addition, your initiative will benefit multiple groups that fall beneath the Atlantic Region; the benefits of each group need to be captured too. Include current customers for the first iteration, and as your work expands, go back and insert any new customers.

Your work group. Do not forget to consider your own group as a constituent. Going back to your firm's organizational alignment, explore whether your knowledge-based initiative is contributing to demonstrating alignment at any plateau. Ratchet it up level by level; start with your work group, and look at every level in between you and the C-level executive you eventually align with.

Indirect Constituents

Entities with sign-off capability. The exact nature of these entities will vary greatly from firm to firm, but at this point, you should have an idea of who will need to sign off on your work. If you have a strong PMO presence in your firm, they would be an entity with sign-off capability. Likewise, if your IT department has levels of sign-off and your solution has a technology element that will need approval, they should be included. When dealing with these groups, you will need to be able to articulate your value proposition from the point of view of your direct constituents; indirect constituents need to clearly understand how your work will benefit your constituents. If any sign-off entities are customers in your work, you have another nuance to include.

Influencers. You may identify, along the way, "influencers" who help form or sway opinion in your firm. Influencers are generally directly and publicly associated with executives. When you engage influencers, share how your work supports your direct constituents, unless the influencers are also your customers. Your direct constituents may also be the influencer's direct constituents.

Beneficiaries of your direct constituents. If your work supports an internal group that in turn supports another internal group, you can claim value based on what the final consuming group will receive.

Identify Friendly Faces

Next, examine your list of constituents and identify friendly faces from each constituency group. Include people you have positive relationships with that you are confident you can corral for a candid conversation. Only include people who are senior or connected enough to be able to give you the correct level of information. For example, a manager of a transactional group three levels beneath a director may be able to tell you less than the administrative assistant of a manager one level below a director.

Step 2: Identify Your Constituents' Value Hot Buttons

After identifying your constituents, the next challenge is to uncover their challenges – their "value hot buttons." Do not expect your constituents to be able to frame their challenges immediately in the context of value. Generally, you will find out what your constituents' challenges or goals are, evaluate how your solution can address or support those challenges or goals, and attempt to assign a value to it based on how your constituents prioritize the challenge or goal you address. You will validate the value you perceive with your constituents.

You will locate your constituents' value hot buttons both formally and informally.

The Formal Route: Alignment Artifacts

Remembering to contact your friendly face list if needed, gather your constituents' alignment artifacts; you may not find alignment artifacts for every group. Look for documented mission statements, goals, strategic objectives, value and beliefs, scorecards, "state of the union" presentations, "about us" presentations, and any other document that may describe your constituents' goals and challenges. If you locate content through a third channel – for example, from your intranet – validate that what you find is current. Particularly with smaller groups, someone may have created alignment artifacts years ago that no one pays attention to now.

The Informal Route: What is Really Going on

The second – and perhaps most obvious way – to identify your constituents' value hot buttons is simply to ask them. This may seem obvious, but it is not always as easy to accomplish as it would appear.

Sometimes, a person who is willing to speak candidly, for example, someone from your friendly faces list, may not have the seniority or visibility to clearly describe their workgroup's challenges. Other times, people may become suspicious and believe that you are angling for a piece of their budget (which you may be, even if you are not doing it intentionally) and clam up. Getting an executive's time can be tricky and something you may not yet be prepared to do.

Whatever route is most appropriate for you, gather hot buttons for each of your identified constituents to the best of your ability. Next, you will call on your executive sponsor.

Step 3: Engage Your Executive Sponsor

This next step assumes that you have a strong relationship with your executive sponsor. If you do not, or have not identified an executive sponsor, substitute a trusted, senior person for this portion of the value prop exercise. We explored the executive sponsor relationship in detail in Section IV.

Set up a brainstorming meeting with your executive sponsor where you will:

- Validate that your executive sponsor agrees with your list of potential constituents. Explain that you won't immediately involve every group on your list, but these are potential areas of alignment.
- Ask your executive sponsor's advice on priority of constituents. He or she may know that a particular group has more urgent challenges, greater funding, or greater influence than others. Divide the list into high and lower priority groups.
- Validate the alignment areas as you have identified them, focusing on high priority groups.
- Share your list of friendly faces, and see if your executive sponsor can add to the list.

- In case of any gaps – areas where you and your executive sponsor believe there is probably strong alignment, but you do not have a person you can validate with – strategize how to gain access.
- Determine which high priority groups you need to speak with to refine, or add to, your understanding of their current challenges.
- Decide who will tackle the remaining high priority groups. Your executive sponsor may be able to casually engage peers that you cannot get an appointment with. If your executive sponsor is not able to participate directly, ask if they can arrange warm introductions, if not to executive-level resources, to people who support those executives and can speak knowledgeably about their challenges.

At the end of this meeting, you should have a list of all direct and indirect constituents, divided into two groups:

- Those you will engage now, or in the near term (high priority).
- Those you may potentially engage at some point in time (lower priority).

For every constituent you will engage immediately or in the near term, you should have:

- Your executive sponsor's validation of that constituent's hot buttons and challenges;
- Agreement on which faces on your list are friendly;

And/or:

- Your executive sponsor's agreement to give you a "warm introduction" to a person in that group who can enlighten you;
- Your executive sponsor's agreement to do some sleuthing and uncover hot buttons and challenges.

Step 4: Assemble Additional PMO Artifacts

Depending on your PMO, you may be required to submit significant paperwork that can contribute to your value prop. If you have not begun working with your PMO yet, getting your value prop in shape first will ease that process. If you have already engaged with your PMO and are substantially along in the process, work you have already done may support your value prop.

Pull out any PMO work that you have completed and look for:

- Value statements.
- Any numbers you provided.
- Any constituents you identified.
- Any constituents that may be implied.

Step 5: Synthesize Value Prop Components into Value Docs

Before you begin the process of creating what we will refer to as value docs, a coaching tip: remain aware of numerical opportunities that present themselves.

As you first analyze, and then engage with your constituents, you will uncover opportunities to demonstrate value that are anecdotal by nature. You will also encounter value opportunities that are numerically defined.

Naturally, you will treat these two types of value recognition differently to some extent. However, any time you stumble on an opportunity to quantify what your knowledge-based work offers a client – small or large – you must seize it. Whether you are gathering success stories or hard figures, the importance of being able to back up *what you say you will do with results – with what you actually did – is critical*. Both numerical results and anecdotes are proof that you are fulfilling your end of the value prop, and providing the value your constituents seek.

Understanding Value Docs

Value documents, or value docs, are an internal team tool that you will use to map, and then track, the formation, growth and delivery of a constituent's value proposition. If a constituent's value prop mutates over time – as it probably will – the value doc will be updated. When you fulfill a portion or aspect of a value proposition and generate a tangible result, it should be noted on the value doc. Every member of your team should be familiar with value docs and you may choose to use a value doc as an informal client diary.

Value docs are not meant to replace project plans, project charters, or any other type of project management artifacts your firm may require. If elements that we include in value docs can or should live in your firm's project management system, that is no issue. What is important is that you track the elements we mention here, no matter where, or what they are called.

The format of value docs does not matter either, although we are fond of using spreadsheets and grouping topics on different tabs. Each constituent should have its own value doc, although you may be able to group constituents with identical needs and alignment in functional buckets. A value doc will contain, at a minimum, these elements:

- The value proposition components that are important to that constituent group, and that your work fulfills.
- How your work fulfills each component, complete with dates and figures.
- Supporting documentation or anecdotes.
- Key constituent contacts.
- Key dates and timelines.

Note that a valuable bit of information to uncover for inclusion in your value docs are specific terms or acronyms that are unique to a particular constituent.

Step 6: Engage Constituents

The point of this last step is a validation of several items:

- You have correctly identified the major challenges and goals of a given constituent.
- Each constituent agrees with the value that will be gained once a challenge is addressed or a goal is met.
- You recognize the need to remain involved with your constituents.

If you followed all six steps, you have completed an appreciable chunk of work. At the conclusion of step 6, what have you really gained?

- You now have success criteria, directly from your clients' mouths.
- That success criteria can be used to help create your goals, which partially helps ensure your success organizationally.
- Clients know that you really understand their challenges and goals.

The more subtle outcome of validating your constituents' needs, however, is that you have just made a deal with them. You have explored and validated their needs and explained how your solution will fill those needs. In other words, you have committed to fix a portion of their problem.

Timing is Everything

When you engage constituents depends on a multitude of factors. Business – and personal – relationships span a wide spectrum of comfort and familiarity. Some clients may be entrenched in your project from the beginning; you know their challenges, hot buttons, and goals. Other clients may need to be sold, reassured, or persuaded (perhaps more than once) to use your solution or support your work in the form of funding or influence. Timing in relationship to other activities, such as budget planning, is key as well.

As mentioned earlier, you may have some "built in" clients that you do not have to sell. They will participate no matter what. All of your clients might be built in. Half may be default clients, and you will need to sell your initiative throughout the organization to obtain the other half. The combinations are endless.

You must understand where on the relationship spectrum you are with a given constituent, whether they are "built in" or need to be sold, and how to time your activities appropriately given your firm's culture and processes. Particularly when you deal with executives, you need to rely on your executive sponsor or other trusted senior resources for guidance. You may be in a firm where your executive sponsor needs to introduce you to another executive, or you may work for an organization where executives welcome direct contact from any level of employee. Your dealings with top management might begin at the top, or push upwards from a grassroots effort. You might need to begin the conversation with people at your level, who in turn will introduce you to their supervisors, and so on.

Engaging your customer won't be a "one-stop visit and you're done," situation. You are forming a relationship. Although you might only have one face-to-face encounter with a Vice President, for example, you might talk to the people who report to him or her several times.

We explore these topics in detail in several other sections of *Managing Knowledge-Based Initiatives*. Publicizing your work is covered in Section VII, and the importance of working with your PMO is addressed in Section VI. How to analyze your firm from the outside in is detailed in Section II. Depending on your situation, engaging the client may be blended into selling your work, or a different activity altogether. Validate with your executive sponsor to be sure you are approaching your constituents at the right time and at the right level.

Once you have engaged with a constituent, remember to remain engaged. Their challenges may change, so your value prop may need to be tweaked. In addition, they continually need to be reminded of the value they are gaining, or will gain, from participation in and support of your knowledge-based initiative. Use every interaction to update them, no matter how briefly.

Example: Customer Intimacy at Acme Corporation

To demonstrate what a value doc might look like, let us return to the fictitious Acme Corporation. You may recall that part of Acme's Vision Statement is to triple their distribution base and double current sales by 2015. To do that, leadership recognizes that a lot of attention will have to be paid to both existing customers and landing new ones.

Imagine that you are asked to help implement a new customer intimacy program that leadership has considered for some time. The goal is to ensure that current customers are so pleased with Acme that they will never consider going anywhere else. Acme plans to provide its largest customers with access to a sophisticated extranet that offers everything customers have been asking for: "gold standard" immediate customer service via chat, the ability to interact with sales people or engineers and get support when needed, the ability to interact with other people using Acme products, and the ability to search archives when they have issues. Acme hopes its customers will not only be pleased, but thrilled.

Three sales managers that you have good personal relationships with believe in the program and have each volunteered to move one of their biggest customers into the environment in pilot mode. Several engineers are also willing to participate in and lead a community of practice designed to let customers offer product improvement suggestions. Of course, you are thrilled to have "willing victims."

If all this is in place, why do you need a value document, let alone a value proposition?

Think of it like this: you may have great relationships with the three sales managers, but do you truly understand what is upstream and downstream from them and their immediate challenges? Why are they participating? Is it because management said they have to, they think the idea is cool, they get along with you, or they have goals to hit and they believe this will help?

Mapping Bidirectional Streams

A useful exercise we advise you to undergo in value prop development is to map upstream and downstream from the identified, obvious constituent, in this case the sales managers. This does not have to be a formal, time-consuming exercise. In fact, if you completed the alignment exercises earlier in *Managing Knowledge-Based Initiatives*, you will probably see the same high level goals pop up time and time again.

For our purposes, imagine that Acme's reporting structure looks like Figure 6-1. The first thing to notice is that your friends, the Sales Managers, are significantly "downstream."

You already know the motivators of the CEO and the Board of Directors; Acme's alignment artifacts as a corporation represent what is important to them.

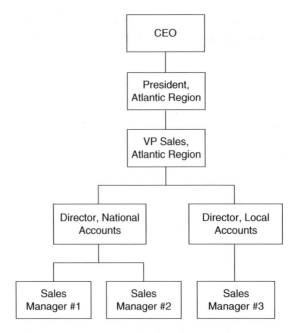

Figure 6-1 An example of bi-directional mapping.

Imagine that after conferring with your executive sponsor and asking some targeted questions, you uncover the following information:

■ The Atlantic Regional President has, among many other goals, to increase Atlantic Region sales by 20%.

■ The Atlantic Regional President determines that the Vice President of Sales is responsible for increasing customer satisfaction by 25% (Acme uses an outside research firm to poll customers, and everyone agrees this is a valid measure), increasing the dollar amount of orders from existing customers by 10%, and increasing the number of Atlantic-based new customers by 10%.

■ The Vice President in turn cascades these goals to each director in the Atlantic Sales organization. Because the Local Sales division is already running close to capacity and has very high scores, the Local Sales Director's goal around customer satisfaction is a 5% increase. The Local group is expected to increase sales by 5%, and the number of new customers by 5%.

■ The National Group has not performed well in past years, so their goals are more ambitious. They are tasked to increase customer satisfaction by 15%, sales by 20%, and new customers by 20%.

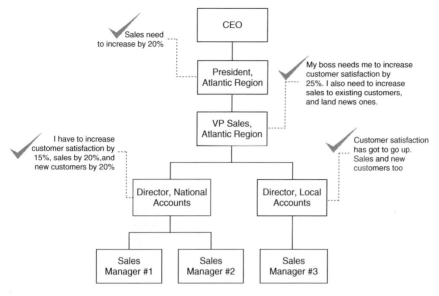

Figure 6-2 New value identified by bi-directional mapping.

Examine Figure 6-2 now, and see how you support activity up and down the food chain.

The thing to remember is that the people you know best, the Sales Managers, may have never had the reason or opportunity to look upstream to really think about their boss' – and their boss' boss – goals. In a well-aligned organization, of course, this would not be an issue. In the real world, however, it is not unusual to find people that are resolutely niched in their part of the company. Even if that works for them, it cannot work for you – you have to know the entire picture. Why?

■ Instead of having a value proposition that supports three members of the Sales Management team, by including the upstream flow, you now have a value prop that supports seven decision-making groups directly – and a multitude of individuals.

■ Instead of being able to demonstrate value to three people who are relatively low on the food chain, who you hope will in turn support you with funding and influence, you can demonstrate value much higher up – where significantly larger budgets and stores of political goodwill lurk. Higher up the food chain usually equals greater access to funding and support.

■ Even though the Sales Managers are willing and pleased to participate in your work, their bosses also need to be on board. Now you know who they are, what their challenges are, and how your work will help them meet their goals.

■ As you engage executives, speaking about their challenges demonstrates that you are aware of the firm as a whole. Even if you do not gain funding from them, getting noticed in a positive light may help you later with influence.

Remember, a value doc includes each group's challenges, how that challenge will be measured, key players that have validated what success measures they will recognize, and a brief diary of interactions with the customer.

7

Using Your Value Props

Once you have developed constituent-facing value propositions, along with your organizational generic value proposition, your work is not done. The care, feeding, and deployment of a value prop is just as critical as the effective execution of other elements of your knowledge-based initiative.

You will:

- Share your value prop(s) – with everyone who will listen.
- Protect your value prop(s) – from anyone who would dilute, reposition, or diminish it.
- Nurture your value prop(s) – by continually shoring it up with examples of successes and victories.
- Honor your value prop(s) – by using it as a guiding mechanism when you are approached with new potential activities, and a measurement when you evaluate your own activities against what you promised.
- Leverage your value prop(s) – by using the facts and figures you will gather and building your own performance scorecard or other vehicle designed to communicate your value. You will also leverage your value prop(s) by continually learning about your organization – its challenges, what works well, what does not work well, the cultural nuances in each group you encounter, and more.

Sharing Value Propositions

You will share value props for general education, proof of your performance, proof of the effectiveness of your knowledge-based initiative, to gain buy in and associated funding and influence, to draw more people into using your solution, and a myriad of other reasons.

Remember, your value proposition contains the "hidden handshake" between you and your customers. While maintaining your value documents, you will track how well you are meeting your commitments. Therefore, as you share value props, you will always have a current stock of success stories to publicize.

Sharing relevant value propositions is critical. You have the chance to share your passion around what you committed to do, how you did it, and the ultimate impact your work had to different audiences.

Current customers. Any time you appear before current customers, open with a recap of the value proposition they validated, what you have done to meet that commitment, and the impact you have seen to date. This can easily fit onto one PowerPoint slide, or be no more than a single bullet on an agenda. Do not spend significant time reminding them, but do remind them. Take the opportunity to harvest new stories and figures.

Your customers should be able to easily describe the value your work provides them. By continually updating them and repeating your value proposition you are not only ensuring that they have the latest progress reports, but you are giving them the language with which to express the value you are adding. In other words, you are doing the hard part for them.

Potential customers. Depending on the nature of your knowledge-based initiative, you will be a salesperson at least part of the time. Therefore, one audience you cannot overlook is potential customers. Sharing sample value propositions with potential customers offers you several benefits:

- They learn about the value you have provided other parts of the firm.
- They see, first hand, the thorough nature of the relationship you have with other customers.
- They see how you fulfill your commitments and track progress.
- They can validate with current customers their experience in participating in your knowledge-based initiative.

Decision makers. You may interact with decision makers, formally or informally, and have the chance to share relevant value propositions with them. Imagine bumping into a Senior Vice President in the break room and having him or her ask what you are working on. Compare these two statements:

- **No/weak value proposition development:** "I'm working with the Pacific region, trying to help them get their teams working together more effectively."
- **Strong value proposition development:** "We have the opportunity, using the virtual workspaces that my team is implementing, to save the Pacific

Region over $180,000 in admin expense this calendar year. We're focusing on helping people collaborate more effectively – no more huge email attachments, phone tag, the usual – and also targeting people who don't collaborate at all today."

Not only does the executive have an idea of the monetary gains that are in place, but he or she also knows who to go to for details: the Pacific Region leadership. PMO representatives may qualify as decision makers too, as might various committees.

Strategy tip: If a senior executive shows interest in your work, even if there appears to be no direct approval or reporting line, keep him or her informed. For more details, see Section VII.

Nurturing a Value Proposition

You must continually update your value docs and in turn, the value proposition itself. Be sure to update the following elements:

- Contacts – who's who for each client, who agreed to key points, who has offered resistance, and so on.
- Changes in client politics or power players.
- Client changes in alignment and/or reporting structure.
- A brief diary of meetings and other interactions.
- The value proposition itself.
- Results of your work – numeric, anecdotal.
- Financial notes – how did any charge backs work? Did you split the cost of any items? Who was your budget go-to person from the client side?
- Client wish list – refer back to this when you look at expanding your work.
- Any problems and resolutions.
- Relevant client language and acronyms.

By keeping information updated, you not only have a record of your work, but you also ensure you are continually in alignment with the customer.

Leveraging Value Propositions

The success or failure of your knowledge-based initiative can influence many things:

- The perception of knowledge-based work inside your firm.
- Your ability to get the support you need to expand current work.

- Your ability to get the support you need to continue your work from year to year.
- Your personal compensation or bonus.
- The perception of you/your professional stature within your firm.
- Your ability to get support for other projects or initiatives.
- Your promotability.

Therefore, it is in your best interest to project a positive image whenever possible. Your value prop, if you maintain it using value docs as we advocate in *Managing Knowledge-Based Initiatives*, can be a rich source of data.

- **Advocates and fans.** Use them for future references, both internal and external. They may contribute to project review or performance reviews.
- **Detractors.** Remain aware of them and perhaps attempt to convert them into supporters.
- **Data and anecdotes about the project and your work.** Data you generate can support project reviews or post-mortem analyses. Both data and anecdotes can be used to support the existence or growth of your knowledge-based program. Both can also contribute to your performance review and resume.
- **Timeline of growth.** Having a timeline is useful for retrospectives and provides a great opening slide when you are later trying to expand your knowledge-based efforts.
- **Your clients.** You have a quick and ready list of all of your clients. Include this list in general presentations about your department or work.

Protecting Value Propositions

The idea of protecting a value proposition may seem ludicrous. If so, consider what a value prop really is – a handshake that says, "This is your problem, this is what I'm going to do to help fix it, and this is what it's worth to you," – and then play out the scenarios that can occur if any of that content is changed. You should begin to see the serious nature of value prop protection.

Value propositions can be damaged in a number of ways. Earlier, we spoke about the importance of identifying initiatives that might be competitors inside your firm and identifying friendly faces. This implies that in addition to competition, you may actually have unfriendly faces inside your firm who, for whatever reason, are not supportive of or actively work to prevent your success. We explore how to deal with naysayers throughout *Managing Knowledge-Based Initiatives*, but for now, let us focus on how a value prop can be damaged. Damage may be inadvertent and easily repaired or averted by education, or might be a concerted effort by an "unfriendly face."

At the heart of any protection scheme you may employ is your ability to remain in control of what is being communicated about your work. Your need to protect your value prop is another reason that knowing your firm inside and out is key; if you do not have your ear to the ground, you may miss the fact that your value prop has been minimized, rebuked, or appropriated until it is too late to make a difference.

Because value prop damage can happen at high levels, it may be necessary to involve your executive sponsor or another trusted senior in this exercise. It is also wise to track "value prop reparation" on paper. Even if you actually correct, for example, an incorrect value prop verbally during a meeting, follow up with an email so that you have a record.

An Incorrect Value Prop

Many elements of a value proposition, when altered, can render it fundamentally incorrect. Elements around who does what, defining the problem(s), the impact of solving the problem(s), or any element that includes dates or figures is suspect to meddling. As mentioned above, value prop damage may be completely inadvertent; the same is true for most of the examples below.

Original Value Prop: *Last year, over $200,000 was charged to mileage in your region, and $180,000 was spent holding virtual meetings using an outside vendor for desktop share. All of that money was processed as administrative expense. If we can eliminate just 20% of the travel, and 80% of the external charges for sharing desktops, that is over $180,000 in savings.*

Incorrect Value Prop: *This initiative will eliminate the need for all travel, thereby saving the Pacific Region hundreds of thousands of dollars each year.*

Response: The response here is obvious: correct the mistake. For example, the response would be something like, "This initiative doesn't eliminate the need for all travel, and from a Knowledge Management point of view, I couldn't advocate for that anyway. People need to occasionally see each other face to face, to establish or enhance a sense of trust. Our conservative estimate is that we can eliminate the need for 20% of the current internal travel. Specifically, these are cases where people are driving to neighboring states just to attend meetings, and usually driving back home the same day. We plan to extend our work and expect that travel can be further reduced once these solutions are fully socialized. We will be in a strong position to do that after this first success."

Finding the Source

If you notice the same mistakes popping up repeatedly, it is possible that they may all originate from a single source. Look for high-volume communicators – administrative assistants, members of your own team that have large networks – as you try to track the source of misinformation. It may be as simple as a misplaced decimal point.

A Rebalanced Value Prop

Imagine that in your original value proposition, a suite of solutions is offered to help associates collaborate effectively, with the full recognition that some groups will benefit more from one tool than the others. Below, see what happens when detractors seize on a single part of a value proposition and blow it out of balance.

Original Value Prop: *The virtual workspaces we plan to deploy can help on both fronts. Your employees will be able to share documents – without emailing them back and forth – so they will always know the latest and greatest version. We will further reduce your administrative expense by in-housing desktop share – no more minute by minute charges to see what is happening on someone else's computer. Instituting secure private chat will help reduce phone tag and is a great way to get quick answers.*

Rebalanced Value Prop: *Sure, some people might use instant messaging for business reasons but most people will just use it for jokes and chit-chat. Maybe even harassment. This initiative is more about enhancing people's social lives than anything else. No way will the company realize tangible gains.*

Response: Your response here will include several different elements. First, you will rebalance the value prop and emphasize that instant messaging is only one of many tools. Second, you will push back against the social aspect as being the most important. Third, you will support that push back with facts and figures, or freely admit that you do not know yet what you will find – but will be open with the results after the tool(s) has been implemented for a given period of time.

For example: "The focus here is collaboration, not chat. Instant messaging is just one of a suite of tools we're using. In other words, it's one of many ways to collaborate. Some groups will benefit more than others from different tools, and we know and expect that. Chat will be archived, and this has passed all compliance committees; chat users know that, like email, nothing is private. Since you've focused on chat, though, let me share some recent industry figures with you . . . ."

A Diluted Value Prop

Imagine your original value prop focuses on collaboration for a single region – and the lever you are using to get executive attention is reduced administrative expense. Remember, before you sold this value prop, you ensured that you had the expertise and resources to live up to it.

Original Value Prop: *Last year, over $200,000 was charged to mileage in your region, and $180,000 was spent holding virtual meetings using an outside vendor for desktop share. All of that money was processed as administrative expense. Since one of your operating imperatives for this year is to decrease administrative expense, our program is a natural fit for you. If we can eliminate just 20% of the travel, and 80% of the external charges for sharing desktops, that is over $180,000 in savings. The Atlantic Region, after participating in our program for just a quarter, has already realized over $50,000 in savings.*

Diluted Value Prop: *Great – these guys have already done this is the Atlantic and the Pacific. Let's target them to immediately take on the North and South regions as well. Looks like this is web-based stuff, and the intranet needs an overhaul. That should go on their plate for this calendar year as well.*

Response: Although this is an extreme example, and one that likely would not make it past the discussion stage, it illustrates a valuable lesson: when you succeed, people will sometimes assume that you can take on exponentially more work. Rarely do they assume that you should receive an equal increase in resources or funding. Perhaps you would be perfectly pleased to take on the North and South regions – as long as you receive four new staff members to help. When you are stretched beyond capacity, though, your ability to deliver what you committed to is severely compromised. At a minimum, that capability is diluted. In the worst case scenario, you may find yourself at the head of a failed initiative.

Well-meaning people may also make incorrect assumptions about the area of your expertise. For example, collaboration experts won't necessarily make great intranet architects. To someone new to the knowledge arena, though, it may all look and feel the same.

This example of a diluted value proposition is clearly being spoken by someone in a position of authority, so you might need to call on your executive sponsor for support. Your response might be something like this: "We're not currently positioned to support the North and South regions, but given some additional funding and resources, I think we could handle that. I'll get those estimates to you later today. I'll also direct you to the intranet team that can help with the redesign. Unfortunately, no one on my team is knowledgeable about our intranet architecture."

Remember, call on your executive sponsor as needed.

A Minimized Value Prop

Sometimes, because of organizational pressure and the speed at which we are accustomed to moving in today's corporate environment, people may brush off your efforts, or minimize them as unimportant. There are several ways to deal with a person who minimizes your value prop.

Original Value Prop: *If we can eliminate just 20% of the travel, and 80% of the external charges for sharing desktops, that is over $180,000 in savings. The Atlantic Region, after participating in our program for just a quarter, has already realized over $50,000 in savings.*

Minimized Value Prop: *$180,000 or $50,000 is a drop in the bucket compared to the $16 million we are supposed to find in our budgets. This may be a "cool new thing" but given everything else on our plate, it is just not that important. I have never even heard of the group proposing it – is this yet another IT project?*

Response: This person is clearly driven by numbers, so that is what you will need to throw back to them. If you have done your homework, you should be able to cite not only your numbers, but those of other firms who have undertaken a similar shift. Again, do not hesitate to call on your executive sponsor or another trusted senior if needed.

Your response might look something like this: "Respectfully, I disagree with your figures. The Pacific region's figures were very conservative – and they only represent one region. That $50,000 savings in the Atlantic represents a single quarter, and we have every reason to believe that the annual savings will add up to over $200,000. Once we get other regions on board, our savings will easily approach a million dollars. In addition, my savings are going straight to the bottom line – no cancelled conferences, reduced headcount, or delay of other planned initiatives needed. This is not a one-time project with a finite start and end; it is a permanent change to how we work together. We will keep reaping these benefits year after year.

"My group, although we work closely with IT, is part of the Enterprise Knowledge Management team. Technology is just an enabler of the bigger picture: getting your staff off the road, back at their desks, and doing their jobs."

An Appropriated Value Prop

You may choose, at some point, to join forces with other projects or programs to pool resources and maximize your impact to the organization. Politically, joining forces may make sense or be something you need to consider to survive. If you join forces with others, trust is key. You both have to trust that your work won't be overshadowed, you will focus on the same goals, and both come out winners.

However, you may find your knowledge-based initiative the target of an attempted "takeover" or "appropriation" by an individual or group that sees the value in it – or is threatened by it. An attempt to redirect your success to their court may seem to be a strange sort of compliment, but such an attempt may also mask the intent to shut your work down.

The tips below assume that an appropriation attempt is not positive or initiated from a genuine business synergy, but rather a power play.

Original Value Prop: *If we can eliminate just 20% of the travel, and 80% of the external charges for sharing desktops, that is over $180,000 in savings.*

Appropriated Value Prop: *My team has an initiative with the mandate of looking for ways to reduce administrative expense. My team should manage this collaborative initiative because it is really just an extension of my work.*

Response: We have seen appropriation attempts happen at both the executive and practitioner levels. Such attempts are generally not a surprise; the person leading the appropriation has probably done it before. Hopefully, in the course of your inside-out investigation of your firm, you developed a list of people to keep an eye on, so you know a little bit about who you are dealing with.

If the appropriation attempt happens at an executive level, it is up to your executive sponsor to counter it. Count on providing your sponsor with any data or arguments that will assist him or her.

At your practitioner level, you can try several tactics that may discourage any would-be poacher. The examples below are provided to get you thinking, but remember to remain true to the culture of your firm and your own personal strengths when stepping into what can be a highly charged political game. If you enter the fray, remember that to many people it is just that: a game. Keep in mind that taking anything personally will hurt your effectiveness. Before you lose your temper, say anything you will regret, or burn bridges, take a step back and call in reinforcements.

Knowledge-Based Work Needs to Remain Autonomous

Sometimes, you can espouse the reasons that knowledge-based work needs to remain autonomous to succeed. If you convince poachers that your work is about far more than the one successful initiative they may be eyeing, they may quickly back off because of the additional work. Even better, they may seek to form a genuine partnership, reasoning that partial glory by association is better than none at all.

Your explanation might look something like this: "Well, we are a freestanding unit for a number of reasons. We serve different businesses units around the company, and we are pleased to serve yours as well. But, you can see how altering our alignment – restricting it to one business unit or one region – would not work well." Smile at the poacher. "Unless, of course, you are prepared to support [put the number of people in your company here]."

Not Today, Buddy

Some would-be peer poachers will stop cold when they realize you are not an easy target. Generally, these people – even if they are your peers on paper – will interact with you as though you are junior, in over your head, or out of the loop with what is happening in the company.

Obviously, those assumptions are wrong, because you have done your homework. Your challenge is to diplomatically let them know that you know their angle and you are not interested. Diplomacy is important because you do not want to create an adversary if you can help it.

For example, imagine being approached with this: "You poor thing! I just heard that you lost two people and your project has slipped into yellow status. You know, I can help. Let me talk to my PMO rep about adjusting your milestones so we can get you back into green status on paper at least. In fact, I have been thinking for a while about inviting you over to my team. I can help with your headcount problems."

Even if some of what the poacher says is true, do not validate it. You might respond like this: "Well, two people rolled off the project as planned – in fact, a little early because we are ahead of schedule. I have never been in yellow status. It is green light all the way. We are actually waiting on another group to move forward. Isn't that just weird, how you got the wrong information? I wonder how that happened!" Smile nicely and walk away.

My Executive Sponsor is Bigger . . .

Another tactic you can take with peer poachers is to let them know up front that you maintain a close and candid relationship with your executive sponsor. If your executive sponsor outweighs theirs, they will back down quickly.

Even if not, dropping your executive sponsor's name may help, because chances are good they are making a poaching attempt without their executive sponsor's blessing. The last thing they want is to have to explain it. If you suggest a roundtable including the poacher, the poacher's boss, and your executive sponsor, he or she will probably decline very quickly.

I am Not Sure I Understand

This last tactic involves, to a degree, playing dumb. The power of a "poacher-bully" is that they intimidate without actually saying anything that you can push back against or escalate for executive intervention. Particularly if you have a mild personality and avoid direct disagreement whenever possible, this tactic can be powerful.

Remember, a peer poacher is probably operating without his or her boss' blessing. These mini-tyrants succeed by intimidation, and by never spelling things out to a degree they can get in trouble for.

Therefore, in this tactic, force poachers to be very specific as to their goals. While appearing to be open to the idea of appropriation (although not understanding it), keep asking for clarification. Chances are good that the poacher will give up. If he or she persists and finally spills the beans, saying something like, "OK, I will make sure your life is easier if you report to me – and I will get the headcount I need to be promoted to director," end the discussion with a smile, and an invitation to take up the poacher's promotion with your executive sponsor, since it will come at your expense. What is key here is to either (a) exhaust the poacher or (b) find out what the poacher is really after.

A Repositioned Value Prop

Using the same example as before, you can see that a repositioned value prop has also caused the knowledge-based initiative to no longer be about connecting people – now it is all about administrative expense reduction.

Original Value Prop: *If we can eliminate just 20% of the travel, and 80% of the external charges for sharing desktops, that is over $180,000 in savings.*

Repositioned Value Prop: *My team has an initiative, and one of its mandates is to look at administrative expense. My team should manage this initiative because it is really just an extension of my work.*

Response: "The reduction of administrative expense is just one outcome of this knowledge-based initiative. It is one of many benefits that we will gain, including [list benefits here.] Repositioning my work beneath this single mandate – reducing administrative expense – compromises my position to be holistically effective, and live up to the value prop I have in place with my other customers. Over the next year, we plan to [other initiative], [other initiative], [other initiative], and none of these are related to reducing admin expense."

A Rebuked Value Prop

A rebuked value proposition refers to cases where one or more people argue against your value proposition. Generally, the "rebuke" will come around the value you state will be derived from your knowledge-based initiative.

People who disagree with your value proposition will have many different motivations. Some will genuinely disagree with you. Perhaps they do not understand your work, or misunderstand the situation. Or, they may have a more holistic picture of the situation than you do. Often, a "rebuker" will dislike the funding or degree of importance that your work is receiving, so they will push back against anything they can. Remember the importance of knowing the history of your work, the people around you, and committee members – it will help tremendously in a situation like this.

It is important to understand individual motivations, because working through genuine concerns with a caring business partner can make your value proposition that much stronger. Addressing unreasonable complaints is an entirely different issue.

Original Value Proposition: *By providing virtual workspaces that will allow associates to share documents, share their desktops, and instant message, we will enable teams to collaborate more easily. This will reduce travel and the associated administrative expense and lost time. We ill also provide an avenue for people who do not collaborate today to do so. Countless avenues for new efficiencies will open up.*

Rebuked Value Proposition: *Let me make sure I understand this. People are not working together today – they do not even know each other. And somehow giving them instant messaging is going to help? Why would you instant message someone you do not even know? It is ridiculous.*

Response: In this case, the "rebuke" centers around an incorrect cause and effect assumption. The trick to dealing with people who form incorrect causal relationships is to refute their claims calmly and systematically. Do not let them interrupt, or talk over you. If they seem determined to start a fight, walk away before you join it. Evaluate whether you really need people's support, and try to gauge how much damage has been done or could potentially be. If you determine it warrants pursuit, coordinate with your executive sponsor as needed. Another option is to bring in a satisfied customer – preferably a business partner the skeptic deals with, and has a degree of respect for – who understands what you are doing and will back you up.

Honoring a Value Proposition

We spoke earlier about a diluted value proposition, where external pressures can force you to dilute the value of your work by broadening your focus to an unmanageable level. *You can inadvertently dilute your own value prop.*

It is easy to:

- Revved up from success, expand your work too quickly, and take on more than you can handle. New and old clients suffer, and your value prop is compromised.

- Agree to expand your work without insisting on additional funding or resources. Doing so may jeopardize your ability to deliver what you promised to your earlier clients.

- Give in to needy customers. It is easy to stray beyond the borders of your value proposition agreement. Using the example from earlier, imagine that a valued client needs some pointers on revamping an intranet site. Since you used to do that, you agree to help – but before long, you are not only offering tips but managing the entire effort. Not only are you spreading yourself too thin, you are failing to honor your value proposition. When your clients think later of the value you delivered, will they recall your knowledge-based initiative? Or the intranet effort? Albeit from good intentions, you are muddying the waters and diluting the impact your work will deliver.

- Stray from your value prop by under delivering ("I know I said we'd have this done, but my team has been swamped by all this extra, unplanned and unbudgeted work") or extra/over delivering ("Sure, we can look at your intranet site, too"). This will almost certainly compromise your value proposition.

Section VI

Executing on the Groundwork

8

Committees, Committees, Committees

One of the most weighted, and perhaps dreaded, terms in the business world is "committee." You may try to avoid participating in voluntary committees or groan about the time wasted in mandatory ones. You might have belonged to a committee that was highly effective, where you learned good team management skills. Or, you might freeze at the thought of having to engage with, or present to, a committee. An ill-informed committee decision may have slowed, or stopped, your work in the past.

Committees come in all sizes and shapes and are called by many names. Some people serve on committees in addition to their regular jobs and rotate in and out after a given length of time. Some seats on committees are sought-after honors. Other people's primary job function includes running or devoting a great deal of time to one or more business-based committees.

Committee Tips

Committees are Just Human, After All

There are no hard and fast rules around governance, purpose, structure, tenure, or perception of committees within or between companies. To complicate matters, the character of a given committee may be entirely different from year to year. Why? The people who comprise the committee may cycle out as new people cycle in. The first thing to remember when dealing with committees is that they are made up of people and reflect the beliefs, culture, values, and behavior of the people who belong to them.

Therefore, statements like, "Compliance committees are always tough" or "No one ever makes it past the IT change management committee," are inaccurate. If you understand the people who make up the compliance committee, for example, its history, and their requirements, the tough committee will probably begin to appear manageable.

Moreover, the rules about which committees you will need to engage, what they do, and what they are named are very different from company to company. Even with the guidelines and methods we provide in *Managing Knowledge-Based Initiatives*, you will have to work through the process of navigating committees relying on your judgment and help from others in your firm.

Search Proactively

Following a common theme in *Managing Knowledge-Based Initiatives*, we believe that finding and subsequently engaging committees, groups, advisory councils, or boards – whatever they may be called in your organization – is a task you should undertake proactively. You have probably discovered by now that there is no cut-and-dried roadmap for your knowledge-based initiative's implementation, so this is one more discovery path you need to undertake.

What are You Looking for?

If you are in a large organization, the chances are good that there are far more committees in total than there are committees relevant to getting your project off the ground. Target your efforts, and look for:

- Committees that have sign-off control over activities that originate from your work area.
- Committees that have governance over the activities of your prime customers as you have identified them to date.
- Committees that control any supporting resource you will involve in your work, such as technology.
- Committees that deal with compliance.
- Committees that deal with projects, which should include your PMO.
- Committees that deal with funding escalations and approvals (e.g., a group that must approve your work if the cost goes over $500,000).
- Committees related to the "how" and "can you" around spending money. This should involve procurement and is addressed in Chapter 10.

- Committees that have a degree of power or influence because of ongoing initiatives that are specific to your firm or industry.
- Ancillary committees that are not required, but are "nice to haves" in the way of influence, such as leadership teams that oversee any of the previous committees.

Along the way, you may find other committees with which you need to interact.

Help is (Hopefully) Nearby

If you work for a firm that has a strong PMO presence, or offers Business Analysts who interact with business units on behalf of other units, ask for help. Like most other things we discuss in *Managing Knowledge-Based Initiatives*, networking is key. Before you start mapping out committees, engage people who can help and see if you can get a head start. Do not forget about your executive sponsor.

One key group that can assist you and may be a stakeholder in your work is the Legal department.

Engaging Your Legal Department

A knowledge-based initiative and the drivers that underlie it are very likely to make sense to a corporate lawyer. A person who has spent a career researching – often online or via CD-ROM – what happened before, why it happened before, and the final outcome will understand challenges around, for example, information codification, defining context, post-event analyses, effective search, and the desire to avoid recreating work already done. Even if the Legal department is not on your list of stakeholders, we advise that you consider placing them there for multiple reasons:

- When it comes to understanding your firm's current challenges, Legal staff can offer a different and well-informed viewpoint.
- A friendly face from your firm's Legal department can validate your list of committees and identify any gaps.
- When planning for the future, a Legal advocate can help you be realistic about six-month-out scenarios.
- Many high level committees have a member from the Legal department that holds a permanent seat.
- An advocate on the Legal staff can likely connect you to executives that may be hard for you to reach alone.

- If you are actively seeking participants for your knowledge-based initiative, a Legal supporter can potentially point you in the right direction.
- The Legal department itself may be a good fit for your initiative – and they probably have alternative buckets of funds from which to draw.
- Final judgments on what is compliant and what is not often come down to Legal staff. Keeping them informed of your activities early on can be valuable.

Your Committee Scavenger Hunt

In a corporation, hundreds and hundreds of committees may exist. How do you know which ones you need to engage? It may seem like a scavenger hunt.

Follow the Headcount and the Money

Whether you need to engage a particular committee depends on a few things. Are people from an area the committee oversees, such as a workgroup or region, going to participate in your initiative in significant numbers? And is that workgroup or region going to contribute to your project in the form of dollars or other resources, including tradeoffs? If the answer is yes to any one of these questions, the chances are good you will have to get an OK from someone who oversees that area.

Keep your eyes peeled for committees that fall into one or more of the following categories.

Sign-Off in Your Work Area

Before you look attempt to locate unknown committees, check in with committees in your own work area that need to know what you are doing. For example, does your boss, or your boss' boss, belong to a leadership team that controls where resources in your division are allocated? Is your department or division contributing funds (other than those represented by your headcount) to your knowledge-based initiative? If so, check with your supervisor to validate whether there are entities in your area that you need to engage. You may find that keeping your boss' boss up to date on your activities is a necessary activity – but not committee-driven.

Committees that Govern the Activities of Your Prime Customers

Your customers may be responsible to committee(s) that need to approve their participation in an initiative, funds they contribute, or both. To make matters more complex, there may be "tiered" committees that function at different levels. Particularly if you start small and grow, you might have to engage with multiple tiers. Tiers are often number or geography-driven.

For example, imagine that you worked with a local Marketing group while piloting your knowledge-based initiative. At some point, someone from that group gave a thumbs up, whether formal or informal, to the local marketing group's participation. If you expand your work to now include 50 participants from Marketing, you may have to get additional sign-off because of the number of people involved. Ask; do not be blindsided.

In addition, if you expand your work from the local Marketing group to include the state, and then the regional Marketing group, you may have to get approval at these different levels. In some firms, you might be able to get the highest level approval (regional, in this case) and that would cover the lower level approvals. In others, you may have to engage with all three committees.

Supporting Resources

To identify supporting resources, close your eyes for a moment and picture your knowledge-based initiative running successfully at full capacity. Put yourself in your customers' shoes and imagine their daily activities. Try to answer these questions:

- Who will your customers call when something is not working?
- Who will they call with questions about how to do, or initiate, something?
- Who will they call with requests that the program or tool do more?
- Who will they call to add or remove people from participation in your knowledge-based initiative?

Think about the programs you participate in today. Whom do you call with these types of questions? Every area you identify is a supporting resource you may need to engage in the course of launching your knowledge-based initiative. Later in *Managing Knowledge-Based Initiatives*, we discuss how to work with your organization's support structures, such as a Help Desk.

Technology-Related Committees

Compliance, standards, and security. IT compliance committees may or may not be related to an IT standards committee. The linkage seems obvious – after all, if you are using in-standard tools, you should be largely compliant – but the committees that govern both may operate separately. In addition, you may find that compliance happens at different levels (e.g., local vs. regional, 10 people vs. 100 people, pilot vs. production), while IT standards tend to cut across all levels. Security may be driven by a desire to comply with corporate guidelines, but security is not compliance in and of itself. Likewise, security does not necessarily represent a standard. If it seems that the three should be closely related, you are right – but they are not identical.

Actual technology used. This includes software, and potentially hardware if your software requires a certain hardware configuration, or an eager vendor is willing to donate hardware to help you get started. If your knowledge-based initiative includes introducing new technology into your firm, seek out any technology standards committees early on.

Security. The people who ensure that you are using approved hardware and software are likely different than the people who ensure that what you are using, and how you want to use it, is secure. First of all, they determine what secure means in your firm. Because of external events in recent years (think of everything from hurricanes and changes in technology to multiple data thefts and Sarbanes Oxley legislation), most IT departments pay more attention to security now than they did a decade ago. If you are in a regulated environment, such as healthcare, you may have another layer of security that is necessary to meet government requirements.

In addition, because the Internet and its associated protocols offers numerous new ways of sharing information – which, after all, is part of what a knowledge-based initiative usually involves – if you do not build a good working relationship with your firm's security people, you could be a collision course with them.

Count on investigating whether you need to involve IT security if your knowledge-based initiative:

- Introduces new software into the firm, particularly if it is web-based;
- Opens up information that was previously inaccessible to users for any purpose;
- Involves sharing outside of your company by opening up part of a current system (e.g., providing valued customers with their own portal);
- Involves allowing outside people to tunnel into your existing environment (e.g., providing valued customers a way to log into your systems to check invoices);

- Runs on devices other than a computer, like a Blackberry, cell phone, or other hybrid;
- Uses technology that does not allow for transaction archiving. For example, if your solution includes an instant messaging component, investigate whether there is a way to archive those conversations for business compliance. Even if you are not a proponent of conversation archiving, it may not be optional from a security and compliance point of view. Just make sure you heavily publicize the fact that it is archived with your end users.

The number of seats. Your firm may have number-driven standards. The number of people that participate in your knowledge-based initiative may become a standards, support, pricing, or hardware standards trigger. In one firm we know of, a knowledge-based initiative remained in "pilot" (instead of production) status although it grew exponentially. When the number of participants topped 2,000, the project leader got a call from the IT standards committee. By their rules, the software tools used in the knowledge-based initiative had to be declared a corporate standard because of the number of people using them. This entailed a new and separate chain of committee appearances. The point to take away is that the knowledge practitioner was not aware and did not proactively engage this committee.

If you encounter a similar situation, even if you do not call the standards committee first, be prepared to answer their questions. Incidentally, the declaration of this knowledge practitioner's toolset as a corporate standard also led to the pilot being declared a full-blown program. The bureaucracy helped shake loose a process roadblock that had resulted in the work remaining in pilot mode long after it had proven its business value.

The number of seats can also have a backlash effect on the cost of the software and associated hardware. Using the example above, the technology being used had, like most technologies, recommended and supportable hardware configurations. In that solution, there was an instant messaging component and the software configuration supported up to 2,000 users on a single server. Therefore, when the 2,001th person joined the environment, a new server had to be purchased, configured, and put into production – and all of these activities required time, expertise and money. If your knowledge-based initiative grows at a furious pace and you expand the number of participants faster than you originally planned, do not overlook that this growth may consume resources in the background if you are using any sort of technology. Frequently, if you stray "out of bounds" from planned activity, even because of positive growth, you will need to explain yourself to – you guessed it – a committee.

The number of participants may also trigger a support avenue of discovery. Behind the scenes, there are multiple pockets of IT support of which you might not be aware. Adding a new server, for example, means that someone, somewhere, has to support that server. There may be pushback if that support was not planned or budgeted. In addition, someone will also have to support all the end users that your knowledge-based initiative creates. We will dive further into the question of working with IT in Chapter 11, but it is something to remain aware of when you set about discovering IT committees you may interact with.

Assorted change control committees. Although we explore change control later, it is worth noting that different areas may have their own change control mechanisms. Using the example above, imagine that the increase in users means that software must be installed on all the new users' computers. In many corporations, even if the software is approved, perhaps even a standard, and sufficient licenses have been purchased, the act of installing the software itself might be governed by change control.

Proprietary systems. Are you touching a proprietary system? By proprietary, we mean a system – software and perhaps hardware – that has been customized heavily to meet your firm's unique business needs. Talent in your firm may have created a proprietary system, or altered a system purchased from outside. Often, the system's vendor or externally retained consultants may have performed these customizations. A proprietary system may be functionally or geographically based, or a combination. For example, imagine that you work for an insurance company. Your firm may have a proprietary underwriting system. There may be an Atlantic Region underwriting system that is completely different than the one used in the Pacific Region. While this would not be an ideal situation, you will find it often in companies that have grown rapidly, particularly by acquisition. Try to understand if you are touching any proprietary system, because it may very well have its own level of governance, particularly if the activity it supports – such as underwriting – is heavily governed.

Non-IT Compliance

Compliance lives in your corporation in more areas than just IT. Depending on your corporation, being declared "in" or "out" of compliance may be a general and not terribly serious statement, a non-negotiable loss of job declaration, or somewhere in between. For example, a person who leaves a company-issued laptop unlocked at his or her desk may be out of compliance if protecting company property is a compliance issue – and be in no trouble whatsoever. A person who fails to accurately report vacation time may also be in violation of compliance, and this could result in him or her immediately entering the ranks of the unemployed.

The compliance committees you need to seek out are the ones that will impact your ability to deliver and execute your knowledge-based initiative. There are likely to be compliance committees that are completely irrelevant to your work; you will have to do some sleuthing to determine which ones you need to interact with in the near future and which ones may have to get involved later on.

Funding Escalation Committees

As we mentioned earlier, you may have to deal with tiered committees that have influence over your customers' participation. We offered examples of tiered committees around headcount and geography. There is another tiered element you may need to consider: financial sign-off limits.

In general, corporate leadership, whether managers, directors, or vice presidents, have "sign-off ceilings." For example, a manager may be able to approve expenditures up to $25,000. A director might have a $50,000 ceiling and a vice president might have a $150,000 limit. Sign-off ceilings will vary greatly from division to division and firm to firm. You can almost think of sign-off limits like credit card limits with one huge difference: even if the money is available, when it moves to the next sign-off level, you can count on having to explain yourself all over again. It is precisely for this reason that partners in an initiative will often work to keep single contributions below that ceiling.

For example, imagine that you and your executive sponsor have secured funding for a $500,000 project. You brought together several business units, IT, and your own group to contribute the funds. Business Units A and B are contributing $150,000 each. IT and your group are contributing $100,000 each.

At the last minute, Business Unit B has to drop out because of budget cuts. Luckily, Business Unit A views your work as critical and can step in with an additional $150,000. Here is the tricky part: the Vice President from Business Unit A that you have been working with has sign-off approval up to $150,000. Since Business Unit A is going to pick up an additional $150,000, for a total of $300,000, a Funding Review Committee chaired by the President of that business unit must now sign off on the work.

Gaining the support of that Funding Review Committee is definitely not a bad thing – but it becomes a question of risk and timing. There is the risk that the committee might not see the value of the knowledge-based initiative, particularly if the value proposition is not presented to them in the strongest possible fashion. They could demand further investigation, lower the amount the business unit will contribute, or stop the expenditure – and possibly the project – entirely. Even if the committee can be convinced of the value of your knowledge-based initiative, getting meeting time to sell/explain your work, and then getting the actual sign-off, could consume months that you may not have.

You might not have to juggle the demands of gaining and managing funding from multiple areas. However, even if you have a single funding source, it is probable that sign-off limits exist.

Strategy tip: Be sensitive as you ask questions around sign-off limits and the funding escalation path; in some firms, this is like asking about a person's salary or performance reviews.

Incidentally, in the scenario above, you might attempt to avoid the involvement of the Funding Review Committee using a couple of tactics:

- Find other business partners so that no one maxes out on their sign-off limits.
- Investigate opportunities to barter, or trade off work to entice other business partners to support your initiative.
- Attempt to phase the work so that half of it can be charged back in the next fiscal year, which again lowers the immediate sign-off amount to within current limits.
- Attempt to get the direct support of the President in the above scenario, hoping that if he or she signs on as co-executive sponsor, your work will be rubber stamped or the President's personal sign-off limit will take care of it.

If none of those scenarios is possible, it would be time for a full out investigation and frontal sales attack on the individual members of that committee and their influencers. We investigate selling your work in Section VII. Be sure to check out Chapter 9 for more insight on what really happens behind the scenes when projects are prioritized and funded.

Ongoing Initiatives

Industries, and the companies that comprise them, face unique challenges. For example, the healthcare industry was turned upside down when HIPAA became law. Whether insurers or healthcare providers, people had to learn to communicate differently, use new procedures around patient information, and deal with reams of new paperwork. Other industries and individual firms have their own challenges.

To answer these challenges, companies frequently form committees, whether called a committee, task force, center of excellence, or other name. A committee that is formed to answer a challenge specific to your firm or industry may have a degree of sign-off in your work.

You will become aware of committees like this by performing the "inside-out" and "outside-in" scan of your firm as we discussed in Section II. In addition, networking with people with experience launching initiatives in your firm and coordinating with your executive sponsor are important.

Making Sense of the Committees

If you have scanned your corporation for the areas we identify above, and potentially identified other areas unique to your situation, you may have quite a list of committees. Grouping them will help you determine the right way to approach them. It is wise to engage your executive sponsor in validating your conclusions.

Grouping Committees

Before you engage any of the committees you identify, you need to determine which ones are crucial, procedural, optional, or irrelevant. Furthermore, you must identify which committees a defined process will steer you towards and which committees work outside of processes.

Independent or Defined by Process

Loosely group the committees that you uncovered as "defined by process" or "independent."

A "defined by process" committee is one that you would have discovered while following your company's processes regardless of your sleuthing. These committees tend to be process-driven and are probably plugged into your PMO. Note where and when in the chain of events you will engage with defined by process committees.

An "independent" committee is one that operates outside of your PMO(s) or other processes. For example, a Center of Excellence that was recently established to help combat concerns about customer privacy in your organization might have a stake in your knowledge-based initiative if participants touch customer information or your initiative offers a vehicle where they could exchange customer information. If it is a relatively new group, it may not be fully plugged into the PMO yet. If its lifecycle is expected to be short, it may never be integrated into your firm's processes deliberately. By calling out independent committees, you ensure that you do not miss them. You will likely have to make yourself known to them, since a process won't guide you to them – or them to you.

Strategy tip: Independent committees often have deep pockets underwritten by the uppermost levels of senior leadership. Can you identify a synergy between their goals and your work?

Crucial, Procedural, Optional, Irrelevant

Now categorize the committees by how important they are to your work.

Crucial committees: These are the ones who can stop or delay your work. Without approval, or with veto, from crucial committees, your initiative can cease to exist. "Without approval" or "with veto" does not necessarily mean the same thing. For example, a review committee might have veto power on your work. A failure to veto does not mean they actively support your work. It just means that they choose not to stop it at this time.

Procedural committees: These are committees that you have to appear before to show that you have done your legwork – dotted the "i"s and crossed the "t"s – but there is little to no question that your work will be approved. In a procedural committee, if you follow the procedures and answer questions correctly, an approval stamp is a sure thing.

Optional committees: These do not have veto power over your work, but it is generally wise to engage them. If an optional committee chooses to actively oppose the launch of your knowledge-based initiative it could prove problematic – but they do not have to vote "yes" either.

Irrelevant committees: These are committees that have nothing to do with your work, or the work of your customers. They are in no way touched by your knowledge-based initiative.

You may identify other buckets unique to your situation.

The Working Mechanics

Now that you have not only located the committees you need to work with, but categorized them into groups, the true legwork begins.

Beginning with the highest priority committees (crucial, if you used our suggested groupings), gather the following information:

- The committee charter and who the group is ultimately accountable to.
- When the committee meets.
- Any voting/decision schedules that could affect your initiative.
- What you have to do to get on their agenda.

- The information they will require from you.
- Who sits on the committee, and where they fit into the larger hierarchy.
- Who you know in the committee.
- Who the power holders are in the committee.
- Any special, undocumented hot buttons of the power holders of the committee, or the committee as a whole.

Administrative Details

You should be able to gather administrative details about a committee without much difficulty. The trick is to begin not with the committee members themselves, but with administrative support staff. Support staff are probably the only people who really know when every meeting is and if not, they can refer you to the people who do. If possible, try to engage administrative resources in-person rather than on the phone. You can learn a lot by watching non-verbal clues.

Once you find the right source of information, whether it is the administrative resource or someone else, explain that you anticipate the need to appear before the committee. Emphasize that you want to do things the right way, and this is why you are speaking to him or her (the administrative support) first. People who are detail-focused and on the hook for making events run smoothly appreciate people who recognize the value of planning; you should win an advocate.

Be prepared to do a "mini-pitch" to the support person, and do not, under any circumstances, discount how important this person could be to getting on the committee's agenda, getting enough presentation time, and succeeding overall. If your engagement with this committee is a predecessor to another activity, make sure that the administrative resource knows that your appearance needs to be "hard scheduled." Also be clear about who your customers and executive sponsor are. Otherwise, like many things in the corporate world, your appearance may be bartered, delayed, or cancelled.

Request or validate the following information:

- Who sits on the committee.
- Meeting schedule, including voting/decision timelines.
- Any forms you must complete or the preferred formats of presentations.
- Whether you need to provide your presentation for review before the meeting.
- Request a copy of any successful presentations others have done.
- Explore the possibility to appearing the week before the formal presentation to conduct an informational session.

- Think about other creative ways to get to key people to share information with them before the meeting.
- Ensure you have the name of the committee correct. Particularly if your firm uses acronyms, it can be easy to make a small mistake that has huge consequences.
- Ask if there is an easily accessible copy of the committee charter available (check your intranet first).
- Ask whom the committee is ultimately accountable to, if there is any gray area.
- Find out where the meeting will be, if it is in-person. Will you need an Internet connection? Projector? Make sure one is available.
- If the meeting is virtual, will you present your materials using a desktop share tool? Who will set that session up, including dial in numbers and password distribution?

Fishing for Details

If you establish a good rapport with the administrative resource, try to find out as much as possible about the following:

Power holders. Scan the list of members and simply ask questions. For example: "Ah, this is chaired by the Vice President of Administration? I have heard that he is great to work with but haven't met him yet." You may get a statement like, "Well, he is in charge but never comes to the meetings – he sends someone else instead." Then, you know to target that someone else. Or, the administrative resource may shoot you a warning look when you mention that the Vice President is great to work with, which can be a sign that he is difficult or unpopular with some people. Learn as much as you can.

Hot buttons. A statement like, "I bet these guys are neck-deep in that new synergy savings initiative. They must be incredibly busy," may net you a confirmation, or an explanation of what the committee is really involved in.

Dynamics. Are committee meetings argumentative or do the members laugh a lot? What is the general tenor? Do meetings frequently run over? You can find this out by asking the administrative resource when he or she would suggest you arrive, and when you can count on being free. If the resource cautions you to leave an hour window around a 15 minute appearance, you can anticipate that meetings do not always stick to the suggested times on the agenda. A good way to find out committee dynamics is to confess that you are nervous and ask for suggestions about how to engage the committee. A sympathetic support person will probably share what he or she has seen succeed – or fail.

We offer detailed guidelines about engaging executives in Section VII. The tips you will find there will be useful in dealing with any appearance. Be aware, though, that you may appear in front of committees of peers. Not every committee that you deal with will necessarily be comprised of senior staff.

Who is Who?

Once you have learned as much as you can from people who support the committee, it is time to look closely at the individuals who make up the committee.

Remember the friendly faces exercise you went through earlier? Examine the list, preferably with your executive sponsor, and identify any people that are supportive of your work. Also, look for people who, if engaged, would probably become advocates of your knowledge-based initiative.

With your executive sponsor and/or any friendly faces, validate your understanding of the committee along these topics:

- Power players.
- Hot buttons, both of the committee as a whole and of the power players.
- Dynamics.
- What to expect when you engage them.
- Tips for succeeding.
- Legwork you should do/things you should know before appearing.

You should find that you are developing not separate points of view around engaging a single committee, but rather a holistic, balanced view.

The Importance of Timing

You may discover that one or more of your crucial committees meet perhaps once or twice a quarter. Imagine the following scenario.

Your knowledge-based initiative is going well, so well that you picked up a region that previously had opted out of participating as a new customer. They even have funds to contribute. Everything is in place: you can support these new customers, technology components do not factor in, and they are excited and ready to join your knowledge-based initiative.

However, the region itself has a review board that holds the reigns on all expenditures over $200,000. Your primary customer in that region is very senior, so you do not expect a problem in getting approval. However, that approval has to be in place before you can proceed.

You track down the support person who sets up the meeting schedules for this committee and discover, to your horror, that the committee only meets twice a year and renders its decisions 30 days after each meeting. Even though it is only January, the March meeting agenda is completely full. The October meeting only has a single slot left. Will your new clients have to wait 11 months to participate in your knowledge-based initiative?

In this extreme example, a solution will probably require personal intervention by your customer, executive sponsor, or a supportive PMO; there is little that you can do alone. However, remaining cognizant of when crucial committees meet and render decisions is key to your success. A situation like this can become more complicated if, for example, this committee's approval is a predecessor to another activity.

Post-Committee Engagement

After you engage with a committee, do not forget the routine details.

Before you leave the meeting:

- Reiterate any to-do items that you have and commit to when the committee should expect them.
- If you are waiting for a decision from the committee, validate when and how you should expect to hear.
- Do you have any leave-behinds? For example, a pamphlet that details your pilot results? If so, distribute or arranged to have distributed.

Back at your desk:

- Consider following up with a brief thank you email to participants. This depends heavily on your corporate culture; in some firms, it would be considered internal spam. What is appropriate in any culture if a follow up note that asks or answers a question, or offers a thoughtful solution to a problem the committee raised.
- Validate with any friendly faces how it went from their point of view, and ask for coaching.
- Debrief with your executive sponsor and determine next steps.

9

Working with PMOs

PMOs are arguably not committees. However, to a person implementing an initiative in a firm, PMOs are one more group, potentially among many, that must be engaged. If you are lucky, your PMO will guide your interactions with committees, or at least point you in the right direction so that you can plan what you need to do, and with whom you need to do it. On the other hand, if your PMO or the segments of your PMO you must work with are not mature, interacting with them may feel like one more check box on your list of to do items.

Throughout *Managing Knowledge-Based Initiatives*, we reference PMOs frequently because most of the activities we discuss can be framed in a PMO context. To get an insider's look at PMOs – Project Management Offices – we talked to John Collier. John spends his days juggling an over $60 million budget on behalf of a segment of the IT PMO organization for one of the world's most successful direct-sale vendors.

If you are new to the idea of a PMO – or multiple PMOs – that govern your work, John can sympathize. After years of working as a functional project manager in the consulting world, he moved into the PMO at a non-consulting firm. "I'd never had to get projects chartered before. Then all of the sudden, I'm at this huge company that owns their own IT group and has a $300 million IT budget in place." The big numbers do not mean that every potential project gets funded, though. "It sounds like a lot," John says, "but it goes really fast. You have to figure out how to get a part of that budget."

Keep these points in mind as you begin to decipher the existence of PMOs at your company, their level of maturity, and potential project impacts.

- More than likely, in a large entity, you will have a somewhat mature IT PMO, if for no other reason than Sarbanes-Oxley.
- Do not assume that your work does not qualify as a project. Even if your solution does not have a significant technology element, it involves people

139

that will use your solution. For example, your participants' man-hours in building and testing your solution could push your knowledge-based initiative into what your firm considers to be a "project."

■ Successfully engaging your PMO depends on multiple factors: your networking ability, strong executive support, the compelling nature of your business case, and your willingness to deal with the details.

■ If your firm has a strong PMO presence, not engaging your PMO will probably lead to the eventual failure of your project.

■ Business PMOs, as well as IT PMOs, will exist – but which came first? Figuring out the relationship matters, because one may drive the other. Who is the boss? You need to understand your firm's PMO history.

■ There are no guarantees. Your company's priorities shift as market conditions do. Stay on top of them, and what is important to your company, and you will be prepared to respond to challenges.

More Knowledge, Less Paperwork

Knowledge Management practitioners tend to be an enthusiastic bunch of people. We love what we do, believe intrinsically that it is the right thing to do, and may become frustrated when we perceive a bureaucracy standing in between us and our vision of a knowledge-enabled enterprise. Collier has been on both sides of the fence. "Before I moved into the PMO, my attitude was, 'Just give me my project, get out of my way, and who cares about your paperwork? The company is going to do this project. It's not optional.' But I moved from not having to worry about any sort of priority – the CEO said we're going to do this, so we are – to having to figure out how we get everything done."

As you engage with seemingly entrenched project bureaucrats, consider this: they were probably driving, and managing, projects that they were as passionate about as you are about your own at some point in their career, or they would not be in the position of responsibility they are now. How can you engage them? How can you make them as infected with enthusiasm as you are?

Accountability, Sarbanes-Oxley, and PMOs

It may seem that your firm's PMOs exist to make your life more difficult. Justifying your work multiple times can be exhausting, particularly if you are confronted with people who are not as enthusiastic as you are about knowledge enabling your firm's work environment.

It is key to understand that PMOs do more than just present a wall of bureaucracy that stands between you and your goals. PMOs exist, in part, to make sure your company continues to exist. "Part of the reason that PMOs got so big and centralized is because of increasing regulatory requirements. SOX (Sarbanes-Oxley) audits, for example," John said. "If you're decentralized, it's hard to pass audits later. If you do a project just because it feels like the right thing, there's no trail that shows there's any accountability on *how you are spending the company's money*. It looks like you don't have any oversight on how you prioritize and spend funds. You need the paper trail – for example, charters – to prove it."

The people who comprise your PMO may not like wading through process any more than you do. However, the rigor around priority and funding is not just good business practice – depending on your company, it may be the law.

John expanded on how his role ultimately is accountable to stockholders. "While it seems like there's a lot of paperwork, there are good reasons when you understand it all. My group reports to a global management committee. They report to the Board of Directors, and they're accountable to our stockholders. Having a structured PMO shows that we *try* to have the right processes in place to lower risk, get projects delivered on time and on budget, and improve the probability that we're working on the right things. This is why there's so much rigor around the prioritization process."

In other words, engaging with, and playing by the rules of, your firm's PMOs is not optional.

What is the History of Your PMO?

We have already addressed the importance of understanding the history – how the organization got to be the way it is – at your company, and the formation of your firm's PMO is no exception. "About four years ago, we started building out stronger Project Management organizations," John explained. "At our company – and most large companies – PMOs just mushroomed. They were self-created to support executive needs. In my situation, the business side PMO is what I call 'the right hand of god.' Although I don't report to them I have a dotted line to them in the hierarchy. I make sure they get what they need from my organization."

Do not be surprised if one area of your firm's PMOs is more built out – and has substantially more rigor around processes – than other areas. Look for heavy PMO involvement around strong leaders that have significant financial responsibilities and accountabilities. As you identify the key players in your initiative's successful implementation, map out the PMOs they belong to, and look for friendly entry points into that PMO. Anticipate the potential need, depending on how synchronized your firm's PMO efforts are, to provide slightly different information to different PMOs.

Natural Affinities Between PMOs and Knowledge-Based Work

PMOs, like any other area in your company, have their own challenges. Those challenges are very often the same challenges that your knowledge-based initiative may address. "In big companies," Collier says, "PMOs will be segregated, matrixed, and reorganized a million times, along with the rest of the organization. A lot goes into building out Project Management organizations. You'd be surprised how much we have to do 'below the line.' We put a lot of rigor into trying to build out repeatable processes. We focused on improving communications, documenting process flows, building useful templates, and a calendar that shows you how and when you need to interject yourself into our roadmap."

As a knowledge practitioner, your ears should perk up at several of John's points. Repeatable processes. Improved communications. Building useful templates – which implies being able to find, distribute and share them effectively. Building a common calendar – which again, implies being able to find, understand, and share it effectively. All of these can be interpreted as knowledge-based challenges. In other words, if you pitch it right? The PMO could become your best friend and perhaps even drive adoption of your solution.

Strategy tip: If your solution involves an element of enhanced remote collaboration that can be adapted to fit project teams that work together remotely, exploit it. Likewise, if you have been knocked down trying to get a platform, or the correct support, for your knowledge-based initiative, consider asking one or more PMOs for support. You may gain a new executive (or co-executive) sponsor.

Making It to Your Corporate Project Roadmap

Although John works for IT, that does not mean he is disconnected from business. He, like most people working in IT in organizations today, recognizes that IT exists to support, serve, and enhance the business of their companies. A large part of John's job is to stay on top of the needs of the business partners he represents. "Particularly in large organizations, business partners generally have their own IT representatives," John explained. "If you're trying to get something done, the key is to find your IT team. You may not even know you have one – but you do. In a large company, there must be some sort of centralized organization."

Although some elements of John's PMO activities may be company-specific, most of them can be generalized to any large firm. The concept of a "roadmap" is central to how John works with his business partners. "We do annualized roadmapping with quarterly refreshes, and use change control review boards to manage the processes. Every few weeks I work with a business PMO – they are now as centralized and organized as the IT PMO. I work with hundreds of business partners. Each one of them thinks that their projects and priorities are the most important."

Strategy tip: Now that you know business partners compete over whose work is most important, why settle for one business partner? Look for synergies across multiple, unconnected areas. Each one comes with its own executive sponsor; each one has bargaining power; the combined influence of many sponsors is nearly always greater than having a single, albeit powerful, executive sponsor.

John defines roadmapping as, ". . . the process of prioritizing and selecting work, and an integration of IT and business. We allocate the work that IT will be doing for the year. In a business, IT is an expense, although theoretically we're saving more than we're spending, usually around a 10:1 ratio. During roadmapping, a whole lot of ideas are thrown around. When something makes it to the roadmap, it's been approved and it's in budget. Until then, it's just an idea. A proposal."

Although your firm may call it something different, it is safe to say the equivalent of roadmapping exists somewhere. You will face multiple challenges in getting your project on the roadmap of an IT and/or business PMO. As John notes above, until you are in your company's roadmap, your idea is just that: an idea. Transforming that idea into reality requires action on your part, and ensuring that you are on the right roadmap will require attention to details. At John's firm, business and IT build a common roadmap together. How does it work at your company?

Once you make it through the initial prioritization exercise at your company, do not lose contact with PMO representatives you formed a relationship with. "Stay in touch with what's going on," John cautions, "and don't assume you're safe because you made it through the roadmapping exercise."

A Strong Business Case Increases Odds of Longevity

Creating a business case may be new to you – but if you are in a firm that has a strong PMO presence, the PMO is there to help you. In some companies, you may be asked to package your business case in a PowerPoint presentation. In others, you may have to input key metrics and descriptions and justifications into a software tool.

Although the names and formats of the elements that will make up your business case will vary, when it comes to dealing with your PMO they support a common cause – to secure funding and a slot in your company's roadmap, then ensure that your position and priority remain rock solid. Two elements that you should anticipate building, at a minimum, are the project charter and a cost-benefit analysis. Your analysis, attention to detail, and conformance to PMO standards must be meticulous, even if you are certain your project is a "shoe in" for support.

The Importance of a Comprehensive Cost-Benefit Analysis

John outlined how things work in his firm. "If you approach our PMO, you'll have to do a charter request – a project request – and it will always have a scope statement, a vision statement, and a CBA (cost-benefit analysis). The part that the businesses own is really the CBA." It can be tempting – especially if budget dollars are plentiful and your project has executive blessings – to scrimp on the details. "A weak CBA might make it through the process depending on the people in power and amount of budget scrutiny that is going on," John continued. "But, the stronger you make your business case early on, the better off you'll be when bargaining around the roadmapping process gets tough."

"It's possible," John explains, "that my budget my shrink. We re-lock on our budgets at least every quarter, and projects may be pulled, or traded, off." If your project is pulled off, it could be shelved indefinitely; if it's traded off, it could be delayed. John continued. "If we end up with, for example, firm-wide challenges to the bottom line, I'm going to inherit part of those challenges. I may have to figure out how to travel less or cut consulting dollars – and still get work done."

If financial challenges force people in John's position to trade off projects, the survival of your project may depend on the compelling nature of your business case – and strong, demonstrable, executive sponsorship. Even if you have that strong executive sponsorship, do not skip the steps necessary to propel your case from being interesting to irresistible. Irresistible may be a minimum standard if budgets are later slashed. And, who knows where your executive sponsor will be in six months, let alone a year?

ROI Figures in Prioritization

ROI is historically a challenge for knowledge-based initiatives, and it is one that you will have to face when you engage with your PMO, as well. Early ROI figures will actually be derived from your cost-benefit analysis. In John's firm, the formula works like this: "For example, if IT says your project will cost $600,000, and you can say the annualized benefit of your project is $300,000 over the next five years for a total of 1.5 million dollars, your ROI is about 2:1. It all comes down to that: having a good ROI. If your project has a 1:1 ROI and there's another project that has a 10:1 ROI, you can imagine where our attention is going to be focused."

As you are putting together your CBA, leave no rock unturned. You may be able to point to hard dollar savings, but have you also included soft dollar savings? Have you created a linkage from your firm's current challenges to the solutions you offer by your choice of language and presentation? Map the language in your CBA to the current buzzwords in your firm. For example, if the phrase "enhancing customer experience" has shown up in every executive presentation for the last six months and your solution addresses that issue, use those words when you create your cost-benefit analysis.

John says that from the PMO point of view, "There are hard benefits and there are soft. The soft benefits might be things like cost avoidance, avoiding being fined, or ensuring compliance. For example, imagine a process improvement. While it's not going to hit the bottom line exactly, extrapolate it out. If you can save ten people ten hours a week and translate that time savings into dollars, you'll get your benefits in a row."

Some firms are skeptical of soft ROI; some are not. Some PMOs will challenge and require proof of claimed ROI figures; others leave that up to the business partners that sponsor work. Your individual situation will vary, so it is important to understand all the variables. For more information, see Chapter 10.

Juggling Multiple PMOs

As you work through getting your knowledge-based project funneled through your PMO, remember that you need support from your business PMO as well as the IT PMO that coordinates with it. Even if your knowledge-based initiative does not have an IT component, as you move to enterprise focus, the chance that it will involve multiple business areas increases. "The business partners I work with *prioritize their own things,*" John explains. This reinforces the need for you to get your work in front of – and keep your work in the minds of – the key players in your organization. If your business sponsor sits down for a negotiation with someone in John's position and does not lobby for your project, you could find yourself in the traded-off or shelved position.

There is a delicate balance between who pays for what elements of a project as well – and if you are leading a project implementation, you need to know how those transfers happen. John's experience is standard for large firms, and the organizational workarounds that can be facilitated by augmenting IT funds with business funds are worth noting. "When we work with businesses, they might provide us extra funding that doesn't have to go through the approval process up to the CIO because it's coming from their budget," Collier explains. "If we need bonus consulting or capital, for example to make a project come in on time because our resources are tight, the business partner might cut a PO out of their own cost center."

Make sure you know where the funds that will fuel your project come from and explore any hidden pockets of revenue. Assuming that your project has any IT component, at a minimum you will need IT resources and potentially associated hardware and software. Do not assume IT can – or will – pay for it all. Your business unit may be asked to kick in some funds too.

What to Think About First

We asked John to think through the steps that he would go through if he were new to executing a project that has an IT component in a large organization.

"The first thing to figure out is if you need IT resources. *Somebody* in your organization owns them and there's going to be a formal process around getting them. Even if IT people in your organization really want to support you, they can't just do it at will. Find out who your IT contact is. Moving up your chain of command should take you straight to the right person. Then, use this information to plug into your PMO. Most PMOs will have documented processes, templates, procedures, etc. that will tell you how to plug in. The key is really having good communication. Once you find the right people, find out how things are getting prioritized in your organization."

Can You Just Ignore the PMO?

We asked John about the temptation to skip the PMO/prioritization process altogether, and how likely a project that is completely grassroots is to succeed in a large organization. Does flying under the radar actually work in large organizations?

"It happens," John says, "and you might even be able to get *part* of what you need done. But you won't get all of it. Where it comes to a grinding halt is at the point that you need to get your systems into the data centers. That's when it will catch up with you – *fast*. Everything there is so locked down and so secure, that the processes will stop you if you haven't followed them."

Barter, Trade, Delay

A recurring theme in *Managing Knowledge-Based Initiatives* is that understanding your relationship with your executive sponsor – and capitalizing on it – is key to your success. When it comes to navigating PMOs, it is no different. The lesson for you, though, is that simply gaining an executive's support is not enough. You have to maintain that support, and be ready, at every turn, to educate and reinforce that how your initiative will help the executive is still true. When funding gets tight in the PMO, executive support can make the difference between your project being executed, delayed, or bartered off for another project that is perceived as more valuable.

It is useful to know what the process looks like from John's point of view. "You really have to find something that executives care about. For example, imagine that you're going to need some IT resources that I control, but you haven't engaged me yet. I go through my standard roadmapping session at the beginning of the year. I have $60 million to spend, and there are 80 projects in line. I allocate everything. A few months later, you pop up with a brilliant idea. Unless you have strong sponsorship, I'm going to say, 'Sorry - see you in eight months.' If a new project is coming onto my plate, something else has to come off. If you don't have an executive sponsor with the power to do, or influence, that trade off? It's very easy to look you in the face and say, 'No.' It's a whole different enchilada if you're an executive. An email can change everything."

For projects that he knows do not have strong backing, John won't even initiate a sizing effort. "People have to follow our processes before we'll size the effort. If I know something isn't going to work, I'm not going to waste the resources to size it."

Collier continued. "You have to recognize that executive clout won't necessarily get you on my roadmap. But it *will* get you listened to, and at least sized. If your executive wants it – and has a lot of clout – then it's my job to go toe-to-toe with him or her. The executive will help me decide what comes off the plate, or agree to pony up additional funds."

Funding Creativity: Not a Bad Thing

Creativity in getting your projects funded is perfectly acceptable, and does not count as "flying beneath the radar." "Once you're plugged into the right people," John advises, "look for another project you can bundle yours with. Can you add your work as a small scope item to someone else's project that has already been roadmapped? It's even better if you can find a trade off that's within the control of your executive sponsor or your business unit PMO. When you get cross-functional and have to ask people in other areas to give something up, it gets very tricky."

Another place where you may be able to get creative is with IT itself, perhaps even the PMO as an organization. "IT will always hold out a portion of their budget to get their own work done," John explained. "We always have a little soft spot. You might be able to get IT to trade off against their own work if your solution will help them."

The Early Bird

If you accept that PMOs are in business to keep your business in business, then it should not be a surprise that you need to be as prepared and proactive as possible. Earlier, we mentioned that your willingness to pay attention to mundane details, which you might view as pointless and even contrary to the goals of your knowledge-based initiative, is a building block of your success. Likewise, being prepared to engage with your company's PMO counts.

"Be as ready as you can be," John cautions. "If it takes you a while to get your footing, your project could get cut for something that is ready to go. Have your ducks in a row, pre-document your business requirements, and you'll be way ahead of the game. Sometimes the first person that's there, and ready, gets a little bonus. Don't ever make someone wait on you, because you may get de-prioritized."

Relationships as Key

A common theme, and one that is important in any knowledge-based initiative, is the importance of people.

John explains how important relationships are when working with a PMO. "Truthfully, networking is the most important thing in locating, and then dealing with, a PMO. Go up your chain of command. Ask who they worked with the last time they did a project. Find out who your PMO representative is. Ask someone two cubes over who their IT contact is, and how they plugged into the organization. Be prepared to do a road show. And if you – or your executive sponsor – doesn't own all the things that will need to be traded off? Get co-sponsors who will agree to trade off your work."

You may wonder where you are supposed to find all this information. The answer is simple: from the PMO contacts you have cultivated, and from any initiatives you have identified synergies with, or identified as competitors.

If your firm has a strong PMO component, you do not have to go through this exercise alone. John says, "In my organization, although we're an IT PMO, we try to be business-centric. In other words, we'll help you. We'll reach out to other groups in IT that we know may be impacted that you, as a business person, might not realize. We develop our own networks so that we can play nicely with each other. For example, I'll usually keep a certain amount of work 'soft' so that I can help in case of a bind. Still, it's also your job to ask: does this impact any other groups? Do I need to start talking to anyone else? Your PMO person will either know, or can point you to someone who does."

The importance of relationships comes into play as your project executes, as well – particularly if you impact other parts of the organization that you did not anticipate, and identify, up front. "Theoretically," John says, "as soon as your project is chartered, you're interlocked with groups. So often, though, until you know the solution to a problem, you don't *know* the impacts. When this happens and you need additional help, networking is key. Like anything else, people work harder for you if they know you and like you. Networking is everything. If you're not good at networking, you better get good at it. Otherwise, if your solution has impacts that weren't expected and you need support? That support might not be available for another year."

How Much About Project Management Do You Need to Know?

Managing Knowledge-Based Initiatives is focused towards people who are executing knowledge-based initiatives in a large company, so we assume that you are familiar with the basics of project management. We also assume that you have investigated the standards that exist in your company and the specific methodologies involved.

If you find yourself at the low end of the learning curve on project management, the Internet is the quickest way to self-educate. The Project Management "gold standard" in many firms is the certification available from the PMI, the Project Management Institute. The PMI offers multiple programs; you may have heard of the PMP, or Project Management Professional, certification. To obtain certification, applicants have to successfully complete an exam and submit documentation that proves they have worked in the field for a specified amount of time. Many take preparatory courses and study extensively in order to pass the exam. In order to keep their certification, PMP holders must participate in an ongoing continuing education program.

Keep in mind that any outside course in project management, even a highly regarded program like the ones offered through the PMI, may not reflect how things actually get done in your company. "What PMI teaches you," John says, "is not real world. It's *perfect* world, so it's helpful to know – but organizations just can't afford it all. All the overhead is very expensive. In the PMO, every activity and how PMOs work is a judgment call."

Understanding your company's language around PMO activities is helpful, though. "One place you could start is the PMI website," John advises. If your solution is technology heavy, you might benefit from investigating the SEPG, Software Engineer Process Group. "Any place that you see 'SEPG' – Software Engineer Process Group – might be useful. Your IT people are there to be translators. People like Business Analysts and Project Managers are supposed to help with this – but you don't want to sound like an idiot, either," he said.

Triple Constraint: The Questions You Should Always be Able to Answer

One way of framing project management activities is the "triple constraint" theory. It is useful to understand as you work with any PMO.

John explains. "You have a schedule – that's duration. And you have the amount of resources that are going to be used. Last, you have scope: what you want to get accomplished. Given enough time and money, you can have any scope. If you have a set amount of resources, you need to figure out how much scope is possible, and how much time."

As projects are reprioritized and bartered, be prepared to answer the question: what is your most important constraint? "For example," Collier said, "imagine that your company is going to launch a new product and that date has already been determined." In other words, one of the three constraint elements is set, and cannot be moved. "If I have a set amount of time, what's more flexible to you: resources or scope? I've got 10 people and 6 months. I can only do what those people can do in that amount of time. In general, we say that IT is a constrained resource. We have a specific budget. Although the budget can get added to, the business needs to prioritize their requests."

Get on Board: The Customer Experience

John advises that if you are looking for a place to investigate ROI, you investigate how your knowledge-based solution can enhance the overall customer experience. "Customer experience is a hot topic right now. Maybe you're not selling more of your product, and maybe it's not a specific 'thing' you can point to, but by virtue of a salesperson having more information at their fingertips, perhaps there's a gain to be had. How would you quantify it? Get with the sales guys. They're the best at making business cases. Look at trending, repeat business figures, show how much it costs you to gain or regain customers. If you can show over time that we get market growth instead of decline by providing a better market experience, your project can claim part of those dollars. Then, you have cost avoidance."

Before you think of PMOs as an obstacle, consider this: a recurring issue that PMOs address is trying to pull together efforts across large organizations to avoid re-inventing the wheel, and standardizing project experiences. As a KM practitioner, you already know those challenges can frequently be addressed by Knowledge Management solutions. Forming a strong alliance with your PMO(s) is one of the smartest things you can do at the onset of your knowledge-based initiative, depending on which profile your PMO fits.

10

Making Sense of Dollars and Cents

Like many of the other elements we have discussed in *Managing Knowledge-Based Initiatives*, activities you will undertake around managing your firm's funds and resources are intertwined with other activities, and heavily governed by process. The exact activities, what they are called, and the processes that govern them will vary from organization to organization and sector to sector, so you will have to do some sleuthing to make sure you are correctly plugged into how things work at your firm. Like other paths we have identified in *Managing Knowledge-Based Initiatives*, assistance from a strong PMO and executive sponsor will be helpful.

Finance, Procurement, and ROI

In this chapter, we will focus on the areas you need to investigate around money.

- In your firm, how do you get money?
- Assuming you have money, how do you spend it?
- What accountabilities do you have around spending money in terms of showing the wisdom of your investment?

For our purposes, we will assume that getting money will involve your firm's Finance department; how you spend money is governed by the Procurement department. Accountabilities around spending money – ROI – may be spread over multiple areas. For example, Finance may have a policy in place that prioritizes activities based on their projected ROI. Your PMO may require ROI projections as well, and the formulas used to calculate ROI may vary slightly between the two. Your executive sponsor will almost certainly require some sort of ROI as well.

In essence, the questions you need to answer and the information you need to synthesize is the *same data that you must have to construct a project*. These areas – finance, procurement, and ROI – should not be viewed as separate from PMO engagement, assuming you have a strong PMO. They may all be rolled up into one thing.

Before You Begin

You have three distinct, yet interrelated areas to attack around money: how to get it, how to spend it, and how to account for it. Frequently, you will find that in order to execute against one of the areas, you need to know information about the other two. For example, in order to calculate effective ROI, you will need to know how much something costs, and the most accurate cost figures will come from Procurement. As Procurement purchases goods or services on your behalf, it must be plugged into Finance to ensure that invoices are paid out of the correct bucket of money. In the course of building your business case, if you are investigating cost avoidance or showing how your solution will be more cost effective than another solution used in the past, you will need to know what money was allocated, what money was used, and how it was used. These facts all come from both Procurement and Finance.

This means that when you encounter a person or process that governs one of the big three areas, you should look carefully because chances are good that person or process actually influences *all of the areas,* just in differing degrees.

Locate Support in Your Network

How much do you know about how your firm handles budgets, purchases, and ROI calculations? Do you have a friendly face in your network who can guide you through how things work at your firm? If not, ask your executive sponsor to arrange for a tutorial.

Locate Pre-Existing Staff

You will probably find "liaison" staff, although called something else, whose job it is to help you through the three processes we discuss in this chapter. Sometimes staff is attached to projects; other times, a resource might be assigned to an executive or workgroup. See if your executive sponsor, boss, or PMO has a designated Finance or Procurement person or team that you are supposed to work with.

Get Organized

Get organized administratively. Devise a system to keep all of your facts and figures straight. If you tend to be scatterbrained with details, enlist someone's help. Your executive sponsor's administrative support might be a good place to start.

Here is some of the information you will need to keep organized:

- Which groups or entities are funding your knowledge-based initiative? Who is your primary contact in each area? How much have they committed? Is any of it "soft", meaning it could go away with little notice?
- What numbers – probably cost center or purchase order (PO) numbers – are associated with each of the funding areas?
- Do areas that are contributing funding have a resource from your firm's financial operations assigned to them? If so, who?

Finance and Budgets: How Do You Get Money?

Your PMO, boss, or executive sponsor is the best source of guidance about how to ensure you are included and well represented in the budgeting process. Your firm may have one central Finance department that governs everything. Or, there may be multiple smaller, semi-autonomous Finance departments who work together at the highest levels, but also have their own policies and procedures. If you are in an educational or government institution, the equation can become convoluted.

The key to conquering the finance and budget question is to first identify the people who will be contributing funds to your initiative. Then, trace back every activity and detail for each group and its individual budget process. If a significant number of groups are financing your work, you will likely encounter a small number of structures that you find again and again.

High Level Guiding Principles

There are several guiding principles around Finance that we have found to be true across multiple firms:

- Finance activities are highly process-driven – but executive intervention can change everything.
- Different divisions within a single firm may have different budget calendars and processes, even if the activities all feed upwards to a single source.

- Persistence and visibility are key to prevent being dropped off the budget radar screen.
- Successful persistence and effective visibility are politically charged activities, and most likely to succeed when your executive sponsor plays a leading role.
- Ignorance of Finance policies and procedures is no excuse for not conforming to them.

Questions You Must Be Able to Answer

- How much money do you need?
- If you need headcount (staff), is that translated into a dollar figure and budgeted for like other expenditures? Are different levels of staff budgeted for differently, generally hourly vs. salaried? Can you "divide" people? For example, can you estimate 1.5 people will be necessary?
- Which groups will be paying for your expenditures, including the person, department, and cost center?
- What are the key budget dates for each group that is contributing money to your initiative?
- What administrative work and process participation does each group require in order for you to be considered for budget dollars?
- Do any allocations from the groups contributing to your work roll up into larger buckets?

Unwritten Rules

Are there unwritten rules around how budgets work at your firm? Unwritten rules are an important part of a firm's culture and day-to-day activities. You must be aware of these unwritten rules before you can determine the wisdom of following them, or factoring them into your planning.

Use of Surplus Funds

If projects or initiatives have surplus dollars at the end of the year, how are they treated?

- Spent as rapidly as possible, possibly pre-paying for activities in the next year.
- Left committed to the project – but the project is extended allowing the funds to roll over.

- Spent on "luxury items" such as additional software licenses, conferences, or classes.
- Traded off to another area.
- Buried, so that the surplus does not show up easily.

Surplus Consequences

If a project, workgroup, or initiative has surplus budget at the end of the year, are there consequences?

- The budget will be reduced by a proportionate amount the next year.
- The initiative leader will take a hit as a "poor planner."

Intentional Overestimation

Does the credo, "Ask for more than you need, because you won't get enough otherwise," sound familiar? In some firms, it is routine to pad project financial estimates. The logic is that what you ask for will be reduced no matter how carefully you estimate; asking for more than you need is the only way to make sure you have enough.

Note that padding may take place not only in straight finances, but in head-count (which equals out to finances at some point) or level of effort (LOE) estimates as well. Whether you pad or not is up to you – but you should be aware if everyone else is.

Intentional Underestimation

Perhaps less common than intentional overestimation is *intentional underestimation*. You will probably encounter intentional underestimation in firms that do not have strong project management processes and accountabilities in place, and there is little negative consequence around having to return to the money bucket to ask for more.

One activity that, for our purposes, could be considered intentional underestimation is the deliberate funding of small segments of a larger effort as separate projects. When a $100,000 project is divided into buckets of $20,000, it may become far more palatable to your firm's financial controls. It may even fall below the level of serious scrutiny.

This can be an intelligent strategy if you ensure that at each juncture, you are delivering something measurable, or your customers understand that this is the first step of many. It is a dangerous strategy to execute the starting activity – for example, the first $20,000 project – and then back peddle by promising that the impact your customers are looking for will come after the next $20,000 project.

You must be aware if intentional underestimation is the way that business is done at your firm. If you submit a completely level, holistically inclusive budget, and everyone else comes in at half the cost of yours, you may be left wondering why your initiative was not funded.

We do not advocate doctoring financial projections, but you must be aware of how things are generally projected at your firm, if for no other reason than to provide pushback. Ultimately, that knowledge can help you create a level playing field.

Procurement: How Do You Spend Money?

In your firm, Procurement may be organizationally related to Finance, or a completely separate entity. You may discover that different portions of your firm have their own procurement organizations. For example, IT might have one procurement entity, while manufacturing has another.

What Procurement Does

In general, Procurement gates what a firm buys, how, and from whom. For example, Procurement may negotiate rates with vendors based on the aggregate amount spent with the vendor each year. A vendor who underperforms or breaches an agreement may be blackballed. Procurement may set a ceiling on what your firm will pay for hourly consulting. They may choose from whom to purchase goods, and may issue request for information (RFIs), request for proposal (RFPs) or request for quotation (RFQs). Procurement policies may also reflect the values and beliefs of an organization. For example, a firm may set a procurement goal of purchasing a certain percentage of "green" or recycled materials.

Typical Procurement Areas of Influence

The degree to which Procurement can influence or control how you initiate and execute your project varies depending on your firm and the type of project. There are multiple areas to investigate around procurement that can influence your project.

Preferred Vendors

Does your firm designate preferred vendors? Does it use preferred vendors for goods and services? Although employing a preferred vendor framework is hugely valuable to large companies, it can also make your life, as someone who is trying to introduce something new into your firm, difficult. Ask for a listing of preferred vendors before you get your heart set on working with a particular consultancy or using a certain product.

It is possible that the skills you need may not be available from the list of pre-approved vendors at your firm. If you anticipate the need to add a vendor to that preferred list, start the process early, and involve Procurement immediately. If you find yourself caught in an argument loop about the value of the new skill, new product or way or looking at a situation, take the time to explain and try to cultivate an advocate, but do not hesitate to involve your executive sponsor if necessary.

If you identify a vendor that is not currently preferred with your firm that you would like to do business with, do not assume that the vendor necessarily wants to do business with your firm. As part of the preferred vendor negotiation, companies may specify a rate ceiling that they are willing to pay. Some vendors – particularly small firms – may walk away from doing business if they cannot turn a profit.

Subcontracting Relationships

What if you have identified talent that can help you meet your specific needs, only to learn that they are not a preferred vendor, and you do not have time to wait for their firm to navigate the process of becoming one? Simple. Have the new company subcontract beneath a vendor who is approved.

The preferred vendor will take a cut of anything the new vendor makes from your firm because typically billing will be run through the preferred vendor's systems. Both parties will have to conform to any ceilings your company has in place, but it is one way to work around the preferred vendor system.

Make sure that subcontracting relationships are acceptable with your Procurement staff before you suggest this solution.

RFP/RFQ Process and Timelines

Understanding the process around requests for proposal (RFPs) or RFQs in your firm is critical as you try to plot a timeline for your work. Failure to manage this process appropriately can derail a project completely.

For example, imagine that as part of your project, you need to hire a handful of consultants, and purchase computer hardware. Other hardware and software components of your solution will be outsourced.

What may happen is that some or all of the elements you request will be wrapped into an RFP or RFQ and distributed to multiple vendors. Project managers new to working with Procurement often do not budget enough time for this process.

- The construction of the RFP or RFQ could take weeks.
- The response window could stretch over weeks or months.
- It might take additional weeks for procurement to evaluate the responses to the RFP or RFQ and make a decision.
- Even at that point, additional negotiation may happen.

If you allocated a few weeks for procurement activities and it actually requires a few months? Your schedule could slip.

Single Sourcing

Note that procurement may use, on occasion, "single sourcing." What this means to you is that instead of soliciting quotes from perhaps dozens of vendors, your firm decides to go to a "single source" for a price. This can speed up the process considerably. If you find that the RFP/RFQ process puts your project in jeopardy, it may be worthwhile to ask your executive sponsor about single sourcing. Your executive sponsor's influence will likely be necessary to create a single sourcing arrangement.

Supporting Documentation

You will have to provide information from multiple sources to Procurement before any purchase is made on your behalf. There is a good chance that the type of information you will need to provide overlaps significantly with information you may have provided at budgeting time, or to your PMO, so reuse is possible.

Make sure you understand exactly what is required, and realize that the information you must provide may vary depending on the nature of your purchase. For example, if you want to hire consultants, procurement may require a detailed breakdown of the types and levels of skills required.

Procurement as a Supporter

Procurement can be one of your most influential supporters. They are well connected with virtually every area in the firm – after all, they control what gets purchased, when, how much, and for how much – and typically have close ties with everything that happens with budgets. Remember that where there is money, there is often influence.

Procurement can help you in a number of ways.

■ They are often aware of larger movement that your firm's leaders or vendors are undertaking.

■ In case of difficulties with performance by a vendor, procurement can generally intervene both formally (refuse to pay the bill) and informally (speak with their contacts and try to resolve the situation).

■ Procurement is aware of upcoming projects, purchases, and trends around management priorities; they can help you find projects, or offer advice about an executive sponsor.

Vendor Relations

As you work with Procurement at your firm, keep in mind that they may have strict rules around your interactions with vendors. The reasons are not hard to understand.

■ To maximize relationships with vendors and get the best possible deals for your firm, Procurement must maintain a consistent dialogue with them. Anyone who inserts himself or herself into that dialogue (like you) can cause ambiguity, or risk agreements that have been reached.

■ You may inadvertently tip your firm's hand around areas that should remain confidential to offer leverage in future negotiations.

■ The vendor may have the impression that you are the "final word" on purchases, when you actually are not.

■ The vendor may not be clear on whom they need to work with.

Any differences between what you say and what procurement says can open a crack in the relationship that someone will have address. Although it may seem silly, before you engage heavily with vendors, ask about any guidelines your firm's procurement personnel may have. For example:

■ Can you talk about money – hourly rates, purchase prices, bulk discounts – at all?

■ Can you solicit demonstrations from non-preferred vendors?

- What happens if a vendor solicits you? Are you supposed to refer them to procurement?
- Can you commit to, or offer any indication that a future relationship is likely to occur with a vendor?
- Can you involve procurement in escalations around service from a vendor?
- Can you accept gifts – even as small as a pen or solar-powered calculator – from vendors? What about free training, or entry into contests?

Purchase Order Process Details

Every firm, large or small, uses POs (purchase orders). How does the PO process work in your firm?

- Who can initiate a PO? Do you have the authority? Or, will your boss or executive sponsor need to be the formal "author" of the PO, even if you do the legwork?
- How do you initiate a PO? A paper form, a phone call, an online system?
- What information will you need to provide? Likely candidates include the amount of the purchase, who is paying for it, the vendor, and associated cost center numbers. Some PO or procurement systems may require that you delve into detail or provide high level ROI figures.
- Does anyone other than you sign off on the PO? What is the process for that – do you specify the chain of "sign-offers" or is it somehow hard coded into the system?
- If multiple people need to sign off on the PO, who are they, and are they appropriate? Do dollar thresholds dictate when different people become involved, or is it because of the reporting structure?
- Double-check the roster of people who must sign off to make sure it is what you expected. Furthermore, make sure that every person who will need to sign off on expenditures for your knowledge-based initiative knows what it is, why they are signing off on it, and all of the other approvals you have obtained. You should have already dealt with this issue in the course of value prop development, but the sign-off process is one way to double-check your work.
- In case of staggered sign offs, can you monitor where the process is? If so, you can proactively reach out if your PO remains in an individual's queue for any appreciable length of time and offer a nudge if it seems to be stuck.
- Can you monitor POs after they are cut?

- Do you have any visibility into who, on the vendor side, will manage the PO process? Can you engage with that person directly in case of questions or problems, or does Procurement need to be involved?
- Does your firm's PO system link related POs? This can be valuable if your project requires the generation of multiple POs. An activity that seems like a single "thing" to you may actually result in the generation of multiple POs. Do not let a chunk of money get assigned to a PO that you are not aware exists.
- If you get any bills directly, how do you charge against POs?
- Will you have an approval opportunity for every charge that goes against a PO associated with your project? Do you receive periodic statements?
- If you do not have an approval opportunity, who does? Can you request visibility into all expenditures?
- Are there different rules around spending money for capital expenditures compared to consulting expenses, or staff additions? Be aware that it is often easier to get funding for consultants than to add full time staff to your company's payroll.
- Do you know how to handle split funding sources? If you have multiple cost centers funding your efforts, there may be small variations in paperwork you should be prepared to address.

ROI: What was the Return on the Money You Spent?

There is probably no topic more despised among knowledge practitioners than ROI. Historically, ROI has been painful for knowledge practitioners because when ROI is executed, or derived, as a formulaic numbers-driven exercise, knowledge-based initiatives come out the loser (nearly) every time.

Increasingly, executives recognize that the value of knowledge-based activities do not lend themselves to traditional measurement, and this is good news for all of us in the knowledge field. Throughout *Managing Knowledge-Based Initiatives*, we hear from executives about what constitutes success for them, and how they decide what to support in an organization.

However, if you work in a large firm, you will probably be required to undertake some sort of ROI analysis, *even if you have an executive sponsor who realizes that it is not going to paint a genuine picture of what your work will truly do.*

The purpose of this portion of the chapter is not to tell you how to derive ROI around your work, but offer you different ways to think about approaching the issue. If you are fortunate, demonstrating traditional ROI is a non-issue for you, or your work will lend itself to traditional evaluation.

Executive Point of View: Jane Niederberger and ROI

Jane Niederberger is an executive who understands that the solution to a problem, even a critical problem, may not offer hard dollar savings. "I see a value proposition as very much equal to ROI," Jane said, "although differences may come from the type of issue you're addressing. For example, if you're solving an important problem, the ROI may not be in hard dollars. You might be preventing me from investing in another area or going down a path I shouldn't. For things like that, you can't measure a hard ROI."

That does not mean you are off the ROI hook entirely, though. "Even if you can't measure a hard ROI," Niederberger said, "you can still make a case for it. Establish core milestones, and make sure you understand when your supporters need to see those milestones fulfilled. Meet expectations, and that's your ROI."

So, does that mean that Jane never expects to see a concrete dollar savings? No. "In other instances," she continued, "I want to see hard dollars. If I'm shelling out money, I want to know how fast I'm going to get it back. A couple of hundred thousand? It may seem like a lot, but in a budget for a large company, it's not – and it's pretty easy to justify. I'd expect to see ROI on a small figure like that within a year." The larger the dollar figures, though, the more complicated the equation becomes. "If it's a multi-million dollar investment? It's a whole different thing," Niederberger said. "It will involve finance people and the process will become much more rigorous and formal. I call it the hallway chat vs. the sit-down meeting with the CFO."

Throughout *Managing Knowledge-Based Initiatives*, we have advocated starting small and growing your work. Not only is it easier to jumpstart a smaller initiative, but as the leader you have a degree of latitude that you may not have once the dollar figures grow. Jane noted that, "One of the interesting things is that the bigger we get as a company, the more formal these processes become – and we lose some innovation as a result."

In cases where outcomes may be softer, such as with knowledge-based initiatives, Niederberger recommends acknowledging uncertain outcomes up front. "Approach it like a science project," she advised. "Lay out your hypothesis. And let the executive who is supporting you know up front that your first attempt may not be perfect; it may not go exactly as you hope." In Chapter 15, Dave Snowden explains how positioning your knowledge-based work as fail-safe or safe-fail is critical, partially because that determines whether you can capture hard ROI on your effort at all. This is the same idea.

"In corporate America," Jane continued, "you can make a project plan for a server migration. You know the milestones, expected results, etc. But in KM, if you want to increase collaboration and communication, it's an *effectiveness* measure. Admit that you don't know exactly what to expect, but you believe your work will improve effectiveness."

One measure that Niederberger recognizes as valid when evaluating new tools is how employees actually integrate the tools into their daily routines. "Years ago, as part of a Knowledge Management initiative, we brought in instant messaging. Anyone who watched saw how quickly it became part of our associates' daily workflow. And now? We use 'click to chat' to service our members. The process took years. Making a change like that takes a lot of diligence – and a lot of courage."

ROI Standards

Do you know what constitutes ROI at your firm? You have two paths to investigate: the formal definition of ROI and the informal. Both are important to satisfy. Your firm's culture and history around ROI, as well as guidance from your executive sponsor and any ROI gurus, will let you know to what degree they must be satisfied.

Creativity in ROI?

The contemporary knowledge practitioner often faces a difficult decision: is it better to manufacture ROI figures that while factually accurate do not portray the true intention or value of knowledge-based work but will satisfy the bureaucracy of your firm, or refuse to supply ROI figures at all and consequently never get the chance to execute your work?

In *Managing Knowledge-Based Initiatives*, we do not presume to serve as your corporate conscience around this issue. However, there are a few high level boundaries we have found to be consistent:

- If you choose to "game the system" make sure your executive sponsor knows about it. Document your activities in an email.
- Make sure you understand the gates/paths/consequences around any gaming you might do. For example, imagine that you need to get your ROI figures above a certain percentage to be even considered for next year's projects. If you survive that cut, in the next round of presentations, the inclusion of soft ROI is accepted. In such a case, "gaming" the figures and benefits might be more palatable to you and your executive sponsor.
- History tells you a lot. Related to the involvement of your executive sponsor is understanding how similar activities have turned out in the past. Can you identify any past project that that offered hard-to-quantify ROI estimates,

but moved forward? Is it still in existence today? Check with your PMO
rep or the project owner to see how they handled ROI.

■ Attitudes towards ROI, and proving it, change greatly with leadership. If
the firm's new PMO guru or head financial officer has been presenting on
the importance of payback in all new initiatives, the chances that you will
be required to demonstrate hard core ROI are greater. `

What ROI Means at Your Firm

To determine what ROI means at your firm, first, locate your firm's ROI expert.
Your boss or executive sponsor may have a designated resource from the Finance
Department who can help. Your PMO should also be able to assist you in getting
started with ROI at your firm.

Next, learn how ROI is calculated. ROI may be figured using a simple formula
that derives the ratio of the cost of an activity against its benefit – or it can be
quite complex. Make sure you understand how the figures that your firm will
use are reached.

In addition to how ROI is calculated, investigate the following:

■ What counts as ROI at your firm? Is cost avoidance or savings a valid
measure?
■ Is a direct impact on profit the desired ROI measure?
■ Are effectiveness measures considered valid?
■ Is there any bias against small savings multiplied by large numbers of
people? Will executives scoff if you predict a savings of one minute a day for
each of your firm's 40,000 employees, and then convert that into dollars?
Particularly because knowledge-based work often lends itself to numeric
benefits that are derived this way, ask.

Who Cares About ROI at Your Firm

Who do you anticipate will ask you to provide ROI figures or efficiencies? You
must have at least a general list in your head, because as you will see in a moment,
different groups may ask for very different information. Likely candidates include:

■ Finance.
■ PMO.
■ Procurement.
■ Any executives who are stakeholders.
■ Any committees that approve you for anything.
■ Detractors.

When and What is Actually Used?

The next area thing you need to understand is when you will be required to provide ROI figures, and which ROI metrics matter. You may find, particularly if you are using ROI to garner executive support or gain approval from unrelated committees, that expectations are different from group to group. The more centralized projects and spending are at your firm, the fewer parties you should have to satisfy.

The "when" matters because being asked to predict what you think will happen before you undertake an activity compared to measuring actual results against a prediction, company standard, previous experience, or sometimes nothing is hugely different.

If you are asked to provide predictive ROI, when in the feedback loop will you have to report results? When dealing with individuals, or ad hoc groups, do not be surprised if the answer is perhaps never. Sometimes, people use ROI figures as a preliminary "can you cut the mustard" tool and never follow up. Other times, an executive may need to understand how you anticipate effectiveness ROI will be generated, but does not expect formal, point-by-point proof that the effectiveness measures have been obtained. However, expect that when you deal with a PMO or Finance department, formal follow up will likely happen. Never provide figures based on the assumption that you will never have to prove them.

You may also be asked to report ROI on activities around your knowledge-based initiative– perhaps an analysis of results from a pilot – after the fact, even though you never predicted or committed to any ROI at all. If you find yourself in a situation like this, be sure to differentiate pilot results from the results you expect to find in the larger deployment.

The second half of the "when" equation is to understand at what point in a process you may be asked to provide ROI. For each of your major stakeholders, trace critical processes that will involve ROI. For example:

- Do you have to meet a baseline ROI figure to be considered for approval, funding, or inclusion? For example, do you have to show at least a 3:1 return ratio to even get on the master project list during the budget process?
- Assuming you make it past the entry ROI requirements, will ROI figures also be used to prioritize projects? Will a 10:1 project always beat a 5:1 project?
- Are different types of projects bucketed in competition against each other and can you find out who your competition is? Are "softer" projects bucketed together? Is there any chance of putting your work in a "foundational" or "infrastructure" bucket, where expenditures may be less formally scrutinized?

- Are you competing with projects that offer more concrete ROI than yours?
- Be aware that if budgets are divvied up by reporting structure, your closest work colleagues may also be your primary competitors.

Playing Both Ends

One model that we have seen used involves recognizing that traditional ROI measures do not tell everything about the value of knowledge-based initiatives, and working with leadership to gather new proofs of value while conforming, at least on the surface, to traditional measures. The "playing both ends" model will work best when:

- Your executive sponsor is completely on board, and will defend your work against pushback, including at budget time.
- Others who hold the purse strings – such as your PMO or Finance representatives, including your firm's ROI guru – are also aware of what you are trying to do, and agree to give it a chance.
- At least one high level person besides your executive sponsor is willing to voice support for the softer measures, such as the effectiveness measures that Jane Niederberger mentioned earlier.

To make this model work, you will essentially keep two sets of ledgers: one that reflects the traditional ROI figures your firm demands and one that measures more knowledge-friendly aspects of the value your initiative is adding to your firm.

For example, imagine that your firm requires hard numbers around expense reductions that your project will effect. The aim of your project is not to reduce expense reductions at all – rather, your knowledge-based initiative's goal is to help several newly merged groups collaborate more effectively. Keeping two sets of ledgers might look like this:

- The "on the record" ledger would reflect expenses that are impacted. Dig deep and leave no stone unturned to come up with some hard-core savings. Examples include reduced mileage and other travel expenses (less traveling due to your solution), reduced meeting time (possibly put towards administrative expense), reduced miscellaneous process time (possibly because of using fewer tools due to the merger of groups).
- The "off the record" ledger contains the other benefits that are not quantified easily by numbers, or are not recognized in general as valid. For example, perhaps you survey all participants in your knowledge-based initiative after they have been using your solution for three months on a number of topics.

You also survey their supervisors and executives. You discover that there is an increased feeling of camaraderie, a reduced feeling of frustration when it comes to performing routine activities, and an increased respect for their new team mates.

What is key in keeping a dual entry benefit ledger for your knowledge-based initiative is that your executive sponsor validates what you are doing, why you are doing it, and agrees that the softer ledger is valuable. Through your executive sponsor's influence, you must both be able to "sell" both ledgers as valuable, particularly at budget time.

Get Help from the Outside

One of the nicest things about working in the Knowledge Management field is interacting with the other people who work in it. We are all knowledge practitioners. What other group is more likely to share what its members know? Do not overlook the power of what people outside your firm have done in regards to ROI.

The KM Community at Large

If you are not yet plugged into the Knowledge Management community at large, it is time to introduce yourself. Even if you cannot afford to travel to conferences where you get a chance to meet in-person, you can interact with some of the field's brightest thinkers online with a click of your mouse. Investigate user groups, forums, and web sites. Do not forget to look for expertise that may not be branded as "Knowledge Management."

Vendor Assistance

Your vendor(s) may be the best help you find around navigating the ROI question at your firm because vendors know that in order for them to sell their product or service, their customers must be able to demonstrate ROI. Vendors may offer free frameworks, tools to gather and calculate ROI, or provide you with "arrows in your quiver" in the form of whitepapers, articles, and other statistics. Vendors can also tell you how other people are handling the ROI question and may even be able to put you in touch with other customers over the phone.

What the Joneses are Up To

It is an unfortunate truth that sometimes value is placed on an idea, product, process, or methodology only because someone else has placed value on that idea, product, process, or methodology. In a corporation, often the "someone else" that counts is the corporation's chief competitor.

What can you find out about how your firm's competitors calculate ROI? You might be surprised at how much people are willing to tell you. Reach out through the firm's network, your personal network, contacts your executive sponsor has, via your PMO, and through the larger KM network. Even if you cannot attend KM conferences, you can frequently obtain lists of presenters online; you might even be able to get a copy of their presentations. You can learn a lot reading in between the lines. In addition, though, do not be afraid to reach out and simply ask how ROI is handled by a competitor.

11

IT – Friend or Foe?

In this chapter, we focus on working with the technology group in your firm. Although we will refer to "computer people" generically as IT staff, please remain aware that they may be called something different in your firm. In addition, the types of people, attitudes, and associated skill sets that you will find in an IT group inside a huge firm are as varied as those you will find looking across the entire firm.

This section assumes that your knowledge-based initiative has some degree of technical dependence. As knowledge practitioners, we know that technology can be an enabler of our work – but it is never the driver. As enablers go, though, in our view, technology is usually at the top of the list. Even if you are confident that your knowledge-based initiative has no direct ties with technology, it is still worth turning your firm's IT professionals into advocates of your work.

In this chapter, we will explore why you need IT in your court, how to work with people whose focus is very different than yours, and some tips for learning enough to be able to engage very technical resources. IT architect and developer Joseph King is our inside informant and offers guidelines around working with project teams that have an IT component, including pointers around commonly misused terminology. We also speak with Brandon Goldfedder, Vice President at IET, a technical services firm, and gain some insight into motivating IT staff and building IT partnerships.

But My Solution is Not About Technology

Even if your knowledge-based initiative does not have an obvious emphasis on technology, in some way technology will probably play a role. The thing about technology is that even if that role is small, it may be critical. Pesky technical details behind the scenes can make or break any initiative.

For example, imagine a knowledge-based initiative that has the goal of capturing the expertise of retired engineers by bringing them together for a series of sessions. The retired engineers will discuss their careers, decision paths around historic critical initiatives, and attempt to recall instances where their findings were counterintuitive to prevailing scientific wisdom. In addition, they will demonstrate, hands-on, how to assemble and disassemble several pieces of equipment that, although discontinued, are still present in your firm's manufacturing facilities. Corporate Communications will film the seminars, and all key parties – junior engineers, senior facilities representatives, human resources, etc. – will be present.

As a knowledge practitioner, you are thinking ahead about how to share and reuse the sessions. If you examine the following Table 11-1, you will see that some fairly basic questions will lead you back to dealing with IT. In your firm, some of

TABLE 11-1 Non-IT questions that may require IT answers.

Question	IT Implication
How – what container and what method – can we share the taped sessions? Can the film be digitized and made available over the intranet?	Who has the equipment to digitize the film, both hardware and software? Is there a preferred format that your firm supports? Does your firm have experience with video? Who will create an area on your intranet where you can post the clips? Who will train you on how to post them?
Who will be able to access the clips?	Can you protect, by password, visibility, or other method, who can view the clips once you post them? Will some people be able to post and delete content, while others can just read it?
How will people view the clips on their computers?	Is video player software installed on end users' machines? If not, what do you have to do to get it installed? Is there an associated cost or timeline to the software installation? Can you predict who will need the software, or will it need to be distributed and controlled by a request process?
How will people know which clips are relevant?	Will end users be able to browse or preview video clips? Are they searchable? What is the search technology and how will content be tagged? Can search terms be weighted? How often is content indexed?

TABLE 11-1 *Continued*

Question	IT Implication
Can people just listen to, or read, the sessions?	Is there a way to create transcripts automatically using software? Can you strip audio out of the existing film and create a voice-only file? If so, what format is supported and how can it be shared?
How will the video clips be protected?	How is content archived and backed up? What is the SLA (service level agreement) around restoring lost or damaged content? Will someone be charged for archiving services?
Is there a way to target people with a certain job profile and suggest to them, via the intranet, that viewing these clips would be useful?	What core systems categorize which employees fit a certain job profile at your firm? On your intranet, do you use a tool, or a flavor of portal, that allows for pushing targeted content?
Can we track how many people are browsing and downloading the clips?	What tools are in place to track navigation and/or usage of the intranet?

the activities referenced in the implications column may be handled by non-IT staff, but this line of questioning should get you thinking in the right direction.

As you can see, the success of a project with a non-IT focus, such as getting together retired engineers to learn from them, can end up heavily reliant on IT.

Why You Need IT in Your Court

Our point of view is that you not only need a level of baseline cooperation with staff in IT, but active advocacy for a number of reasons.

People do not always separate KM from IT. As a knowledge practitioner, you are certainly aware that the failure to separate Knowledge Management from technology is a historic source of frustration. This confusion may exist within your firm, through no fault of yours, or the IT staff. Establishing a good relationship with technology resources in your firm will make it easier for both of you to refer people correctly. A good relationship may also help you drum up business.

IT may be aware of changes in supporting technology that affect the capabilities you can offer your customers. IT staff's input in product capability and growth paths can be invaluable and prevent you from making substandard, unwise, or unsupportable decisions. Their expertise will primarily come in three areas: helping you choose the correct toolset at the beginning of an initiative, keeping you appraised of larger changes in the marketplace, and ensuring that you make wise, supportable choices around technology.

- **IT input at the beginning of an initiative.** Using an example from Chapter 3 in *Managing Knowledge-Based Initiatives*, imagine that it is your job to help several newly merged groups in your firm collaborate more effectively. Collaboration can mean many things; you have narrowed it down to shared document repositories, threaded discussion groups, instant messaging, and desktop share in this situation. Does that mean that you will purchase four separate tools? If you do buy four separate tools, will they integrate with each other, or other packages your firm already uses? Alternatively, should you purchase a single tool, or suite of tools, that can do everything? Does your firm already own tools that do one or more of the desired functions?
- **IT input as to changing technologies.** Later in this section, we will discuss Brandon Goldfedder's view of how technology is changing. Building on the example above, imagine that you are supporting an initiative focused on collaboration that was built using four separate tools. IT input can help you determine the "when and if" of vendors' plans to expand or enhance those tools. For example, you might learn that a piece of functionality is scheduled to be added to the next software release of one of the tools. Perhaps one tool can do the job of two, or you will have significant new functionality to offer your customers. On the other hand, perhaps that new functionality will offer nothing to your customers. In addition, because technology changes so quickly, things that were not possible (or easy) a handful of years ago are quickly becoming both affordable and supportable. You may not be aware of these changes but an IT person who knows that your passion is around collaboration can spot developments and explain what they may mean to you.
- **IT input in supportable and wise decisions.** The software world is different from other disciplines to the outsider. For example, one question an IT person might ask in relation to a software purchase is about scheduled releases. The idea is that software vendors periodically release product updates; a

vendor who offers updates every three years may appear stagnant, inattentive to customer requests, or a sluggish responder to changing technology capabilities. On the other hand, a vendor that issues new releases or patches every week might have suspect change control procedures. A vendor's track record is also important. In the past, did major releases of the vendor's software offer customers a smooth migration or upgrade path, or was it a disaster for IT and end users alike? This can be critical if you are making a decision that will touch many people in your organization; the last thing you want your knowledge-based initiative to be associated with is an "upgrade" that does not work the first dozen times it is attempted.

Understanding a vendor's plans for a software product or suite is critical as well. For example, investing in a suite of products that is about to be retired would probably not be a good decision. A vendor might not freely disclose this information, but an IT person would proactively know to ask that question; they would discern the warning signs.

You should also cultivate a degree of sensitivity to how things actually work inside your firm, including relationships that your firm already has. For example, imagine that you are investigating collaborative software and have narrowed the field to two vendors. From your point of view, they are equal. You like the features both tools offer end users, both of the interfaces, and have used both tools. IT input might uncover additional information that will tip the balance in favor of one or the other. Will either of the tools integrate with systems already in place, for example, email? Do you already own, anywhere in the organization, software developed by one of the firms? If so, Procurement/IT might be able to negotiate a favorable price. Is support free, or does it come at a price? Are there different levels of support? Do they offer free training classes? Will the software run on a wide variety of machines, or does it require very specific conditions to succeed? What do expert reviewers, like the Gartner Group or Meta, have to say about the tools and the company? These are just a sampling of the types of questions an IT resource might ask.

In addition, IT staff probably have a good sense of where your firm is headed technologically. Imagine that one of IT's internal goals is to decrease the number of locally installed (meaning, each person who uses software has it installed on their desktop or laptop computer) software packages in favor of web-based packages, the rationale being that it is easy to administer, allows for increased security, and is less expensive. There is probably little reason for you to be aware of, or involved in, that goal. However, if you are investigating software solutions and want to purchase a tool that requires desktop installation as opposed to running over the web, you might wish you had known about that goal up front.

IT may be aware of other groups in your firm that your knowledge-based initiative can help. Particularly if your IT group has a heavy business focus, they may be able to point you to groups that would greatly benefit from your knowledge-based initiative. Although you have other methods to identify potential customers, do not discount IT input. Try to build the type of relationship where IT staff feel free to drop you a casual email or phone call, alerting you to customer developments.

They may be aware of similar or competitive projects. As we discuss in several areas in *Managing Knowledge-Based Initiatives*, you may find yourself unknowingly in competition with other projects, particularly projects that do some or all of what your project does, or have the same or similar customers. Finding those projects in a large organization can be difficult, although a strong PMO should be able to assist you. However, if the other projects have a technology component, IT staff can also be invaluable.

IT can help you safely cross compliance and security waters. If you are introducing a new product or way of doing something into your firm, you may have to meet compliance requirements or engage your firm's security team. Therefore, IT-specific compliance or IT-specific security may factor in. IT allies can help you prepare for those meetings, gather the necessary information, and explain things you might not understand.

IT has its own grapevine. We mentioned earlier that being aware of the happenings of your company, including the latest office gossip, is necessary when it comes to determining your firm's internal landscape. Although you never want to be considered the spreader or primary source of gossip, being plugged into the IT grapevine could prove beneficial. They have different sources of information and different ways to sleuth out what may be happening inside a company.

You may be a single face to the customer. If you get any degree of support from IT in your knowledge-based initiative, in case of problems, an IT support person may be called on to assist your customer. It is best to have support personnel be cheerleaders of your knowledge-based initiative rather than detractors. After all, the customer may not know who is who.

IT has its own pockets of funding. We have emphasized the importance of understanding all the moving pieces inside of an organization in *Managing Knowledge-Based Initiatives*. Funding is certainly a key part of continued and large-scale success. IT probably has its own pockets of funding that are managed completely outside of the business. If they are advocates, actively invested in the success of your knowledge-based initiative, you may be able to access some of that funding. Do not forget to investigate whether IT might be a good customer for your initiative.

IT has its own channels of influence and support. Chances are good that if you work in a non-IT portion of your firm, your ultimate boss – the person with a "C" in front of his or her title – is different than the corresponding "C" position for IT staff, which is generally the CIO. If IT leadership firmly supports your knowledge-based initiative, that means you have at least one additional "branch" of support at the highest levels. We have touched on the importance of working with your executive sponsor around funding, alignment, and support issues; explore whether a strong partnership with IT might help address any problem areas.

IT can make or break a knowledge-based initiative. This final reason you need IT in your court is perhaps the most important. A technology element that is arguably small in the overall mission of your project may factor in hugely around how end users will engage in your knowledge-based initiative. Referring back to the collaborative example used earlier, the instant messaging component is small from both an importance and a technology point of view. Small, that is, until it does not work, works intermittently, or is delayed six months. Then it becomes huge.

When things go wrong – for example, the instant messaging component mentioned above is delayed – it could be for many reasons. Perhaps the product itself is flaky; maybe the IT staff assigned to you has too many other commitments. Your project might not be as "cool" as other projects – or you might not be perceived to be as cool to work with as other people. Whatever the reasons, whether personal or business, the end result of non-functioning or non-present technology is the same: failure.

Learning to Speak IT's Language

Throughout *Managing Knowledge-Based Initiatives*, you will see that we advocate not only dropping KM jargon, but actively working to adopt the language of your customers or other key entities. You may need to tweak your understanding of IT's role in your firm in order to effectively communicate with them, as well.

Your Company Standards

One of the first things you should know is your company's technology standards for both hardware and software. You do not have to understand every finite detail, but you should know, high level, what those standards are and whether a solution you may propose complies with those standards. That is not to say that a solution outside of standards should not ever be considered, but be aware that there will be substantially more activity required on your part for any solution that is outside of your firm's current standards.

Not only do you need to be aware of current standards to understand where any knowledge solution might fit into them, but you also need to be able to speak with some degree of knowledge to IT staff.

Discovering Standards

Look around you. On your work computer, what software is installed? What product do you use for email? What browser does your computer use? Do you have instant messaging installed? If so, can you message with people outside your company?

When you boot your computer, what is displayed? If you use a PC, something about Windows probably splashes across your screen – and that splash screen tells you about your computer's operating system. That is more than likely a standard inside your firm.

How locked down is your computer? In other words, can you install and run programs without contacting anyone from IT? Or, do you have to open a helpdesk ticket (or your firm's equivalent) to get new software installed? Does anyone else have to authorize your request, and is there a charge back that you know of?

Now, compare your machine with someone who works in an entirely different area. You will probably find that the core software is the same, although any "specialized" applications may vary. More than likely, you have just created a thumbnail sketch of your firm's software standards.

Find an IT informant. IT people, in general, enjoy explaining how things work, and like all of us, are pleased when someone expresses interest in their field. If you have a good relationship with an IT resource, no matter how junior, ask them what your firm's hardware and software standards are. Even if your informant cannot recite the standards from memory, he or she can certainly point you in the right direction; this is baseline information for most IT resources.

General or compliance documentation. Browse publicly available information on your intranet, and see if you can locate the latest version of your firm's standards. Particularly if you have a "locked down" computing environment, unauthorized change of that environment is probably a violation of compliance. If so, you may find information about your current environment embedded in compliance documentation.

Commonly Confused Terms and Definitions

We asked Joseph King, an Atlanta-based IT veteran at working with non-technical project managers on internet, intranet, and extranet solutions, to talk us through some commonly confused terms. You may find different usage at your firm than we have included here.

ASP. The acronym "ASP" means different things to different people. "In the web world," Joseph said, "an ASP page is a web page that has code on it to do a specific function." You can tell if you are looking at an ASP page because the address of the page will end in .asp. Joseph advises that you think of ASP as a way that things get "done" over the web. "There are really two types of code on web pages," he said. "There's markup language (HTML) that tells the web browser how you want things to be displayed. The other type of code *does* something. For example, submits your name to a database. ASP, or Active Server Pages, are one way to do that. The page actively talks to a server to do something."

You might also have heard of the "ASP support model," a vendor who is an ASP, or ASPs related to outsourcing. This is the second meaning of the acronym. "You'll also hear about ASPs, or Application Service Providers," Joseph said. "They are companies that provide a service using the web. One of the biggest one is PayPal." Another one you may have heard of is Salesforce.com.

Desktop. Desktop is a term with multiple meanings. "If you're talking to developers," King explained, "the desktop is the place from which you, the end user, can access all or any of your applications. An infrastructure person, though, would consider a desktop a small machine. A personal computer. So, as an IT person, if I hear end users complain that they can't access their desktop, I have to be careful. Do they mean the machine itself? Or a specific application?"

Encryption. Some organizations choose to encrypt content such as files or email. "Encryption," Joseph said, "is essentially a code that translates data on one side, and then un-translates it on the other side. Behind the scenes in computers, everything is a one or a zero; there are only two choices. When you hear about 128-bit encryption, imagine taking those two choices to the 128th power of possible combinations – that's what it means. Non-IT people won't have to be concerned about encryption or encryption methods, because organizations usually outsource the software that generates encryption keys." However, you may have to be concerned about how things are secured within your internal networks, extranet, or knowledge-based system.

Enterprise. You undoubtedly have your own definition – as does your firm – of the word "enterprise." Your IT staff may think of it a little differently. "Enterprise," Joseph said, "describes how all of the applications fit together within an entire organization. What enterprise means is not only does an application touch more than one department, but more than one *application*, which in turn supports the enterprise." Do not assume that enterprise software is the biggest, most complicated or expensive software you will find in your firm. "Enterprise doesn't mean," Joseph concluded, "that the application itself is large."

Extract, export. To a non-technical person, extracting information may seem pretty much the same as exporting it. Both of these may seem identical to creating a report. The fine differences matter in the technology world, though, and can potentially trip you up if you do not pay attention.

According to Joseph, "A data extraction isn't meaningful in and of itself. It's the equivalent of a data dump. If I have a database, and I pull some information and display it in a report or something, the pulling part is *extraction*. It's an un-meaningful data dump from a bigger data source." Exporting is a little different.

"One way to think of an export," Joseph continued, "is that an export is a *meaningful* extraction of info. Perhaps an extraction plus some massaging will mean something to someone. A good analogy is RSS feeds. They are extracted in XML. If you look at the base XML (and you don't know XML) it looks like a bunch of code. However, when you see it displayed in your web browser, it's fine. Exporting, in that case, is taking the RSS feed, massaging it through the web browser and then displaying it."

J2EE, .NET. As you begin to interact with technical people, whether outside vendors or your own staff, you will hear lots of acronyms thrown around. Two of the most common are J2EE, and .NET. Note that .NET is actually pronounced "dot net."

King explained what those terms should signify to a non-IT person. "J2EE stands for Java 2 Enterprise Edition. It's just a programming language. .NET, in and of itself, is a framework that Microsoft uses to support its products. The equivalent of J2EE isn't .NET. When a non-IT person hears 'Java vs. .NET' *what it really means is whether the organization uses Microsoft or something else.*"

Open source. Particularly in the Knowledge Management field, you will hear a lot of news about open source software. The idea of open source fits nicely with many practitioners' views on knowledge itself; it would seem like a natural fit.

If you are instituting a knowledge-based solution inside a corporate environment through, open source software may not be an option. The problem lies at the heart of what makes open source special: the fact that it is open means no single person or firm is responsible. And that makes corporate types, both technology and business, very nervous.

"The definition of open source software is any piece of software that is built or enhanced by more than one person," Joseph said. "The source code is open, so anyone can contribute. The community works together to make it better. However, open source in a corporate environment is unsupportable. My advice to a non-IT person in a large corporation is not to pursue open source tools."

Operating system. Understanding operating systems might matter to you on several fronts. First, when you familiarize yourself with your firm's standards, operating systems will almost certainly come into play. Additionally, if you investigate software on your own, it might be beneficial for you to understand your firm's standards around operating systems. Joseph pointed out a third reason: the type of operating systems your firm has in place may tell you about the level of complexity your IT staff have to deal with behind the scenes.

"Think of an operating system," Joseph said, "as the layer between the user (you) and a machine (your computer). It shouldn't affect a non-IT person to a large degree, but it's not bad to know. See if you recognize the names. For example, your desktop may use XP as the operating system and servers might use Windows 2003. If you start hearing terms that you've never encountered – like Linux, AS400 – things like that, take it as a red flag that you're in a very complex environment. It may not be structured in the most logical way. At the very least, there are a lot of pieces and parts to consider."

Query/Report. It can be easy to confuse common English language definitions for terms like "query," "report," or "export" with what they mean in the IT world. Although the differences may seem picky to you, remember that your goal is avoid misunderstandings between you and technical staff.

For example, a query is not a report. "In IT speak," King explained, "a query is a SQL statement that returns a specific set of data. A report is a defined object that shows you the *results* of one or more queries."

Server. Server is another term that can mean different things depending on whether infrastructure or applications people use it. According to King, "To an IT infrastructure guy, a server is a physical box with, for example, two gigabytes of RAM and a hard drive. However, a server is also *an application* that is used to serve up information. So, when you hear 'SQL server,' that doesn't necessarily mean there is a physical piece of hardware that supports only SQL. You might have multiple pieces of server software running on a single physical box."

SQL. A non-IT person should think of SQL (pronounced sequel) as the language that is used to retrieve data from a database. "SQL," Joseph explained, "stands for Structured Query Language. IT people use SQL to get – or extract – information." SQL is not used to display information.

SSL. SSL matters only in the web world and stands for secure socket layer. If you bank, manage investments, or purchase goods online, you have encountered SSL technology. Joseph explained. "Essentially, SSL means that I've stored information on my site in such a way that you have to trust me, and my site, to access this information. If you see 'https' show up at the front of a web address instead of 'http' and a little lock appears in the lower right corner of the screen, it means that you're in a special secure web site. You have to trust that site via a digital certificate; it's a file that equates to a handshake between your browser and my site that says, 'OK? Right. Everything is OK.' It's like using a card badge to access a secure area in a building."

Web service, SOAP. To a non-IT person, web services are pieces of functionality or code that perform a specific function that is application independent.

Joseph offered the example of a spellchecker. "The thing about web services," he said, "is that it doesn't matter whether you're thin client, full client – any client. I could be anywhere – for example, using an application inside a web browser, and I can call Google's spellchecker. It will work the same as if I call it from any other place, perhaps a full client installation from a desktop." An acronym related to web services is SOAP – simple object access protocol. SOAP is the way that machines call web services.

"If you're working with technology people," Joseph advised, "don't be afraid to ask what something means. And don't be afraid to ask why. You have a fresh set of eyes that can be useful. Just because you don't understand the technologies in depth doesn't mean your input isn't valuable. Failing to ask *why* is the reason so many processes never get improved upon.

"Work your way through the IT ego part of it," King continued. "Find out why you do something in that particular way. The answer, 'It's always been that way,' or 'That's the way it is,' is never good enough. Perhaps something has happened; someone dropped the ball. Continue to probe and ask why. Why, for example, can't we upgrade? Is it funding? Training? Bandwidth? Were you bitten by this consulting firm in the past?"

Key Areas to Investigate

Just as you have investigated a number of areas of your company, your executive sponsor, committees, and the people who comprise them, and how you and your work are regarded firm-wide, you should investigate parallel areas inside the IT organization.

Perception of Your Work

One of the personal antennas that should remain on full alert is the one that sniffs out clues regarding how your work is perceived in the organization. Earlier, we asked you to take an honest look at how your work group, you, and the field of Knowledge Management are regarded inside your firm. Now it is time to narrow your survey to how your work – and you – are regarded by the IT branch of your firm.

We also emphasized earlier that you need to become a firm historian with a broad understanding of why things are the way they are. Again, it is time to narrow your vision to understand the history around knowledge-based work and IT. Often, IT staff have developed their own internal knowledge-based solutions, although they probably won't think of them in that way, and may not intuitively see what is unique or exciting about your solution.

Welcomed. If you are extremely fortunate, your work may be regarded as welcome. IT staff are ready and anxious to support it and perhaps use it themselves. This scenario is most likely to occur when your solution includes:

- Elements that IT wants to use for themselves.
- Elements that IT has been trying to get buy in and/or funding for and has been unsuccessful (probably because they did not tie it in with a business need).
- Elements that contain building blocks they will be able to reuse in ways not related to your knowledge-based initiative.
- Technology they want to learn, or get hands-on experience with.
- An injection of cash into infrastructure.

Challenger. You may be regarded as a challenger of the *status quo*, which is not bad in and or itself. The question, and associated risk, is whether challenges are welcome in your IT organization. Change is inherent in most IT organizations; the question is whether your technology group welcomes change initiated from the outside rather than the inside.

There are multiple ways to address a challenger perception. Converting enemies into allies is always effective. We also advocate a grassroots approach where you engage multiple IT people who are open to your solution, and let them spread the word. Your executive sponsor and IT leadership are key too; if IT leadership sends the message that you are a welcomed challenger, the tone of your interactions with IT staff can change overnight.

You and your knowledge-based initiative will likely be regarded as a challenger if:

- Your knowledge-based solution includes technology elements that have never been used before (for example, instant messaging).
- Technology elements in your solution were created by vendors the firm has never used before.
- Technology elements in the solution will be deployed in a way that has never been used before (e.g., over Blackberry).
- Your work will require any other "first" around technology in your firm.
- Your solution will require that an existing technology standard be re-examined.
- Your solution will displace an existing solution.

Competitor. The competitor perception may be the most difficult perception to change. It is likely that you will have to find ways to work with people who hold this perception without expecting to win them over. Frequently, those who regard you as a competitor may be dissatisfied with leadership decisions or alignment (why did you get funding and they did not?), see your initiative as the result of crafty politics (your boss is bigger than my boss and you shut down my other project), or believe that your firm should be involved in more cutting-edge technology than it is.

Another possibility is that your firm's IT staff may be very interested in developing a solution to support your knowledge-based initiative from the ground up. Albeit unwittingly, your project may have brought the classic "build vs. buy" debate to a head inside your organization. A buy decision (even if you did not make it) around your solution may have sorely disappointed firm developers.

Some signs that you might be considered a competitor include:

- IT has tried in the past, or may be trying unsuccessfully, to address the same or a similar challenge.
- IT staff successfully addressed a knowledge-based issue and that success led to it being handed off to dedicated staff (you).
- IT staff have a genuine desire to become more involved in the business side of things and feel they should have been the party to bring this solution to the customer.
- IT staff have an internal solution that they use and have perhaps spread to a few customers.
- IT staff are very interested in a new technology that your knowledge-based initiative will force a decision on – and probably not in their favor.
- Your solution will displace an existing solution.

Tactics to combat a competitor perception are much the same as the ones you should use to combat a challenger perception. Try to win over those who view you as a competitor. Learn as much as you can about the history of their work and the tools involved. Give them credit for their past work in front of leadership. Acknowledge that you wouldn't be where you are now, or that you will not succeed in your efforts, without their expertise. Ask their opinion and try to involve them in areas that they enjoy, even if you do not have to.

Irrelevant. If you and your work are regarded as irrelevant inside your IT organization, you have an opportunity to change that perception – hopefully. If all business requests, including yours, are regarded as irrelevant, the best you can do is locate a few confederates that you can get excited about your work.

If other business people have strong ties with IT, they might be able to coach you on how to engage IT and succeed. Try to discern whether there are IT leaders that seem to engage best with the business, and who they are. If you are forced to work with a team that regards your work as irrelevant – and the support they give you is grudging at best – be sure and document everything, set or negotiate firm deadlines, involve their leadership as far up the reporting hierarchy as necessary, and check in with them frequently. Share victories and positive feedback with them, even if you do not have to. For more suggestions on working with IT staff, read Chapter 12, where we interview IT thought leader Brandon Goldfedder.

You are likely to be regarded as irrelevant if:

- IT support in your firm is very disconnected from business needs.
- General morale in IT is low.
- IT staff are overloaded and constantly swapping priorities.
- The existing perception of you, your work, or the field in general is very low.

Consultants – Can They Help?

The use of IT consultants in firms has positives and negatives. Note that in this sense, consultants are different from contractors; consultants are used to perform a well-defined and finite service that is probably strategic to some degree and requires technology expertise that your firm does not have, or does not have enough of. Contractors (sometimes called "staff aug," short for staff augmentation) may be brought in to bulk up staff numbers and essentially function like a regular member of staff.

Countless variables can influence whether consultants succeed in any firm, including how well the project is defined, the firm culture, the talent and maturity of the consulting team, the involvement of the client, and many others. In the technology world, though, another factor heavily influences their success: the cooperation and involvement of the local IT staff.

It is relevant to discuss whether engaging outside consultants can be helpful in the context of IT's perception of your work. It is not unusual for individuals trying to launch a project, when confronted with IT hurdles, to consider going outside and hiring consultants to do the work. If funds are not an issue, it may seem to be an ideal way to speed up the process and avoid frustration. Before you do, consider the following:

Who do the consultants work for, you or IT? In this section of *Managing Knowledge-Based Initiatives*, you have been exposed to many facets of technology and the people who manage it that may influence your knowledge-based initiative. Technology environments, particularly in large firms, are tightly controlled "process houses" that tend to be logical. When this happens, that happens. If A, then B. The environment may be extremely complex, but the one thing it generally is not is uncontrolled.

When you consider it like that, it should seem unlikely that your bringing in a group of outside people, no matter how expert, without IT's involvement or blessing, will result in a warm welcome. Or the project's ultimate success. If you believe that bringing in outside technology help will be of assistance, pursue that avenue – but involve IT at the beginning of the discussion, not the end. Even if you are willing to manage the outside consultants yourself with no IT assistance, you cannot; they will have to be involved at some level. Count on sharing management of the outside IT consultants with your internal technology staff.

Consultants are temporary. If you envision using consultants as a conduit – even if only for communications – into your firm's IT staff because of general frustration, remember that they are only temporary. They will leave eventually.

Consultants will consume IT time and therefore resources. If you are considering bringing in consultants because IT does not have the resources – and therefore, the time – to support you, remember that consultants will still consume their time. Consultants need access to the systems they work on, which IT staff will have to grant and configure. They need input and guidance from your firm's IT experts regarding your firm's setup, processes, and procedures. They might need a physical location to work from inside the IT department and access to email and other network resources. If they will be doing development using your firm's software, they might need software licenses that are not available.

It is important to keep this in mind as you come up with creative alternatives to help (or nudge) an overloaded (or uncooperative) IT staff. Even if you provide the bulk of guidance for external IT consultants, IT has a valid point if they claim there will still be time, and therefore resources, required of them.

IT may be left supporting consultant work. Someone will have to maintain the work products that consultants leave behind. In some firms, there may be an explicit agreement that IT will not support certain environments that are created or purchased without their involvement or blessing, but in reality such environments often end up on their plate, anyway. It is a valid point that is easy to overlook if you come from the business side of the equation.

Consultants may – or may not – help combat a perception issue. Any core problems between you and your firm's technology staff will remain long after the consultants have gone. A high quality consulting team will ensure that the environment, including processes, is sustainable after they leave. However, if your internal resources simply refuse to cooperate, even the best transition plan in the world won't help.

In no way should you shy away from considering the involvement of consultants if it will help your knowledge-based project – but do not use consultants to try and get around fundamental disagreements with your firm's IT staff. In the short term, it is just a band aid; in the long run, it won't work.

Operations

Take a moment and think about what happens every morning when you sit at your desk, turn on your computer, and log in. To you, it is trivial. Behind the scenes, you are probably hitting a number of different systems that are configured, monitored and maintained by your firm's IT staff. If, one day, your password is rejected, that routine morning activity will balloon in importance immediately: you cannot work until you log in.

If your knowledge-based initiative has a technology component, it will probably be much the same. End users, including you, will see one face of the technology component. IT staff will see a completely different face. This is appropriate, of course; end users do not need to know how software works. They just need it to work. At a minimum, though, you should understand that there is a potentially large and complex set of activities behind the scenes that must work in order for your knowledge-based initiative to function as planned.

Throughout this section, we have encouraged you to get to know your firm's IT support along several lines. Understanding how operations in your IT department are divided, particularly if you work for a very large firm, is important for multiple reasons. If you do not, you may not involve the correct resources in project planning and forecasting, budget the correct amount of money for activities, miss activities, or not know who to call when something goes wrong.

How Much Do You Have to Understand?

Here is the good news: you might not be responsible for determining the details like how many IT resources you need, what activities need to happen, or who to call. Earlier, our PMO expert, John Collier, discussed something called a "sizing effort" where IT staff size projects that are under consideration. In other words, they forecast the activities that need to happen, the amount of people that will be needed, any associated costs, and timelines. If your PMO, or IT itself, conducts sizing efforts (or whatever they are called in your firm), your need to understand IT operations at a finite level is less than we describe below.

If you do not have strong institutional support when tackling the technology portion of your knowledge-based initiative, such as a heavily involved PMO, at a minimum you must have an IT partner, particularly if technology – and how your firm's IT area works – is new to you. You cannot, for example, single-handedly forecast what it will take to build a server. However, you may need to aggregate information around server construction to derive cost and time estimates. Count on learning a great deal about how your firm is structured as you investigate IT operations.

Not understanding IT operations may leave you open to the following areas of risk:

■ **Headcount projections might be inaccurate.** If you need to project headcount or LOE (level of effort), you can miss people if you do not understand what goes into an activity.

■ **Activities might not cascade automatically.** Activities that may seem to be the same thing to you – such as installing software on a server – might be far more compartmentalized than you realize. Using server activities as an example, we know of one firm where determining which server to purchase ("speccing out") involves one IT team; receiving and physically setting up the server involves another. Installing the baseline operating system on the server requires yet another group's involvement, and finally, installing the task-specific software is performed by a separate team. This does not even take any monitoring or maintenance setup into consideration.

This matters to you because in a perfect world, these activities would cascade without your involvement or knowledge, and all fall into a bucket you might think of as "get the server ready." If they do not neatly cascade in your company, you might have to pull some activity triggers by hand, so you need to know what the discrete tasks are. In addition, if timelines slip, you will need to find out where the activity derailed before you can intervene.

■ **Missed activities.** Taking the time to understand your company's IT operations will also minimize the possibility that you miss an activity that you need to budget time, staff or money for – or one that is a predecessor to another activity in your knowledge-based initiative.

For example, large firms typically try to minimize the necessity for IT support staff to physically visit an end user's desk for routine maintenance or troubleshooting. Tools that help IT staff administer and access machines remotely (meaning, they might be in another room, building, city, state, or country) can be used for many activities, including software installation, inventory, monitoring, and troubleshooting. Similarly, companies try to ease support by making machines as similar to each other as possible. Machines that are similar in hardware (the same type of laptop or desktop, with the same amount and type of memory installed, for example) and software (with the same email, word processing, and spreadsheet software) are desirable for this reason. Generally, a firm will use multiple configurations; they may be called profiles in your company.

If your knowledge-based initiative will necessitate the installation of a new piece of software on any end user's machine, IT may have to create an entirely new profile, or alter existing profiles. Those updated profiles will then have to be installed – sometimes called "pushed" – onto end user machines. More than likely, there will be not only a timeline associated with the updating of profiles, but potential change control implications as well. If you are responsible for pulling together all the moving parts, something like this can be easy to miss. To the uninitiated, installing a small piece of software does not look like a big deal.

Methodologies

You may find yourself at the center of different, and perhaps conflicting, ways of doing things if your knowledge-based work brings together multiple areas that have strong methodologies. In particular, investigate whether your PMO and IT staff use the same methodology, or at least complementary ones.

Joseph King shared a story about a situation he once encountered where the PMO used one type of methodology, and IT used a completely different one. The result was that the two were so out of alignment nothing could get done. "Imagine this," King said. "One group – the PMO – was using a traditional waterfall methodology. In waterfall methodologies, there's lots of analysis time up front. More than one thing runs at a time; tasks overlap and begin before other tasks are completely over. It looks kind of like a Gantt chart, and it's pretty common.

"On the other hand, you may find developers that use agile methodologies. There's not much analysis; every feature that's needed is its own little development effort. Someone like me, a developer, sits with a business sponsor and we hammer out one little piece of the overall effort. Then we make another little piece. Eventually it all comes together. The argument is that if the business changes, we only have to alter a few of those small pieces – not everything from the beginning. In the waterfall methodology, you're really dependent on the business. If something changes there, you usually have to start over again at the beginning."

Which methodology your PMO, or a developer you work with, prefers is probably largely irrelevant to your efforts. However, as you begin to work out who will do what in your knowledge-based initiative, take the time to ask about methodologies and how they might factor into task or activity handoffs.

Service Level Agreements

Service Level Agreements, or SLAs, are agreements about how things will be done – how service will be provided – between affected parties. In business, they often indicate how things will not only be done, resolved or addressed, but how quickly. SLAs are common in technical environments.

For example, a request to generate a new user account for your knowledge-based initiative might have an associated SLA of 24 hours. Restoring data that was accidentally deleted may have a different SLA of three days. The amount of time it will take to restore a server that goes down will likely have a third and different SLA.

Your Role in SLAs

Many of these SLAs do not involve you; even if it would be your preference to provide immediate service in all cases, it is probably not your call, and not realistic in a large firm. Because SLAs affect the users of your knowledge-based initiative, you must become well versed in the relevant SLAs and who to coordinate with in case they are not being upheld.

The reason is simple: *you are the face of your knowledge-based initiative to your customers*, not the IT staff that may ultimately be responsible for creating a new account, restoring a server, or installing software. Your customers have the right to know what to expect from their participation in your project or program. They will probably, at least during early stages, rely on you even when they should call the Help Desk or other support area. Like it or not, as the relationship owner, you may receive the brunt of frustration when things do not go as planned, even if you cannot fix the problem.

Violated SLAs May Trigger Other Inquiries

It is also important to understand that if SLAs are not met, an entirely new trigger may be pulled (or gate opened) that kicks off a process designed to get to the root cause (often called RCA, or Root Cause Analysis) of what happened and why the SLA could not be upheld. Depending on how your knowledge-based initiative is structured and the role you play, you may be part of that RCA process. Depending on your firm, the methodologies it embraces, and the amount of process in place, RCAs can be simple – or a major paperwork nightmare. Keep this in mind because staff will typically do everything possible avoid having to conduct RCAs; meeting SLAs is preferable to not meeting them.

SLAs as a Compensation Factor

SLAs, and the degree to which they are met, may factor into another part of the IT staff's concerns: compensation. For example, if your firm has a centralized network center (perhaps called a NOC, Network Operations Center), they may have a goal of 97% systems availability, meaning that computers are available 97% of the time. How that goal is met or exceeded may factor into the NOC staff's annual bonus. Even if it does not factor into a bonus plan, it may play a part of IT leadership's compensation.

There can be a lot of "fine print" in SLAs, as well. Using the example above, there may be agreed-upon scheduled maintenance windows at odd hours. Perhaps the 97% only counts during business hours, and business hours are defined as 8 AM to 8 PM Monday through Friday. There may be other variables, particularly if your firm spans multiple time zones. Ask to make sure you understand SLAs that are relevant to your knowledge-based solution, and communicate them appropriately to your customers, particularly those that will use your solution for mission-critical activities.

Typical Relevant SLAs

Investigate these topics with IT to determine the SLAs that may affect your end users. You may encounter other relevant SLAs, as well.

- If your knowledge-based solution uses a separate authentication system (such as a password), how long will it take to reset an end user's password?
- If an end user accidentally deletes something from your knowledge-based solution's environment, can they get it back? How long will it take?
- Is there a general SLA around system availability (meaning, the computers and all associated software are functioning)? Are there exceptions you need to be aware of, such as weekends, holidays, or scheduled maintenance windows?
- Is there an SLA around adding new users to the environment? Or, deleting users?
- In case of hardware failure, is there an SLA around when the environment will be restored?

Change Control

Change control can be an activity, a group of people, or a "thing" such as a policy. As you launch your knowledge-based initiative, you may have to engage change control gatekeepers around project initiation. Once your initiative is up and running, and hopefully becomes part of your organization's permanent landscape, you may engage other change control entities as your work grows.

In some cultures, a person touching an area that is governed by change control must get the appropriate change control committee's blessing before any activity happens. Alternatively, employees might be expected to know and conform to change control policies with no intervention or coaching; unless someone points out an infraction, it is highly unlikely a committee will ever check or audit activities. Because change control may mean different things from firm to firm, you must understand what change control means at your firm, and how it is managed.

Change Control as a Committee

As a group of people, change control committees may bless certain activities before they happen or examine cases where change control procedures were not followed (and usually, where something bad happened). Although people who enforce change control and its associated policies are frequently affiliated with project management, change control entities also exist in non-project, production environments, especially if technology is involved.

Change Control as an Activity or Artifact

Defining, adhering to, and auditing change control are all activities. When executed, they often spawn other activities. One activity that comes out of, for example, conducting a change control audit is the development of change control policies (written documents). So, in theory, you can sit on a change control committee, vote on whether to allow or disallow activities based on their impact to change control, and develop change control artifacts. Very different things, but in most places, they will all be called generic "change control."

Nearly any activity is a candidate for change control governance. Change control policies are guidelines for how to do perform an activity. For example, consider the activity of granting someone access to a secure area of your firm's infrastructure. If you asked ten password administrators how they would do it, you might get ten similar, but different answers. One thing change control helps ensure is that activities (like granting access to sensitive data) are done the best and the same way every time. If a change control policy around granting access was developed, no matter who executed it, the steps necessary to grant access would always be done in a specific order, with signoffs and controls in place.

An additional benefit that following change control offers you, as an end user, is the fact that change control policies have the additional stamp of approval from some member of upper management who has mandated that the policy is the preferred and correct way of performing a prescribed action. By following change control policies, you can be sure you are doing things the right way.

When Change Control is Violated

The penalty associated with violating a change control process varies greatly according to impact, the culture of your firm, and the type of change control violated. In some instances, you might have to explain your actions to the change control gatekeeper and will perhaps receive a verbal slap on the wrist. In others, an appearance before a senior committee with a written explanation that stays on file might be required. A deliberate violation of change control around a sensitive area, such as security, might escalate into compliance and result in disciplinary action.

One universal unwritten rule is that if change control is violated, and a change control team halts your project to examine your activities beneath a microscope, you should be prepared to locate and resolve other change control issues that will undoubtedly become known. You may have to potentially re-sell or re-justify your work. A close change control examination often leads to the discovery of an assortment of problems.

Typical Change Control Areas

For the purposes of *Managing Knowledge-Based Initiatives*, change control typically lies in a few areas. Remember to validate with others at your firm how things work.

- If your knowledge-based solution requires software development, there is probably change control behind the scenes that dictates how activities will happen.
- If your knowledge-based initiative requires that any change be made to end users' computing environments, change control may be invoked to determine the safety, correct sequence, and timing of such changes. Imagine that your solution requires a small piece of software to be installed on end users' machines. First, you might appear before the relevant change control committee. They, in turn, could kick off an activity to test the new software against all configurations. Once they are confident that other applications are not affected, the committee grants you approval to proceed. If you need to upgrade the software in six months, change control may again be involved.
- Changes in access – for example, granting a group of users new access to data stores – may require change control approval.

Your Role in Change Control

Earlier, we discussed that presenting a united face to your customers is important. The divisions between areas in your firm that support your knowledge-based initiative should appear seamless to your end users. This is one reason that getting IT, and other support mechanisms, invested in your knowledge-based initiative is important.

To gain the investment of IT staff, you will have to invest in them by following established change control procedures. Earlier we mentioned that customers may come to you with IT-related SLA concerns, even though you do not set or resolve SLAs. Likewise, customers may come to you with small requests – arguably tiny things – that they ask you to take care of.

Although it can be easy to offer up an immediate yes, and seem unduly process bound to put a tiny request through formal channels, consider the ramifications of skipping process, particularly if IT will be involved in any way.

Joseph King has experience as someone who sets change control guidelines, enforces those guidelines, and has been guilty of violating change control guidelines in the past. "I call those requests 'bumps in the elevator,' " he said. "You know, where executives mention some small enhancement that they'd like to see. A non-IT PM may get a bunch of those bumps, because he or she is the face of the project."

If you and your IT staff have an agreed upon change control process, it is important that you rigorously follow that process, even for little requests. "You know those small changes?" Joseph asked. "The ones that take ten minutes, and an IT person will often do for you without documentation or tickets? Those are actually *bad*. Every little change adds up. A ten minute change that doesn't go through the correct change control process – and doesn't work or messes something else up – could take weeks to fix."

Joseph shared a story about how failing to follow his own change control procedures cost him weeks of work. "IT people, for the most part, are customer oriented so they'll just do something if they think it will help. I once worked on a project, got an 'elevator bump' and agreed to fix a customer's problem. I didn't ask him to submit paperwork, a ticket, nothing. It seemed simple. We just added a step that allowed them to export files to the existing environment." The small change that Joseph made to the computing environment seemed to work great – until more people rolled onto the solution. Then, the server began running slower and slower. Soon, no one could get anything done.

The slowdown was caused by the change that Joseph had instituted outside of normal change control. The behavior of the software that eventually caused the server to shut down was not insurmountable, or even unusual – it was just unidentified because it had not been through change control. Furthermore, because there was no documentation of that change via change control channels, when the server began slowing down, the team did not know where to start looking. "If I had followed my own change control process, the one that

I implemented, there would have been a statement of work, requirements around the change, I would have tested the software first . . . and none of that would have happened," Joseph said.

Therefore, as the face of the project, make sure you follow change control procedures and do not commit to "elevator bumps" that may cause you to get around them.

Archiving: A Compliance and IT Interdependency

We have already discussed the importance of remaining in compliance on multiple levels. Compliance entities vary greatly from company to company and industry to industry. For example, archiving requirements your firm has in place may be the result of litigation your firm is facing or has faced in the past, where its records come into play. The number of variables is huge, so you will have to seek guidance on what compliance means inside your firm.

However, if your knowledge-based solution involves technology to an appreciable extent, there is a good chance that a product is created, such as an email chain, discussion group, instant messaging archive, or data repository. Archiving electronic byproducts of your work may be a compliance requirement inside your firm.

Recent legislation has changed – and continues to change – how companies must treat historic data, including what they keep, how it is stored, and how long it is kept. Whether or not you are affected depends on many variables, including the nature of your knowledge-based work, and your firm's industry.

You are not the person who will make the ultimate decision around whether you need to archive byproducts of your knowledge-based work. Look to IT and your Legal Department for guidance on that topic. However, depending on how things are set up in your firm, you may have to budget for archiving around your knowledge-based initiative. Budgeting in this sense means both dollars for materials and resources and time to complete archiving activities.

In addition, if you are bringing in a new technology, or an established technology that is new to your firm, you will have to ensure that any knowledge byproducts of your work can be archived to an extent to satisfy compliance. This might mean that during the planning stages of your work, you need to reach out to multiple entities – some that we identified in Section VI – and educate them, perhaps even involving them in solution selection.

You will need to answer a couple of questions: What has to archived for the sake of compliance? Who is responsible for doing that archiving and paying for it?

The Offsite Component

Archiving solutions generally involve an offsite component. Although your firm's members, most likely IT, will be the people who actually archive content that lives inside your corporation, periodically, those backups are moved offsite to a secure location. The reasons are multiple:

- Storing backups onsite does not help if a building is destroyed or inaccessible for any reason, such as a natural disaster.
- Backup mediums take space, space that many organizations do not have to spare. In addition to the additional security offered by offsite storage, it is also a pragmatic space planning measure.

Determining the Cost of Archiving

Determining the cost of archiving is critical because if you do not budget for it, you could be in deep trouble. Because archiving may be tied to compliance, performing it, and performing it in a certain way, is not optional. Therefore, having the funds to ensure that archiving is performed to spec is also not optional.

If you are fortunate, archiving costs and manpower may be absorbed by IT. You would be equally fortunate if there is a trigger around your PMO and its processes that will ensure that archiving activities are taken care of early on, when funds to ensure compliance are perhaps easier to come by. However, particularly because legal requirements around archiving are changing rapidly, do not leave this to chance.

Outputs: What Could be Archived?

When you look at your knowledge-based initiative, do you see outputs that could be archived? Some likely candidates are the following.

Any electronic conversation. This includes instant messaging, discussion groups, email, and desktop share sessions. More than likely, email is dealt with by an enterprise archiving system, so you should not have to worry about that. After all, you did not introduce email, even if your knowledge-based solution includes it. Similarly, if instant messaging is not a tool that you have introduced, but that perhaps your knowledge-based initiative uses in new ways, you are probably not responsible for figuring out how to archive conversations. To be sure, ask.

Any data repository. This could mean a collaborative or team space, any sort of database, or any sort of document share or archive. Think about large data stores where bunches of records or documents live as outputs of your knowledge-based work. Frequently, if your work is around enabling teams, you may find that a team space, for example, encompasses both data storage and the electronic conversations we mentioned above.

Any process and procedure documentation. Make sure that you can point to process and procedure documentation throughout the lifecycle of your work to explain what got done, how, and why. That documentation may live in a data repository – but it is worth calling out as its own area.

Any place customer information is exchanged. With a shifting emphasis on protecting customer privacy across industries, keep an eye out for any place that customer information may be exchanged inside your knowledge-based work.

How Do Things Get Archived?

Once you have determined what needs to be archived, you need to find out how archiving happens at your firm. Expect the answer to be more complicated if any portion of knowledge byproducts created from your work are housed outside your corporation.

Questions you need to ask about process around archiving include the following:

- Do I need to do anything special to get my content archived? Is there a request or change control form I need to complete? How do I kick off the process?
- How often is content archived? Can I get it more frequently if needed?
- Am I billed for archiving services? How much, and how often?
- Who does the archiving? What group, and who do they report to?
- What is the actual process for archiving? For example, what medium is content archived on? Where is content archived? How long does the process take?
- What does archived data look like? What format is used?
- What fail-safes are in place to ensure that archiving happens successfully? For example, are backups periodically restored to ensure they are not corrupted? Is the backup medium ever tested?
- How does medium rotation happen? For example, if you have to keep content for five years, what happens to the medium once it is older than that? Do they reuse it, reformat it, destroy it, or ship it back to your firm?

How Do Things Get Restored?

Similarly, you need to understand how content, once archived, can later be restored.

- Who can request that content be restored? What safety measures are in place to ensure confidentiality?
- Who can request access to the archived content?
- If you need content restored, how long will it take? Typically, this depends on several things: if the content is stored offsite, there is the time necessary to return the medium used to archive content back to your firm. Then, there is the actual restoration time itself.
- Do you have to stick to business hours for restoration requests? Is weekend and after-hours service available, and if so, does it cost more?

How Do Things Stay Safe?

Just as we discussed that you would not be making decisions around what needs to be archived single-handedly, you will also not be choosing the firm that stores archived materials. However, it is worth asking the following questions:

- What environmental safeguards are in place to protect archived content?
- What happens if your firm quits doing business with the storage site?
- What happens to old tapes?

Mediums and Associated Costs

As we mentioned earlier, you are fortunate indeed if you do not have to worry about any details concerning archiving. If you do have to manage the details, however, you need to understand what type of medium is being used, how the storage works, and associated costs.

Mediums come in multiple shapes and sizes. You won't choose which medium is used; your firm's IT staff should deal with that. However, you might have a say in the capacity of the medium, particularly if you are forced to purchase it as part of the larger archiving agreement, and that decision factors into multiple other areas. To get an idea of why this matters, imagine the following scenario.

In your knowledge-based work, you have created multiple team areas. Your IT resources tell you that each team area contains about 2 GB (gigabytes) of content. You calculate that roughly, you have less than 20 GB of content that your firm's Legal Department has advised you must be archived. You know that archived content must be moved offsite bi-weekly, and your Legal Departments expects you to take a daily snapshot of the content.

That means that in a five-day workweek, taking daily snapshots, you will need a medium that will accommodate at least 100 GB of content. Remembering that you have to move the archived content physically offsite every two weeks, having a medium that will accommodate 200 GB of content would seem to be ideal.

One option might be to use 10-GB tapes. If you purchase 20 10-GB tapes, you increase the number of tapes you are paying to have physically transported and stored; you may lose money there. In addition, the chances of someone forgetting to swap out a tape, or losing one, are increased. Restoring the data will also be more time consuming and tedious.

On the other hand, if you purchase a terabyte's worth of storage, which is over 1,000 gigabytes, you are wasting a great deal of space because you have to use a new tape every two weeks. As of now, the maximum that would be used is about 200 GB, less than 1/5 of the content. You would be paying for – and wasting – over 800 GB of space every two weeks.

The ideal solution would be something that would handle the content you have, with some additional space to grow, as well as space that the backup technology itself will require. If your IT department is handling all archiving details for you, you won't have to concern yourself with the math, mediums, or process. However, if it directly impacts your bottom line, you must be concerned.

Understanding Offsite Storage Costs

Restoration costs. If data needs to be restored, there is generally a cost associated with retrieving the correct medium and returning it to your firm. If your corporation does significant business with an offsite storage firm, they may have negotiated a number of "free restores" per quarter or year. Make sure you know what restores will cost you. Include that information in communications to your customers.

Restoration timelines. Non-critical restorations that can be performed over the space of a few weeks may incur no additional charges, while critical restorations that must be performed within 24 hours may incur a substantial cost. Make sure you understand the difference.

Transportation costs. Transportation occurs both in sending content offsite and bringing content back to be restored. Make sure you know what each trip costs, and whether there are multiple options from which you can choose.

12

Expert Q&A with Brandon Goldfedder

Brandon Goldfedder has nearly two decades of experience in the IT industry and is currently a Vice President of IET, a professional services firm that specializes in research, development, and implementation of knowledge-based expert systems for decision support, information fusion, and modeling of complex phenomena. Brandon's point of view on how to deal with IT staff is valuable for multiple reasons.

Because of his extensive consulting experience, Goldfedder has been exposed to dozens of industries, varied business cultures, knows what works and what does not, and has gained his experience as a team member, manager, and executive. He also belongs to what is sometimes a rare breed: a true "geek" who loves technology for its own sake – but also understands the world of business. Here, he shares his thoughts on what makes IT and non-IT people different to work with and manage, some tips on motivating and understanding different types of IT people, and the importance of understanding your firm and working well with people. In addition, he discusses how the IT industry and people who work in it are subject to extreme and rapid change, something to keep in mind as you engage with IT people and build a knowledge-based solution that may include a technical element.

Dealing with IT Staff

Q: *What does a non-IT person need to know about dealing with or managing IT staff?*
Brandon believes some of the key differences between technical and non-technical staff are how praise and requests for improvements are handled and

the depth of business knowledge IT staff may have, or believe to be necessary. "One thing that occurs to me," he said, "is that IT people tend to rely a lot more on praise. There's a level of praise they want from people that they consider to be peers; they want to be the best at something. They want people to think that what they're doing is cool and neat."

This is important for you to keep in mind when you deal with IT staff, particularly if they are undertaking development for you. A little praise may go a long way, and suggestions for improvement may be best tempered by that praise. Brandon explained. "If you're an IT guy and show your stuff to a business user, and they say, 'Hey! That's great!' – and then follow up with suggestions to make it even better, that works."

In other words, praise, then request enhancements. Failing to recognize progress, even if it seems small to you, can have disastrous consequences. "I was once in a meeting," Goldfedder related, "where the feedback from the non-IT people was that the IT prototype was 'amateurish' and 'juvenile.' I walked away wondering: do they really think these people (the IT staff) will do anything else for them?"

Another key difference between IT and non-IT people lies in their respective levels of business understanding. If you work on the business side of your firm (meaning, not in IT) you might be surprised at how disconnected individuals who work in IT can be from the business as a whole. "I think it's important," Brandon explained, "for non-IT people to educate IT about business. At the same time, don't expect them to care. The more junior IT resources are, the less they think it's their job to understand how the business operates. Their job, in their eyes, is wrestling with technology – not wrestling with a business problem. That's the problem with IT: it's not until a person gains some seniority that he or she understands that the root problem is, in fact, business."

Brandon has seen this change over the years. "In the early 90s, as I visited multiple companies, I noticed that IT people tended to be not very good at the software side, but knew the business inside and out; they understood the domain very well. Towards the end of the decade, what I noticed was that the IT capability had increased – lots of C++, Java, web design skills – but the core knowledge about the business itself had drifted away. Today, IT people tend to be generalists more than business people. A devaluation of IT people has occurred, and part of the reason IT people don't care about the business they support is that there's not an expressed value in it."

While you won't find this attitude everywhere, the lesson is clear: do not assume that IT staff you work with will intuitively understand why your solution matters to your customers. Recognize that they might not be highly motivated by the challenge of solving a customer's problem. You will probably need to connect the dots for them. The IT people you deal with may have entirely different motivators, areas of expertise, and goals than you do, although you work for the same firm.

It is not an insurmountable issue, though. "The way in which I've seen things work very well," Brandon shared, "is if the non-IT person can provide a 'dummy's guide' that simplifies things and explains the business side."

Personality Traits, Strengths, and Weaknesses

Q: *If you could group IT people, what would those groups be? How are they different from each other, and what are their strengths and weaknesses?*

Brandon identified two large groups of people: those that consider technology a job and those that consider it a way of life. Of course, you will encounter people in the gray area between the two extremes, but understanding attitudes and motivators of technical staff can be invaluable, particularly if you have a voice in who is staffed on your knowledge-based initiative.

"There are a large number of people," Goldfedder observed, "who wound up in IT because there was money there, or it let them utilize some other kind of interest. For example, some HTML web development people are failed artists. Even the term "computer science" means different things. It's undefined. The field of Computer Science may be engineering at one university, arts and sciences at another, and business at another.

"There are those who are there to accomplish a job," Brandon continued. "They put in their time, do their job, and have a clear separation of job and life. They seek a healthy balance, and probably aren't reading books about what's going on in the field outside of their job. The bulk of IT resources fit into this realm, and that can possibly be very good for a company because these people are the most able to fit into the business, and handle repetitive tasks well. They're not there to be challenged every day; they have a job to do. To manage them well, task them in a way that's non-painful, and they're happy."

Goldfedder freely admits that he belongs to the second classification. "The other group – I'll call them highly motivated, although you might refer to them as uber-geeks – are IT people who basically blur the line between life and technology. Their mantra is, 'I work hard so that I can afford more expensive toys to work harder.' They probably feel guilty reading a non-programming book. Business users might recognize them as type-A driven people."

Working with or managing this type of resource has both rewards and challenges. Brandon explained, "The problem with managing this type of person is that the bar has to constantly be moving up. They require something that makes them work a little harder – sweat a little more – to get involved. That little extra push. If they're *not* sweating, you lose them. They internalize that lack of challenge as unhappiness, begin to think they're wasting their time, and ultimately their life. This is the group you have to keep motivated with stronger and stronger mechanisms to 'do stuff.' "

One way of successfully pairing up the two camps of IT resources with an activity is to divide them based on the degree that your work is governed by repeated process. "Processes work best with the first group; they like consistency and *want* a process," Goldfedder said. "Processes give them a way to balance out the world."

On the other hand, the second group may chaff if forced to conform to processes, particularly those they do not view as relevant. "Processes don't work well with the highly motivated group. They don't know, when they go into work, if they are going to have a 20 or a 3 hour day," Goldfedder explained. "They can be hyperactive and dangerous to have on projects. However, they are the most likely to have breakthroughs. But," he cautions, "it's very difficult to predict deadlines with a team comprised of the second type of IT person."

Understand that the two groups may have very little in common. "Within those camps of people are those who understand the beauty of software design," Brandon said, "and understand it's an art. And, there are those who hack code together and just happened to wind up in the field to begin with. It's an interesting mismatch when you start putting things together."

Management Tips for the Non-IT Person

Q: *What tips would you offer a non-IT person who needs the support of, will be managing, or is the business owner of a project that requires IT resources?*

Although you may have to work with whatever team is available and assembled, there are some tricks, including shared accountability, carefully managing timelines, and meeting habits, that can help things run smoothly.

If you do have input, understand that from the IT point of view, putting together the best team possible varies greatly depending on the final goal. "It depends on the nature of the project, how much time you have, how important functionality for a prototype is vs. having a staff for a production large scale application – all of these things matter," Brandon explained. "I need a completely different team doing real-time tasks than I would to develop an interactive web piece. They're not the same skill sets at all and use very different techniques when you look at server side vs. desktop applications. Many people don't realize how different they are." Make sure you are clear about your knowledge-based initiative's technology goal and ask pointed questions about the types of resources needed to accomplish specific tasks.

Brandon believes that sharing responsibility can lead to success. "One thing that is essential in managing IT people is a dual accountability model," Goldfedder said. In this model, IT staff help set their own deadlines, and as the business person, you participate fully and are accountable as well. "Specifically, it's rare that I ever set a deadline for IT people," he continued. "I ask, and I might negotiate, but they set the deadline as opposed to me dictating an artificial one. Artificial deadlines don't work. One exception is if you're doing a time-based agile process in which you, for example, define up front that software releases will happen every 30 days. Even in that case, you're agreeing to when – not what – will go into those releases.

"The key is to negotiate up front and then hold IT staff to what they agree to. Micromanaging the process, or forcing overtime doesn't work. Punitive measures don't necessarily work, although I've found it interesting to observe companies that schedule major releases right before a holiday, the idea being that it will motivate the team to get things done before the holiday. It doesn't work that way; I count on working that holiday."

Brandon is quick to point out that you, the business owner, have a degree of accountability as well. This can be a challenge in your role as a knowledge practitioner, because the chances are good that you, in turn, have customers who are the genuine business owners. You may find yourself in a position of being a conduit of business needs, not the final authority. Even so, your participation is key.

"Accountability goes the other way, as well," Goldfedder said. "If an IT person says what they need from you, the end user, you better comply quickly to meet the deadline, or you've just given them a perfect excuse for the work not happening. IT people are often terrible about timelines because they're perfectionists. To the alpha uber geeks, timelines are very gray because they want everything to be done perfectly; they want to raise that bar. They're likely to go after the 'bright shiny objects' and ignore the core business problem. The first group of IT people will tend to go with the simple solution up front; they're there to get the job done, not discover something. They like cool technology, but not enough to miss home time."

Another tool in managing IT people is to stay in regular contact with them, and this means maintaining and establishing effective and regular meetings. "The business owner needs to be part of the team," Brandon advised. "That's key, an essential for constant feedback. Meetings that are driven by actual demos are successful, as opposed to PowerPoint discussions. They provide a mechanism so that you can praise the IT person for the work done and suggest changes. It's helpful to be physically there so that terminology differences don't lead you down false paths." For examples of common misinterpretations around IT related terminology, see Chapter 11.

Brandon does not believe in long and frequent meetings. "Meet often, and in short durations," he advises. "Don't over meet. IT people tend to view a meeting as time away from accomplishing the tasks they have in front of them. A meeting is useful if it helps them accomplish their tasks. If not, it's no longer useful and they might resent it. A daily meeting of ten minutes, for example, checking in at nine o'clock, could be great. A two-hour meeting a few times a week is losing huge productivity."

Brandon also recommends that you, as the business owner, try to keep tasks to a manageable scope in terms of elapsed time. "The shorter the task and its duration, the better," he says. "Use user stories to scope your project small per iteration. The reason is that it's easier to go adrift upstream and get focused on the 'bright shiny objects' the more time you have. If an IT team doesn't meet with the end user for six months, they can get into a whole lot of trouble. If they only have two weeks until the next physical meeting or dog and pony show, they'll steer things back into place. Long cycle projects tend to fail in business projects; there's too much time in the feedback loop," he explained.

Changes in the World of IT that May Affect You

Q: *What's happening in the IT world that might impact a business user?*

"The practice of developing software is changing very fast, which has a tremendous impact on a lot of things," Brandon explained. "Specifically, the use of more dynamic languages like Python and Ruby (and others languages), the growth of open source software, as well as development techniques like several of the agile methodologies allow more common business solutions to be developed quickly. My personal theory is that we're moving towards a model of software development going into two camps: people to build components which will be done by fairly high end development type people, and people who take those components and plug them together to solve a business need. Dynamic languages make a huge difference in the rapid combination of components to solve the business need. The question is, at what point do you need the IT people to do this, and at which point can the business end user do it? As the level of IT knowledge increases in the field, when does the IT person for this aspect become unnecessary?"

External forces are at least partially responsible for the bar constantly being raised in the IT industry. "I remember when people wouldn't use Windows," Brandon says. "What changed? One thing is video games. They raised the bar. Now the bar is so high that a high-end video game has a larger budget and bigger staff than most IT projects. Entire teams of artists design different parts of the screens. Lots of usability people. In an IT project, maybe part of one person is devoted to usability.

"There are a lot of questions around software development right now. What are the new tools available for developers to use? And then, how do we train the developers? There's much more urgency around the need to keep up with what's happening in the field. Of course, that varies according to what business you're in. If you work on large government contracts, you can be two to five years behind. The smaller the company you're in, though, the more up to date you have to be."

Brandon also believes the market around software purchases, and the associated development, is changing. "People buying general software for business or personal use is disappearing. People want to use open source software. And, the concept of buying software will become less and less prevalent as the service model increases. Look at the game, World of Warcraft. Users pay a monthly fee to play. Revenue is generated from monthly fees. Why charge for the software? Almost all web services models out there work like that.

"So, I believe the days of people going out and spending a fortune on software purchases is coming to an end. But, there's more of a need to use high end developers. The fulcrum is larger; there's more of a need to rapidly develop solutions. For example, I can roll out a web application in a week that used to take six months, all because of the components I mentioned earlier. The build vs. buy decision is starting to pivot."

Communications Basics

Q: *Talk a little about communication between technical and non-technical people.*

"I alluded earlier," Brandon said, "that when it comes to managing IT teams, a key aspect is to have someone who can bridge the gap between IT and non-IT people and can communicate with both sides. IT people will respect people who understand their jobs. So, try to understand technologies. Try to understand what you're working with, even if it's not your job. You need to be able to articulate how some of these things work, and if you can't, ask IT to explain it. If they tell you something can't be done, ask questions, and learn." Even if you consider yourself a complete technology failure, do not be afraid to ask questions when you do not understand something. If you do not have time to become conversant on the technology side of your knowledge-based initiative, assign someone on your team to fill that role.

There may be additional help available inside your firm to help with any translation problems. According to Goldfedder, "At a higher level, I generally bridge the gaps between IT and business owners – but people who can do that are often expensive. On the IT side, that type of role will usually be filled by a chief architect, but in a lot of companies, there isn't one. Be sure to ask who is responsible for pulling it all together. You may need someone who will enforce the process, depending on your situation. For example, right now I'm working on a project where my clients are scientists. They're discovering new ways of doing things so there are no requirements. No business driven anything. Supporting this client requires a very different type of IT group compared to working with a business owner."

Organizational Knowledge

Q: *How important is organizational knowledge and facility in navigation to working with IT?*

Goldfedder, like the other executives interviewed in *Managing Knowledge-Based Initiatives*, believes that understanding the organizational landscape is key to your success – and that as a Knowledge Management person, you should be especially good at that. "Know how to operate in a large organization," Brandon advised. "In a lot of cases, the most important thing is to understand the landscape up front, how the firm is set up, what they value, what they do not value, and ensure you're in alignment with that."

Things can vary greatly from company to company. "If you're operating in a start up model," he continued, "it may be free form. In other businesses, you may align heavily with the government. I've worked with coders at a bank where they had to wear a business suit. I've taught in other organizations where people showed up without shoes.

"As a knowledge elicitation person," Brandon pointed out, "that's even more essential because your job is to communicate. You should know things like what is proper attire, behavior, what is OK or not, 'how do you get invited to the cool table at lunch.'"

In Chapter 2, we asked you to identify where Knowledge Management fits into the firm. As you approach working with IT, it is also beneficial for you to understand where they fit. Brandon explained. "Is the IT organization considered a cost center, meaning their job is to support others? Or, are they a profit center? Are they building things and generating revenue? Depending on how the IT organization is set up, you have to operate differently. I've run an IT group that had revenue goals, in which case, the business side was more important to us. I've also run an IT cost center group. We went in, fixed things, and got away from users as soon as possible because they were a distraction."

What to Avoid

Q: *What common mistakes should knowledge practitioners try to avoid when working with IT staff?*

"In my mind, a key mistake to avoid is a failure to show an appropriate level of respect. In fact, it's one of my pet peeves," Goldfedder said. "Once, I was working in an organization that had a 'critical defect.' A true critical defect, if it is raised as an error, must be fixed *before developers can go home*. They might have to stay for two days – no one leaves because if it's a critical defect, it's critical to the operation of the business."

You might imagine that the business owners of the critical error would be right there, alongside the IT staff, but Goldfedder has seen the reverse more than once. "I've seen cases where the business owner went home," he said. The IT response? "We cancelled the critical effort because our thoughts were, 'If it was truly critical, they wouldn't have gone home.' If an IT person is working late on your behalf, at least offer to stay. There are two reasons: the general bonding that can happen, and the commitment level that you will demonstrate. If you're truly committed to the task at hand, an hour won't hurt you. Show that you're willing to put the extra effort in."

Brandon recognizes that this may not always be possible. "People have to make a decision about where they sit on the whole work/life tradeoff thing. If you have two kids at home, maybe it's not realistic for you to work every weekend. There are tradeoffs everywhere."

In Conclusion

Q: *Any final words of advice?*

"Learn how to play nice with people," Brandon said. "There's a lot of common sense things that I've seen people miss completely. For example, don't belittle anyone – especially people with the power to remove your passwords. Make sure you're generally nice to people.

"My theory is that it all comes back to communicating," Goldfedder said. "Do whatever you can to bridge that communication gap. It's a combination of figuring out ways to educate IT people and show that you're open to learning. Keep in mind that if you're junior or new to a firm, company veterans in IT may understand more about the business than you do, even if they don't show it. Learn as much as possible from IT staff. They like to explain how things work to people. Of course, whether they care about the business at hand or not is a whole different question."

Even if you never fully succeed in generating excitement around a business issue that may be theoretical – or irrelevant – to the IT staff that support your knowledge-based initiative, following the guidelines above may help you to glimpse your organization through their eyes. And, as Brandon explained, IT people tend to respect, and listen to, people who understand and respect what they do.

13

Engaging the Help Desk

People who spend their careers focused on knowledge-based solutions are, to some extent, visionaries and optimists. We analyze pain points and extrapolate how to address them from the root up – and that root will, with rare exception, be knowledge-based in our viewpoint. We are optimists because we really believe knowledge solutions can change everything. Knowledge practitioners who operate largely on theory may work towards the creation or nurturing of an "aspirational" knowledge environment. Other practitioners live in an extremely tactical and process-based world. There is a large gray area between the extremes.

At least in part because of our focus, many knowledge practitioners are sometimes not so good at "in the weeds" types of activities, the day-to-day things that, although boring, are critical in a large organization. In this chapter, we examine working with your organization's support structure(s) to ensure that your "in the weeds" execution matches up to the quality of your knowledge-based solution overall. If your participants will call on any Help Desk that you do not personally manage for support, this chapter is for you.

Would You Want Their Job?

Just as people often say that knowledge practitioners are a different breed, so is Help Desk staff. We have all been around – perhaps even been – the person who grouses about the service received from a Help Desk.

On the other side of the phone call, consider what Help Desk employees face:

- People generally contact the Help Desk when something has already gone wrong; the interaction starts on a negative foot.

- Help Desk personnel cannot possibly know every answer, every time. First call resolution is considered by some to be a "holy grail" of Help Desk/Call Center interactions.
- Call center workers have one of the highest turnover rates of all industries. Because of the high turnover, institutional knowledge may be at a minimum. The person who knew everything a month ago is often gone.
- Speaking with outsourced Help Desk representatives can be a hot button for end users if they know they are speaking to an outsourced person. On a personal level, individuals who have been touched by outsourcing may react negatively because of a large set of reasons. As offshore outsourcing has become more common, the combination of impatient, already-frustrated users with non-native speakers has proven incendiary. The target of customers' anger is not the executive who made the decisions – it is the people who are staffing the facilities that are the outcome of those decisions. They take the brunt of anger for multiple situations they did not create.

Defining Support

Support, what it is called, and how it is aligned and socialized are vastly different from firm to firm. For the purposes of *Managing Knowledge-Based Initiatives*, we will assume that support entities include the following:

- Any group that makes your solution work at any level, including technology, process, or education.
- Any group that can, through performing their job function well, help your knowledge-based solution succeed.
- Any group that can, through performing their job function poorly, cause your knowledge-based solution to appear an ill-conceived, badly planned traffic wreck.

Although support mechanisms may not be called "help desks" in your organization, for ease of reference, we will refer to organizational support mechanisms in this chapter as a Help Desk. Similarly, we are excluding the types of help desks that might handle equipment returns or reports of product defects because they are probably irrelevant to your efforts. More than likely, the Help Desk entities that you will need to care about are technology-based.

What Type of Support Will Your Work Require?

Before you engage your Help Desk(s), make a list of areas that you believe they will (or should) support. Because your Help Desk may ask or require that you participate in support, it is good to have a laundry list of potential areas or situations before you divide responsibilities. You may end up bartering. Consider the following areas:

- **Information requests.** Can people call the Help Desk with general "tell me more" sorts of questions? At the very least, will the Help Desk refer callers to you or your team?
- **Processes.** Can people enroll in your knowledge-based initiative via the help desk? Is that how they begin and cease participation in your project? If an enrollment process is kicked off, will it cascade into other processes, such as supporting associated software? Are there seat counts to worry about? Will anyone validate a request for participation with you? Should they?
- **Education.** Does any branch of your Help Desk assist with training, or tracking training requests or class enrollment? At the very least, will the Help Desk refer callers to you?
- **Problem solving.** When things do not go as expected, to what extent will the Help Desk support callers, and when will you be expected to step in?

The Organizational Landscape of Your Help Desk

In Chapter 8 of *Managing Knowledge-Based Initiatives*, we asked you to identify committees that control supporting resources in your firm. As a next step, take that analysis a level deeper and explore the following topics.

- How many individual Help Desks are there in your firm with which you need to be concerned? How are they related to each other, if at all?
- Where do Help Desk personnel fit into the committees you identified as crucial? In particular, look for them around standards, change control, and compliance.
- What is the reporting structure for the Help Desks? Do you have friendly faces in positions of power somewhere in the related organizational hierarchy?
- Is your Help Desk geographically dispersed, centralized, or a combination? Does your company use geographic differences (and therefore time zones) to maximize Help Desk coverage?

- Is any portion of the Help Desks you are concerned with outsourced? For more details, see *Blended Modes of Support.*
- What are the Help Desks' biggest challenges?
- What are their annual goals? In particular, are they working towards any key metrics?
- What are the Help Desks' turnover numbers?

Who Does the Help Desk Work For?

As you delve into the details concerning Help Desks in your organization, remember to keep an eye towards to finding their highest level bosses. You may discover, for example, that technology Help Desks fall beneath IT. Perhaps, the technology Help Desks fall beneath a larger support organization that has a dotted line to your firm's technology group. Relationships may not be obvious.

Blended Modes of Support

In addition, look for unusual or blended modes of operation. You may encounter multiple combinations. The combinations are something to be aware of because they tell you, essentially, who holds the power in the relationship. Often, it can indicate who has funding – and who does not. You also need to know about blended modes of support because you need to know who to deal with in case of difficulties.

Some possible combinations are:

- Part IT, part anyone else.
- Part staff "aug" (short for augmentation). These are contractors who function like full time staff but are not, who work in combination with your firm's internal staff.
- Part outsourced, part "insourced." In a case like this, be sure and determine percentages. It can help you track down who really controls – perhaps even owns – the relationship in the end.

Keeping a Strong Relationship with the Help Desk

You will find that first building, and then maintaining, a strong relationship with the support structures in your organization will require a significant amount of work. However, the benefits are numerous.

Think of working with your Help Desk in phases. First, you will prepare them to support your knowledge-based initiative. This may mean bringing up a large number of people from a no-knowledge level to a minimum-acceptable level.

During the execution of your knowledge-based initiative, you may make significant changes after the initial engagement. If so, you will need to reengage the Help Desk. For example, if the suite of products they support on your behalf expands from two products to eight, they need to know. Likewise, if you had planned to grow by 5,000 users over the next two quarters, but leadership will only fund a 1,000-user expansion, you must communicate that change of plans as well.

In addition, you will maintain the relationship throughout the lifecycle of your knowledge-based initiative by staying in regular contact with Help Desk staff.

Three parties will benefit from a close relationship:

■ The Help Desk itself, because they will be able to do their jobs more efficiently and potentially use your tools.
■ Your customers, because their support will be enhanced.
■ You, because you will get customer feedback from Help Desk staff, and be more likely to have satisfied customers if their problems are getting solved quickly.

Why the Help Desk Must be a Fan

Developing and maintaining a good relationship with the Help Desks that will be supporting your work is crucial for a number of reasons.

Who's who. Customers of your work may not be able to tell the difference between you or someone from your team, and a member of the Help Desk. Obviously, you want any customer-facing interaction that reflects on your knowledge-based initiative to be a positive one. Customers can be left with a negative impression any number of ways, but two of the most common are if Help Desk staff are under-engaged, perhaps even actively opposed to, your work and they share that point of view, or Help Desk staff genuinely does not know how to support your customers.

Can you fix this? Not only should Help Desk staff be generally positive about your tools, but they should be invested enough to actually care if tools associated with your initiative work. Bringing your customers' needs to life, and involving Help Desk leadership during the formation of your knowledge-based initiative is important to achieving that investment.

Free publicity. If you can, gather numbers around a typical day in a CSR's life in your firm. You might be astounded at the number of interactions with people that even the lowest level CSR has in a given day. Each contact is an opportunity for a CSR to say something – and hopefully something positive – about your work.

What You Can Learn from the Help Desk

What is not working. When something breaks, the Help Desk is the first place that end users will go – that is, if they do not contact your team directly. Because of this, you can get a heads up on a small detail that is not working the way you planned, or is causing "pain" for the end users. You may find that pain points have nothing to do with your solution itself, but instead an associated process. Remember that to your end user, it is all your product and therefore, it is all your problem.

Enthusiastic embracers. Those with their "feet on the ground" – such as support people that interact with end users hundreds of times a day – will be aware of groups that are enthusiastic adopters of your knowledge-based solution.

Unexpected ways people use your tool or idea. In the knowledge-based field, we ideally embrace new and innovative ways of accomplishing a task, even if it means moving outside of preconceived ideas. Make sure that as you are immersed in the corporate reality of implementing a knowledge-based solution, you maintain an open mind about people who may use your tools in ways that you did not predict.

View it as an opportunity to show how versatile your tools are, or perhaps drive home a point about how managing knowledge is a slippery, unpredictable process. If people are under-using your tools, which you may view as using them incorrectly, you have the chance to spot the gap that is contributing to under-use and address it. You may find some element of your solution that is unnecessarily complicated, or irrelevant to end users. Whatever you discover, you win in the end. Always remain alert to opportunities to gather success stories or relevant metrics.

Opportunities for improvements or enhancements. Help Desk staff may be the first to notice opportunities for improvements or enhancements to your tool. For example, imagine that Help Desk staff notice that end users regularly ask how to save a favorites list. You may not even be aware that this feature holds value for your customers and your tool, today, does not support that functionality. Now you have an idea of an improvement that may be valuable for your customers. Help Desk staff can help you understand functionality gaps or opportunities.

Opportunities for increased participation. Help Desk staff can also alert you to groups that would benefit from your solution who are not using it today. They may know early on about organizational changes that could impact your work.

Early public relations problems. It is just as important to be aware of poor perceptions of your work as it is to know about positive perceptions. Help Desk staff is often a lot like bartenders or hairdressers: people unload frustrations, stories, and observations on them. While you do not want every comment to be relayed for your review, try to create an atmosphere with Help Desk leaders and senior personnel where they feel comfortable alerting you to problems, even if doing so implies some criticism of you or your activities.

Help Desk and Knowledge Synergies

There may be no other corporately constructed relationship that more clearly illustrates – daily, and repeatedly – the value of quickly connecting people to the information or people they need, than that of the Help Desk and its customers. If you look, you will probably find other synergies between your work and the Help Desks' needs. Investigate whether the Help Desk itself is a good candidate for your knowledge-based work.

Some possible synergies include the following:

- Any tool or process that positively impacts important Help Desk metrics, like first call resolution or dropped calls.
- Anything that cuts down on the number of calls the Help Desk receives, such as effective self-help systems.
- Anything that reduces the number of tools, or ways of doing things, that Help Desk staff have to know or know about.
- Any new tool that helps the Help Desk service customers.
- Anything that increases Help Desk staff job satisfaction.

Engaging Help Desk Leadership

Significantly before Help Desk personnel will be expected to support your knowledge-based initiative, engage their leadership. How you engage with the Help Desk may be well-orchestrated and documented, a known process in the world of your firm. On the other hand, you might be moving into, if not unknown, at least "un-process dominated" territory.

Who, Exactly, is Leadership?

You might need to ask some questions to determine which level of Help Desk leadership you should engage. Consider the following:

- Your Help Desk may have its own change control mechanisms that will determine exactly who you must engage with. Ask for "whoever is in charge of your internal change control."
- Your level of support may very well reflect your scope. For example, if your participants are all from a single state or region, ask for "whoever is in charge of the Pacific Region's Help Desk."
- Do not forget to ask friendly faces, including your executive sponsor or PMO representative, what level of the Help Desk you need to engage with. Depending on your level and your firm's culture, you may need to bring your executive sponsor or a designee to the first meeting.

High Level Leadership Must-Knows

Engage Help Desk leadership with an eye to finding out the following:

- Exactly what they will support; is there any portion of your work that they consider to be out of scope?
- Are you or your staff expected to participate in support?
- Who are your primary Help Desk contacts in sorting out the rest of the details?
- If training is needed, do they have trainers on staff who you can train, or will you and your staff function as trainers?
- Will training be mandatory for Help Desk staff? Who will enforce attendance?
- Any key timeline measurements: is there a minimum amount of time they will need to ramp up?
- What key metrics do they care about that you can affect?
- How, generally, do they anticipate their staff will react to supporting your tools?
- Who will own communications efforts to Help Desk staff about your tool?
- What are the high level SLAs around support?

Be prepared to provide:

- Timelines for your rollout, as you know them today.
- A roster of your staff members (assuming you have any), including who to call for what.
- A high level roster of your participants, including numbers and alignment.
- A generic overview of your project, which should include your primary stakeholders and who you work for.

Hidden Activities

Depending on the information you learn, other gates may open and other paths that you must follow may reveal themselves. For example, in one firm we know of, all new products that the Help Desk is expected to support, and in turn, new processes they will follow, must be documented before the new products and processes can be rolled out to Help Desk staff. A small group of designated technical writers who use a very specific methodology must be engaged to create the documentation. Materials had to be developed both in PDF and HTML format and formally released before the staff could roll onto supporting the new tools. Although a small detail, it was important and took a few weeks to accomplish. Watch out for similar details in your firm.

Planning Support

Once you have established a level of contact, and early agreement with help desk leadership, it is time to begin diving into the details. Some of the details you will need to address include training, communication, process, and support.

Communicating: Who, Why, When, and How?

The importance of communicating in any situation cannot be underestimated; as we explore in Section VII, having a good communications plan and learning the correct methods for communicating are key. In this case, communicating with Help Desk staff that will support your knowledge-based initiative is important.

From your earlier conversation with their leadership, you should have determined who would take primary ownership of the communication. Chances are good that although you will provide the content, messages will actually come from Help Desk leadership, perhaps with a dual signature that includes you at the bottom. The reason is simple: people tend to read, and listen to, information that comes from their leaders.

Even if your name is not on communications about your initiative, remain involved in its content and creation. It is the only way that you can ensure the right things are communicated at the right time. After all, no one cares about your knowledge-based initiative as much as you do.

At a minimum, ensure that your communications efforts:

Are segmented to an appropriate degree. Some probable segments are people who will lead the initial roll-on of Help Desk staff, different tiers of support, Help Desk management, everyone, and new employees.

Include Help Desk staff benefits. What will they get from not only supporting this new initiative – but supporting an initiative that is headed by you? That second part is important, because you may be communicating something of an intangible nature. Perhaps you can tantalize them with the fact that they will know about, and learn what the firm is using to (insert what your initiative does here) first. Or, perhaps your initiative is supporting a larger alignment artifact that the Help Desk has also been charged to support. Point out that alignment. If the Help Desk will actually be participating in, or using, what they are supporting, include that as well.

Detail support they will receive. Tell Help Desk staff about the training they will receive and other resources that will be made available to them.

Explain when to expect what. Let them know any timelines that you are comfortable sharing. Sample timelines include training dates, when they will be "up to speed" on the solution, or roll-on dates for your clients. If you do not have these dates specified, at least let Help Desk staff know when to expect the next update.

Offer immediate Q&A contacts. Make sure your communication includes whom they should contact with immediate questions and answers.

For a sample communications plan, refer to Section VII.

Training: Yours, Mine, and Ours

Calling a Help Desk and being given incorrect information is bad. Even worse is calling for support, only to quickly discern that the person offering support knows substantially less than you do. Engaging and holistic education can help you avoid either situations in conjunction with your knowledge-based initiative.

You have several areas of training to consider:

- Training Help Desk staff on how to support your knowledge-based initiative.
- Being trained on how to participate in the Help Desk's support process as appropriate.

Is There Help Available?

Before you are forced to "become" a trainer, if this is not part of your skill set, look around for help.

Trainers within the Help Desk. You may find that the Help Desk has experienced trainers who can train their staff on how to support your knowledge-based initiative. The idea is that you would train them and they in turn would train Help Desk staff. This is also referred to as a Train the Trainer, or TTT model. The added bonus of having a Help Desk staffer perform the training is that they have an inside perspective of what it takes to support customers, and will spot gaps in materials and flow. Note that if this model is used, you should attend all the early sessions for quality assurance purposes.

Trainers in your own group. Is there anyone in your workgroup, or in your executive sponsor's workgroup, that you could "borrow"?

Dedicated training groups. Is there a dedicated training group anywhere that may be able to help? In particular, check with IT and HR. Your PMO should also be able to point you in the right direction. You may find that leadership is willing to free up resources to help you train if they understand that the material will later be used with their own constituents.

Your customers' resources. In addition, track down resources that your larger customers may have. You may find trainers who are willing to participate if they understand that the material will later be used in their area.

If you and your staff are going be become trainers, look for good examples of training materials that you can follow. Ask for tips and templates from your firm's training experts. Do not start from scratch.

Strategy tip: Logically, the Help Desk will be trained before end users are. Therefore, keep reusable training resources and materials in mind as you train the Help Desk.

General Use Training Compared to Troubleshooting Training

Even if you are an experienced trainer, there is an added element to training a Help Desk that might be new to you. You must train Help Desk staff on not only how to use the product or process they will support, but how to troubleshoot it. If you are deploying a tool that falls within a family of tools already at use in your firm, experienced Help Desk staff will be able to draw parallels. If, however, your tools are new to the organization and have no logical predecessors, developing a troubleshooting curriculum component may be a challenge.

Most likely, you will have to get help from outside entities that are using the same or a related tool, or let your troubleshooting "knowledge base," whether a formal or informal one, grow with usage, as do many other knowledge bodies.

It is nearly impossible to construct useful "artificially engineered" problems to build how-to guidelines for Help Desk staff. Genuine troubleshooting and the subsequent learning occur when problems happen and useful problems won't really begin happening until the end users stretch the tool's limits. Furthermore, it is unlikely that you or your staff would construct a troubleshooting body of knowledge that reaches the necessary level of granularity that, for example, an IT Help Desk may need.

With these caveats in mind, aggregate all troubleshooting tips you and your staff may have uncovered in your early use of the tool. Ensure that some sort of vehicle exists in the Help Desk world to share, contextually, troubleshooting information. If not, you may have uncovered your next knowledge-based project. More than likely, the vehicle will be embedded within or linked to software your Help Desk uses to manage tickets. Contribute any troubleshooting information you have. Check with Help Desk experts to see if any of it is valuable enough to be included in the training materials.

How Much Do You Need to Know?

You should also begin to determine the level of troubleshooting skills that you, or your staff, will need to develop. Most of this will be determined by your comfort level with technology and the relationship that you have with IT staff and the Help Desk. In our experience, it is key to remain aware, at a minimum, of problems at a high level. Understand the issues, even if you would never be the person to solve them, or even tell someone else how to solve them. You may find yourself in the position of passing information between multiple troubleshooting parties, particularly at the onset of your work. It helps to be aware of everything that is going on.

For example, imagine that your solution requires a small piece of software be installed on end users' machines. However, on a number of machines in one region, the software won't launch. Further investigation between the Help Desk, IT, and the software vendor uncovers that there is a conflict due to old video drivers. Those drivers were updated in the latest Windows service pack – but not all parts of the firm have installed the service pack yet.

This would actually be a simple problem from a Help Desk point of view because there is a known cause, a known solution, and no work arounds or specialized diagnostics are needed; the service pack installation was scheduled anyway. In real life, problems will be more complex.

Even our simple example problem and resolution impacts two key activities the Help Desk is responsible for, the installation and troubleshooting of software for your project. The process to install software for your knowledge-based initiative now looks like this: before installation, ensure that the service pack has been applied. If not, install the service pack. Then, install the software.

The process for troubleshooting a software launch failure has changed, too. The first thing Help Desk staff must do is verify the version of service pack software. If the version reflects that the service pack upgrade has not been installed, the next activity is to install it. Then, probably after a reboot, try to use the your project software again.

Should you know the name of the video drivers, the version of the service pack, and who has or has not been upgraded? Probably not, unless you have a strong technology background and find such things interesting. Should you be aware of the issue, particularly in the early days of your initiative launch? Absolutely.

General Use Training Compared to Help Desk Process Issues

Also to consider is that different issues, products, and situations may utilize different parts of the Help Desk itself. Because the Help Desk uses tools that you have probably never interacted with, such as software that helps manage Help Desk tickets, there is an element of process around your solution that you not only do not know, but that you will probably never know.

Because of this, you do not own some of the content the Help Desk needs to be trained on in order to support your tool. One effective way to deal with this dilemma is to include Help Desk management who can speak to these issues in every training session. We discuss this in detail a little later on.

Understanding Tiers

Help Desks typically have at least three tiers of support. The first tier, Tier 1, is the most general; Tier 1 reps answer Help Desk phones, and are often the most junior. Second tier is more specialized, and third tier is typically the highest level of support. Customers usually never interact with the highest tier directly until a problem is escalated to them, and the highest level reaches out to the customer. Problems reach the highest tiers after they are escalated through the lower tiers.

Tiers matter for you for several reasons:

- If you are educating multiple tiers, you may need to tweak training for each tier.
- You may assist Help Desk leadership in determining which questions and therefore resolutions can be handled by Tier 1 generalists, and which need to be escalated to higher tiers.
- If you are playing a role in support, which tier will you functionally fall in? You should fall in a higher tier and be treated as a specialized resource.

Make sure and find out how tiers operate at your firm and where you might participate in them.

Training Details

Mandatory or optional? If you are given a vote, unless your Help Desk staff has supported very similar products, request that training be mandatory to ensure they are ready to support your initiative.

If training is mandatory, then you will need to track attendance, which will in turn be flipped back to Help Desk management. Let Help Desk management be the attendance enforcers – you should not play the "heavy" with people you do not manage. We advise that even if the Help Desk does not ask that you track attendance, you do. Later, these numbers may be valuable in calculating how many end users you have touched – and in resolving issues if support performance slips.

In one such roll-on we managed, when the Help Desk staff was also consumers of the knowledge-based tool, their access to the tool was not turned on until they attended class. We positioned their attendance as a compliance issue, because all other customers had to be trained to meet compliance. In the baseline session – which ensured compliance was met – we also included the training they needed to effectively support customers.

Attendance tracking tricks: Particularly in virtual classes, it can be difficult to track attendance. Your goal is to have people attend the entire session, and participate by visually processing the web meeting content, while also listening to the discussion. Set the expectation up front that attendance will be taken the last five minutes of class and have someone else from your team assist with taking names. If you are using a desktop share product, you can see who is signed into the virtual meeting. The person who is helping you will be able to spot if someone signs in for just the last portion of class. Taking attendance the last five minutes also keeps people from bailing early. Asking for a verbal confirmation helps ensure that students do not sign in and keep the phone on mute the entire session. If people do leave early, pass the responsibility off to Help Desk management to judge whether their attendance counts.

Flexibility is key. One of the most important things for you to remember about dealing with the Help Desk is that they require flexibility. You should count on, for example, not being able to have one large training session for everyone. Even if that would meet your needs (and it is doubtful it would be the most effective vehicle), it is impossible because there would be no coverage on the Help Desk since everyone would be in your class. Multiple smaller sessions are not only desirable, but necessary.

Consider offering both virtual and in-person classes. If class attendance is not mandatory, be sure to create a version of the materials that is suitable for learners who do not attend a formal session. You may need to offer some odd-hour classes, particularly if you work for a global firm with offices around the world, or you will be training any off-shored staff.

Another model that we have used with great success is setting up mentor relationships. Help Desk staff who could not adjust their schedules to attend mandatory training without risking Help Desk coverage were eligible to participate as long as they had their management's blessing. We assigned relatively senior, already-trained staff who we were confident "got it" to train junior staff members as time permitted. Key to the success of this was choosing senior staff that was invested in the success of the training, allowing training to happen in chunks as schedules permitted, and having the senior staff assume responsibility for the success of the junior staff. Everyone agreed that if junior staff members did not perform up to par, the senior trainers would be asked to explain.

Including Help Desk management's voice. It can be a struggle to target general training in such a way that it is relevant to specialized groups, like Help Desk staff. Likewise, it is hard to answer questions that dip into process when you are not a member of that group or an expert in its processes. One simple model that has been very successful is the inclusion of Help Desk management during key portions of training. Keeping in mind that "more is better" it is unrealistic to expect that a member of Help Desk management qualified to answer detailed questions will be able to attend every presentation, particularly if you are rolling on a large number of people. However, you can probably bargain for part time attendance.

In one model, at the beginning of class, the instructor sets the expectation that the last fifteen minutes of class would be devoted to Help Desk specific questions. During that time, a member of Help Desk management joined the class. Setting that time window allowed Help Desk management to allocate their time wisely – and also allowed the trainer to table any issues that he or she could not answer. We have also kept experts "virtually" on call using Instant Messaging programs; they would commit to remain at their desks the duration of class and be ready to join class over the phone, but would be free to continue work until they were needed.

Your Role in Support

Chances are good that you will play some role in support. Curbing the role you play can be hard; you have to "let go of your baby" and allow the Help Desk to do their jobs. In addition, one maturity measure of your knowledge-based initiative is how easily your solution can be expanded and replicated. Decentralized support (meaning, not just you) is key to that.

Your Help Desk will have its own way of categorizing types of issues and whom those issues should be routed to; much of that categorization will depend on any software package or methodology your Help Desk uses. Count on learning some new terminology and processes for handling tickets.

At a minimum, you need to understand the following:

- Who, specifically, will participate in support? Just you, different members of your team, your entire team?
- What level of support are you? The higher the better; you do not want your team to get inundated with calls that the Help Desk can easily handle.
- What is the SLA that you are expected to maintain and what are other SLAs?
- Who will train you in the use of supporting software? Basic skills that you will probably need to have include:
  - ☐ How to open and close a ticket.
  - ☐ How to forward a ticket to someone else.
  - ☐ How to reassign a ticket.
  - ☐ How to return a ticket.

Process

We include this section as a reminder that you need to address the processes that will govern how you and the Help Desk will work together after the initial roll-on is complete. It can be easy to effectively manage the project-based relationship, but let the ongoing relationship slip.

You may find at the onset of your relationship with the Help Desk that these processes are fairly defined; they have done this a million times before. Or, you may find yourself in "pioneer" mode and discover new ground as you go.

Investigate these areas with the Help Desk:

- **How you will engage with them in the future.** Do you have a single point of contact?
- **How you will handle changes you see coming from your side.** For example, if you want to roll on a new group of users that will cause you to exceed the number of users you estimated at the beginning of the project, whom do you let know? Is it a formal process, or an informal email?
- **How new people will be trained.** How will new Help Desk staff and new members of your team be trained?

- **Who helps you resolve problems?** For example, imagine that customers of your knowledge-based initiative alert you to the fact that they consistently receive faulty information from a particular portion of the Help Desk. Who can you work with to resolve issues like that?
- **What happens when things go wrong in process?** If anyone drops the ball process-wise, what red flags are thrown? For example, if you fail to meet an SLA, will someone alert you?

Tips for Ensuring a Helpful Help Desk Relationship

When things change, involve them first. This goes for not only the initial introduction of your knowledge-based tools into a live work environment, but for subsequent changes as well. Help Desk staff need to know about things before they happen. Be proactive about keeping them in the loop even when change control does not mandate that you have to.

Create single points of contact. Appoint a single person on your team, and a single person on the Help Desk side or sides to coordinate activities. This includes communications, training, on-boarding, any tool related activities, and problem resolution.

Stay in touch. Consider meeting regularly in the beginning of your relationship, which is typically while you are planning the introduction of your tool into the Help Desk environment, and the subsequent introduction itself. As you move into business as usual, schedule "checkups" with Help Desk leadership.

Network up. Pull in any executive markers to make sure that C-level owners of the Help Desks express their support of your work. Ask your executive sponsor to work on cementing these relationships.

Section VII

Communications, Salesmanship
and Publicity

14

The Corporate Red Carpet

Understanding the corporate red carpet is only tough if you have never been there. It is that magical place where the key decision makers know who you are and the goal of your work. People approach you in the hall and tell you how much they admire what your knowledge-based initiative is trying to accomplish. Executives begin to ask for your opinion, or inclusion in your initiative. Appointments seem to be somehow easier to get, and phone calls and emails are returned quicker than before.

In a nutshell, the red carpet that we are referring to in this section is the state that is achieved when enough of your firm has bought into your solution (or is at least willing to give it a chance). You have two challenges: how to get to the red carpet, and once there, how to remain as long as you need to. You will address these challenges through a combination of effective salesmanship and top-shelf communications skills.

In this chapter, we focus on several topics:

- The link between effective communications and selling.
- Different types of communications.
- How to build a communications plan.
- Tips for handling in-person communications events, particularly executive meetings.
- What vehicles and events you should consider to publicize your work.
- How to incorporate those vehicles and events into a comprehensive communications plan that will guide and structure your activities.

Later in this section, we discuss:

- KM guru Dave Snowden's point of view about selling your work.
- Examples of real-life salesmanship of knowledge-based work in Australia.

- Executive points of view around sales success.
- Continued sales and publicity success at your firm.

Communications and Selling – the Same or Different?

Selling your work is not only part of what will get you to the corporate "red carpet" but is an activity that you will continue to perform, even while you are metaphorically negotiating the paparazzi gauntlet that accompanies any self-respecting red carpet. Continual and unselfconscious salesmanship will help you remain at the forefront of your corporate public's mind as long as you need to. Selling and communication are so heavily interwoven that they cannot – and should not – be considered discrete activities in this sense.

What Does the Red Carpet Mean?

We define red carpet strategies as those that will place your knowledge-based initiative:

- At the forefront of people's minds.
- In the contender's circle, at the very least, for corporate dollars and priority.
- On the short list of your corporate communications people for reference and inclusion.
- On the short list of your business partners, executive sponsor and boss list for inclusion and reference.

These strategies will be kicked into action, at least partially, by effective communications planning. Some characteristics to keep in mind include:

- Wrapping up your activities into a modularized "story" so that someone five years from now could pick it up a communication and understand what you were doing.
- Using solid communications strategies to ensure that you are communicating the right things at the right time to the right people.
- Using your value proposition as a rudder to ensure that you are staying true to message and are communicating what is important to target audiences.

Communication will happen at multiple levels, and never be just top-down, lateral, or bottom-up. Think strategically about how to place communications at lower levels to be filtered up and at higher levels to be filtered down.

Focus on Communications

Communication is foundational to the success of your knowledge-based initiative. Chances are good that you would not be in the position you are today if you were not at least an adequate communicator.

To move to the next level of navigating in a corporation, though, you will have to become more than adequate: you will need to excel. In addition, the communicating that you do as a stand-alone individual will matter less and less as your knowledge-based initiative grows in size and scope. Even if you as an individual are charismatic and well-liked, you have to shift attention away from you and onto your work.

Communication has popped up again and again in *Managing Knowledge-Based Initiatives*, in different contexts:

- Our executives told us that communication is one of the areas where people underperform and cautioned us that style and tone matter hugely.
- Multiple experts cited the need to work well with and influence people, which partially boils down to being an effective communicator.
- After building value props for your constituents, the key messages behind it must be communicated – effectively and frequently – to truly penetrate.
- The KM thought leaders featured in *Managing Knowledge-Based Initiatives*, Melissie Rumizen and Dave Snowden, cautioned us to tone zone down KM zealotry in favor of language that is relevant to the business.
- Multiple experts also discussed the importance of being an effective salesperson of your initiative. Selling happens, again, through communications.

Clearly, communications matter.

Why More Structure is Necessary Now

If you excel naturally at personal communications, you may never have structured the how, what, or who around communicating into a cohesive plan. You probably never needed to. However, once your knowledge-based initiative moves from small to large, it is likely that people other than you will be communicating about your work. Even if you do remain the primary communicator, you need to structure your work into a plan. The only way to keep everyone saying the right thing, to the right people, at the right time, is to plan it out. Consider the following:

- You will likely be communicating to more discrete audiences than before.
- You may be communicating different messages to those discrete audiences at different points in time.
- Your executive sponsor may require a formal communications plan from you.
- Your PMO may require a formal communications plan as part of standard project documentation.

In this chapter, we take you through the process of putting together a communications plan. There is no single "gold standard" communications plan. Some plans look like a 2 × 2 grid; other communications plans may stretch across 12 tabs on a spreadsheet. We will share several flavors of communications plans with you so that you can determine which best fits your needs.

If your knowledge-based initiative is small and you are the sole communicator, a simple plan that breaks out audiences, vehicles, and key dates might be appropriate. If other people will be responsible for some of your knowledge-based initiative's communication activities, you will need to include a slot to track who-does-what. Other elements, such as plotting recurring communications driven by phase or event, may cause your communications plan to become more complex.

Why Communicate?

It is worth thinking about the reasons that you might communicate, high level, in general terms before you build a communication plan. Work through the reasons we list below, and add any additional reasons that might apply to you.

Build awareness. For example, manning a booth at a road show hosted by your division president might not garner customers or sponsors, but could raise awareness of what you are doing, and the results you plan to achieve or have already achieved. You might communicate by verbally engaging visitors, running a multimedia presentation on a loop, or handing out brochures.

Create understanding. One challenge in launching your knowledge-based initiative might be clarify what, exactly, your work will do for the company. You may need to differentiate your work from other initiatives, gently steer people away from labeling your work incorrectly, or untangle misunderstandings to create realistic expectations.

Educate. Education can be achieved using multiple communications vehicles. It can be overt – as in a classroom activity – or soft peddled, the result of an artful communication that educates without the receiver even knowing it.

Convince. You will need to convince multiple parties of multiple things along the way; some of these activities will fall into a "selling" bucket. You might convince a dynamic executive to serve as your sponsor. You might convince your PMO representative to back you in a tough meeting around prioritizing new work. You might convince your firm's IT staff that your solution not only falls in line with their current standards, but also supports the future direction in which they intend to move.

Reinforce. People generally have to hear something than once before they truly internalize it. Count on repeating your message, although not verbatim, multiple times.

Communications Guidelines

The following guidelines should be kept in mind around communications.

No accidents. Communications should be deliberate – not accidental, incidental, a low priority, or a spur of the moment activity. Build in communications planning at the front of your project and periodically revisit it to make sure you are still on track.

Everyone knows what is coming. Communications should not be a surprise to any of your stakeholders. For example, before you communicate that your firm's IT department will be rolling out the technology portion of your solution on a given date, make sure their leadership agrees on that date and has communicated it to their staff. All affected parties need to be in alignment and agreement on the details before you communicate a message.

Targeting is key. Communications should be as targeted to your audience as possible. For customers, use the value document that we constructed in Section V as a guideline.

Before You Begin

Before you jump in and begin creating your own communications plan, take a moment and investigate the areas below.

Resources at Your Fingertips

What resources are available to you? Does your firm have a central corporate communications department? You may find communications bundled beneath

Human Resources, Corporate Affairs, or Administrative Services, so do not be surprised if you have to look around. If a professional communicator already working inside your firm is willing to advise you, your job will be infinitely easier. You may also find guidelines around communicating to large audiences that you must follow.

Do not forget to look for people who are professional communicators but may not live in a Corporate Communications department. For example, top-level executives may have a dedicated communications person that reports directly to them. People who fit this profile can also advise you on how communications really works in your firm.

Look for both internal and external experts. There is the possibility that your firm divides out people who communicate internally (memos, emails) with those who communicate externally (press releases, magazine articles). If you find one group first, do not forget to ask about the others.

Beg or Borrow

Ask around for communications plans, both from inside and outside of your firm. Inside your firm, think of a recent large-scale communications effort that caught your attention. For example, perhaps your Human Resources department recently communicated a change in benefits to everyone in your firm. Find out who owned that effort, and ask if they will share the actual communications plan with you so that you can learn from it, and adapt it for your own use. Later in this chapter, we provide you with multiple examples of communications plans.

Your Sponsor's Resources

As always check with your executive sponsor or your sponsor's administrative support to see if there is a communications plan that he or she prefers or has used in the past. Depending on your sponsor's level, there is a good chance that he or she may have a go-to communications person who can advise or potentially assist you.

The Source Matters

People are more likely to listen to, and believe, a message that comes from a known and trusted figure. In the business world, this usually equates to senior leadership. In reality, however, you will often find yourself communicating to people who have no idea who you are, or why they should care. Employ the following strategies to take the edge off that degree of separation.

- When presenting synchronously to a new audience, ask for an introduction by a person the audience knows and respects.
- If you are communicating via email, consider asking the audience's leadership to send the message from their account, with a dual signature from you both.
- If invitations to events will be sent via email or a voice mail blast, ask the audience's leadership to originate the messages.
- Try to involve your executive sponsor. Even if they only appear for the first few minutes of the presentation, assuming they are senior enough and well respected, their involvement can be key.

Understanding Communications Vehicles Available to You

Take a look at the list below, and determine which communications tools are available to you in your corporation. The purpose of this list is to get you thinking; see if you can add any vehicles that are specific to your firm.

- Presentations – may be in-person or virtual.
  - ☐ Self-originated staff meetings – your own, or those in your division.
  - ☐ Outside staff meetings – you act as a guest speaker.
  - ☐ Any other scheduled meeting where you will present, but people may not all report up through the same leaders.
  - ☐ Town hall type meetings where speakers are allowed.
  - ☐ Any offsite or large meeting of your constituents.
- Newsletters – may be paper or digital.
  - ☐ Self-originated – you own the effort and periodically publish newsletters.
  - ☐ Outside – you contribute content about your knowledge-based initiative to any internal newsletter.
- Road show.
  - ☐ Self-originated – you organize and "road show" your product.
  - ☐ Participant – you join an existing, larger road show as a participant.
- Intranet.
  - ☐ Place content on your firm's intranet.
  - ☐ Multiple placements are possible: your area, customers' areas, a public news area, etc. Link, link, link.

☐ If blogs are used in your firm, consider asking for mentions in leadership's blogs. If you are comfortable with the effort involved, and the ramifications, consider starting your own.
■ Email.
  ☐ 1-1.
  ☐ Group blast.
  ☐ Co-authored (where the other person is held in high esteem by a given audience).
■ Marketing collateral – may be used as part of road show participation, large meetings or training events.
  ☐ Brochures.
  ☐ Informational leave-behinds.
  ☐ Table tents.
  ☐ Case studies.
  ☐ Multimedia pieces.
■ Live chats – does your firm offer a way to have live Q&A via a chat piece of software?
■ Open web meeting or phone calls.
  ☐ Consider having a day or days of information web meetings or phone calls about your knowledge-based solution. Publicize it heavily, but do not require people to register. Allow them to cycle in and out as desired.
■ Recorded web meetings or phone calls.
  ☐ See if you can record any of the web meetings or phone calls, and post them somewhere for replay.

Building a Communications Plan

Now that you have considered some of the ancillary areas that contribute to a communications plan, you can begin to flesh out what your communications plan might look like. You need to consider all the following areas, but may find that one or two are most relevant to your needs. After working through areas below, you will be ready to slot the information into a communications plan.

Who Do You Need to Reach?

Who is your audience? The chances are good that you will have multiple audiences. Below, we discuss some common audiences, but evaluate your own circumstances for different ones.

Customers. Members of this audience group have already agreed to participate in your knowledge-based initiative. Because you have already refined your value proposition to clarify how your work meets their needs, the "what" around your communications efforts is simple. You will probably reach out to customers multiple times over the duration of their participation.

Potential customers. These are people that you would like to be customers, but have not agreed to participate yet. Your communication to them might fit into multiple buckets: educational, persuasive, or informational.

Executive stakeholders. This group should include executives who have a stake in your work for any reason. Some potential executive stakeholders include the executives who your customers ultimately report to, any executives who have supported your work by influence, funding or headcount, and executives who, although skeptical, have not opposed your work. Because you always want to convert skeptics into allies, targeted communications that celebrate successes are a good idea.

Supporting entities. Do not forget to include the people who make your solution work behind the scenes. This may include Help Desk personnel, IT staff, or administrative support staff.

Governing entities. Think of all the entities that have a say-so in your work and might need to be communicated to at some point. This includes groups like your Legal Department, compliance committees, standards committees, or your PMO.

Friendly faces. Take a moment and consider the people who have supported your work although they may not have benefited directly from providing that support. Continuing to keep them updated on your progress is key to ensuring their continued support.

Messages and Themes

Now, for each audience, determine the key messages you want to communicate and any themes you wish to reinforce. If your knowledge-based initiative is fairly simple, your message and theme might be essentially the same thing. In more complex initiatives, they will be different, although related to each other.

We advocate developing value props for every customer and potential customer, and those value props will serve as the source for your messages and themes. For example, hearkening back to an example we used earlier in Chapter 3, imagine that you are leading an effort designed to help several newly merged groups work effectively together. Management and individual team members have been charged with being able to demonstrably demonstrate an increased level of collaboration and a decreased level of

TABLE 14-1 Themes and messages for a knowledge-based initiative.

Theme	Messages
Participation in the "Regional KM Initiative" will help your group achieve your goals	1. Using our collaborative tools will decrease administrative expense by increasing the use of web meetings, reducing travel expenses including mileage, and reducing the associated travel to meeting time 2. Consolidating tools will decrease support complexity thereby decreasing administrative expense 3. Increasing inter-team connectivity with enhance group culture and increase camaraderie

administrative expense. One element of your work involves instituting collaborate workspaces. The key messages and theme for this workgroup might look something like this, see Table 14-1.

Details

There are a number of details you will need to know about each communication event. Make sure you are comfortable with the following:

- **Dates.** When will you communicate? Will you communicate only once, or multiple times? Do you need to validate your communications dates against, for example, a corporate calendar?
- **Venues.** If you expect to communicate in-person and are responsible for the entire event, remember that all the logistics planning will fall to you or someone on your team. Do not count on anyone else arranging tables, finding chairs, ensuring the projector works, turning on the lights, or setting up a conference call.
- **Vehicles/supporting materials.** What will you use to communicate for each audience? What vehicles and materials best support your message? For example, if you will be presenting at a meeting, you might use a PowerPoint presentation. If you are manning a booth at a road show, you might pass out brochures. If you are distributing a survey, you might send out the link via email.
- **Value props.** Have you developed, and validated, a value prop for each audience where appropriate? Value documents as we have described them in *Managing Knowledge-Based Initiatives* will help greatly in communications efforts.

One or Many?

Do not be surprised if you find yourself developing more than one communications plan. Sometimes it is easier to manage a small number of simple plans than it is to manage one gargantuan plan. If you choose to break out your work into multiple communications plans, consider using the divisions below. One easy way to keep track of an effort like this is to split things up on different tabs inside a single spreadsheet.

Audience. Consider dividing out customers into one plan, executive stakeholders into another, and support staff into another. This is especially useful if different people will be accountable for different audiences.

Phase. You could build one communications plan for everything that has to happen, for example, pre-launch, another for day of launch, and another for post-launch.

Accountability. You could create separate communications plans for different accountable parties, assuming that there is no interdependency among activities.

Vehicle. You could divide out communications by vehicle, as well. This will be most appropriate if the accountable parties can also be divided by vehicle. For example, if Person A is in charge of all print communications, they could be grouped. If Person B leads all communication to internal infrastructure, they could be grouped, and so on.

Theme/message. If you are managing an extremely large effort, you might find yourself communicating markedly different messages to different groups. You could divide plans out by theme or message, as well.

Sample Communication Plans Elements

Below, we have constructed several sample communications plans to give you an idea of what yours may look like. Keep in mind that these communications plans are, by necessity, more cut and dried, and smaller, than yours will probably be. One thing that every communications plan must have is an indication of time.

Mapping Audiences by Value Prop Elements

To create a plan like the sample below, first pull the key elements of your value prop, across all audiences, which you want to emphasize. Then, map those key elements to the audience(s) the elements are most relevant for and indicate how the value prop benefit fills the audience's needs. Note that this plan would most likely include additional columns for timing and method of communication and may include an indicator of completion as well. For an example see Table 14-2.

TABLE 14-2 A communications plan element grouped by value prop elements.

Value prop element to emphasize	Audience	Key benefits that align with audience needs
Enhances protection of firm knowledge	■ PMO ■ Legal	■ Responsible for project generated knowledge ■ Current repository scheme cumbersome ■ Currently in litigation that may require archiving of all content, no existing tools or processes to accomplish that ■ Offsite storage enhances disaster recovery capability
Connects our people to each other	■ Culture Team ■ PMO ■ HR	■ Breaks tradition of giving only executives the "cool" tools to connect – egalitarian because everyone gets the tools ■ Supports new team diversity measures ■ Training on the tools give us an opportunity to socialize how our associates communicate with each other
Stable reliable tool performance	■ IT ■ Procurement	■ Vendor already has preferred status ■ Compliant with firm's current J2EE standards ■ Passed security review by IT

A communications plan element like this can be very useful when you are coordinating multiple presentations or interactions because it clearly spells out the key messages that should be emphasized in any medium. This type of plan element assumes that you have solid investigative work at its foundation, drawn from a targeted value proposition. It can also be useful to identify audiences with similar needs; you may find synergies you were not expecting.

Mapping Audience as Primary

You may choose to break out communications plans by audience. You could also group audiences as shown below in Table 14-3.

TABLE 14-3 Dividing out communications by audience.

Target Audience	Message/Event	Mechanism	Timeline	Owner	Notes
Technical					
Standards Review Committee	Gain approval of our solution	Standards Review Committee meeting	Q2	Joe Project Manager	The SRC must sign off on our solution as a non-security risk to proceed
Desktop Change Control Committee	Get approval for first wave of participants	DCCC Monthly Meeting	Q2	JoAnn Team Leader	Need 2 weeks notice to get on the agenda
Executive Stake holders					
All	We need funding; support us for these reasons	In-person meetings when possible, detailed email if no executive availability	2 months before budget begins	Sally Team Lead and the Team executive sponsor	Informational + PR meetings to gain support
Potential Customers					
West Region	We can help you meet your goals this year	Meeting	Q2	Steve Salesman	If the Pacific Region signs on, the Atlantic will probably follow
Success Celebrators					
All associates	Look what we did!	Company-wide email; plants in executive speeches; intranet	At the end of each quarter	Courtney Communicator	Must be approved by our executive sponsor before they are distributed

Dividing by Responsibility

A communications plan element like the simple one below divvies up responsibilities for certain audiences and vehicles to individuals. An ancillary benefit of looking at communications activities in this way is that you may identify opportunities to collapse responsibilities for more efficiency. For example, does it make sense below that two different people are performing training? Maybe it does – but the overlap may also indicate a redundancy. Looking at your work this way helps shine a light on overlapping areas. Ideally, a column for time would be included in a communications plan element like the one below in Table 14-4.

A Phase-Based Approach

You can also break a communications plan down by phases. You may use generic project management phases, or phases that are relevant to your particular initiative. In addition to the passage of time being inferred by the use of time-bounded phases, you may choose to additionally blow out activities around event timing.

TABLE 14-4 A communications plan element divided by responsible party.

Responsible Party	Audience	What	Vehicles
Joe Communicator	All associates	■ By the end of the year, you will be using these tools. ■ Here is the training schedule ■ Here is where you can test drive the tools	■ Team meetings ■ Newsletter ■ Intranet site
Sally Team Lead	Executives	■ Latest usage statistics, scorecard ■ Selected anecdotes that illustrate efficiencies ■ Continued funding support critical to next year's expansion	■ Monthly executive briefing
Bob Project Manager	Current customers	■ Scheduled outage last Sunday of the month ■ Learn how to do these new things	■ Email ■ Training courses
Kathy Training Manager	New employees	■ You are joining a firm that values collaboration ■ Here is how we collaborate	■ Training/ orientation courses

For example, some messages should be communicated before your knowledge-based initiative launches. Others should be communicated at launch, and others, including debriefs on progress achieved, at strategic junctures after launch. You can nest phases inside of other type of communications approaches we have addressed here. For example, you may expand upon what happens for your customers before launch, during, and after.

Selling Events

Before you consider the specific selling events that are available at and specific to your firm, think about selling events in general. There are a few types that you should be aware of.

Scheduled/planned events. You will have selling opportunities at scheduled, or planned, events. These are live, synchronous meetings that you appear at in-person or virtually. Although selling is most effective in-person, it can also be accomplished via the phone. Note that you may be a guest at a planned meeting – not a presenter – and still have an opportunity to sell your work. For example, during questions and answers that follow a formal presentation, there may be a chance to ask or answer a question in such a way that you have the chance to mention your work.

Note that if you are the primary presenter, what you present should be governed by your overall communications plan.

Casual events. Casual selling opportunities may appear to be offhand, even thoughtless. They are characterized by seemingly unplanned or un-constructed interactions, with another person or group. Hallway chats before or after a scheduled event, for example, are the perfect time for casual salesmanship.

Informational. These are opportunities where you are expected, at a minimum, to inform or educate. Buried inside the information are the key elements of your value proposition, and communicating those elements turns an informational event into a sales event. Examples of informational events include newsletters, email updates, even status reports – anything where communicating facts about your knowledge-based initiative also helps you sell it. Informational events should be included in your communications plan.

Why Publicity Should Start Early

You may be wondering whether you have to have a finished, accomplished "thing" to generate publicity. For example, should you wait until you have actual results from your knowledge-based initiative to publicize it?

246 Managing Knowledge-Based Initiatives

The answer is a resounding "no." Think about it this way: how many movie studios produce flashy trailers after a film is released to the public? None, of course. No one would ever go see the movie if they did it that way.

Similarly, it is to your benefit to generate publicity about your work before it is underway, if at all possible. Publicity, in this sense, does not mean unrealistic claims about how your solution is going to change the corporate world. Instead, it is laying down a foundation for the later communication that will be targeted to specific groups. After all, we have already established that you will be asking a wide range of people in your firm for something – cooperation, support, approval, financing – at different points of your initiative. Approaching an individual or group who has already heard about your work is infinitely easier than approaching an individual or group who has not.

Ways to Generate Pre-Publicity

There are multiple ways to generate pre-publicity for your knowledge-based initiative. One of the smartest things you can do is use other people to generate pre-publicity.

Engage friendly faces. Throughout *Managing Knowledge-Based Initiatives*, we have asked you to rely on your friendly faces for a number of things. Publicity is no different. Ask early fans of your work to help you spread the word.

Pre-educate. Earlier, we mentioned that planned meetings are one publicity vehicle. If you are scheduled to present at a meeting, ask for the opportunity to provide your presentation, or supporting materials, beforehand.

Pick and choose. You know the people at your firm who wield influence over others. Identify a few key people who can generate pre-publicity for your knowledge-based initiative before you appear in front of a group of people. The key people may be members of that group, or might simply have influence over that group.

Your executive sponsor as newscaster. Particularly if your executive sponsor is a frequent speaker, ask for inclusion on his or her agendas under "general updates." Not only does this spread the word about your work, but it firmly entrenches your executive sponsor's ownership role in the minds of others.

Web and print. You may also be able to generate pre-publicity by creating a snappy informational piece to share on your intranet or in a newsletter. Keep in mind that you will offer the piece to other groups for their use; it won't necessarily appear in a newsletter you create. Your goal is to increase awareness about the issue that your knowledge-based solution addresses. For example, a small piece that shares success stories from another firm or industry after enhancing collaboration could be a wonderful lead in to announcing your collaboration-focused initiative.

The Executive Factor

One key group that you will need to publicize your work to is, of course, executives. Throughout *Managing Knowledge-Based Initiatives*, you have heard from multiple executives about how to best interact with them. You also saw that our executives did not all have identical points of view; executives in your firm won't, either. Do not forget to individualize how to approach each person.

What are You Asking For?

Before you engage executives, be very clear what you are asking for. You will always be asking for something. Most likely, you will be asking for support.

Support that requires action. Frequently, you will be asking an executive for support which requires that he or she take an action. For example, you might be asking an executive to defend your work to a committee that he or she chairs. You may simply be asking the executive to publicly state that the problem your work addresses (or even better, your work itself) is a priority for the coming year. You might be asking whether a region or work group the executive heads can participate in your work. Or, you might be reaching directly for the executive's wallet in the form of funding or headcount.

Support that requires no action. On the other hand, you may be asking for executive support that requires no action at all from the executive. Another way of thinking about this is that you are asking the executive not to oppose your work. For example, you might express excitement over the fact that the executive's region is slated to participate in your work next quarter, particularly if you know that the decision-making happened substantially beneath the executive's level. You are not asking for anything overtly, but creating a bond with the executive based on a positive emotion, your excitement.

Preparing for an Executive Meeting

In Section VI, we outlined the considerations and activities that you should address before you present to a committee. The steps you need to take before you present to an executive are much the same.

Before the Meeting

Before meeting with an executive, make sure that you have addressed each item below.

Type of meeting. What type of meeting is it? In-person, virtual, mixed? Will you be speaking one-on-one to the executive, or will others be there?

Audience analysis. Who does your audience, whether it is one person or many, report to? Do you anticipate they will, or will not, support your work? What are their hot buttons and concerns? What other initiatives do they support today? What is the grapevine buzz about the executives with whom you will meet? If you are presenting to a large group, who are the two or three most critical people for your purposes?

Content check. Have you practiced your presentation? Have you narrowed the content that you will present to the most relevant facts? Are you prepared to dive deeper on any topics the executive might hone in on? Is your tone appropriate? For example, are you offering a solution rather than lashing out at a problem? Have you purged broad, sweeping generalizations from your presentation or speech? Have you purged Knowledge Management specific jargon, and are you using the language of your audience whenever possible? Is your presentation as devoid of inappropriate emotion as possible? Can you back up every quote or figure that you present as fact?

General checklist. Do you have the names of all the key players right? How will you address them, by first or last name? Are you certain of everyone's titles? The names of their administrative assistants? Have you allowed plenty of time to arrive at the meeting? Are you dressed appropriately? If you are going to distribute any material, is it duplicated and ready?

Logistics. Can you answer the "who-what-where-when" questions about your meeting? Have you arranged for whiteboards or flip charts – and are there markers? If you will need a projector, is there one present, and does it work? Same thing for an internet connection. If you are using a web meeting, have instructions for participation, including passwords, been distributed? If you are presenting from a computer other than your own, have you copied the presentation to a flash drive or CD? For extra peace of mind, have you emailed it to a location you can reach online as well?

During the Meeting

Control your presentation. How is your pace? If you are nervous, chances are good that you may be speaking too quickly. Are you conscious of – and have you banished – distracting habits you may have, such as clearing your throat, tapping your nails, or playing with your hair?

Relax. While controlling your presentation is important, relax as much as you can. Remember to breathe. Smiling is good, too. Use your personality to your advantage, and remember to express your passion without alienating your audience.

Connect. Do not forget to make frequent eye contact with varied members of the audience. You might pick up visual cues about where they are with your presentation – confused? Intrigued? Amused? – but you can also begin to determine who your strongest advocates are. In addition, you can often locate people who have questions, and sense areas you will need to expand upon.

Speak, do not read. If you read a presentation from your notes or a projected screen, it indicates that you did not rehearse enough, you are nervous, or no one has ever told you that reading to an audience is not only boring but could be considered insulting. Refer to the information on the screen, but do not read it word for word. Reading a presentation is a giveaway that you're a novice.

Timing counts. Have you allowed plenty of time for questions at the end of the presentation? Do not count on speaking until the very end of your allocated time.

Open and close the sale. Earlier, we asked you to be very clear about what you were after. Funding? Headcount? Political support? At some point early in your presentation, share what you need with your audience. Then, preferably close to the end and after you have offered the reasons that they should support you, directly ask for their support.

Listen well. When your executive audience offers comments, or has questions, listen carefully to their feedback. Listen not only to the words, but also to the tone to see if you can discern the speaker's attitude. Particularly if you are answering a sensitive inquiry, rephrase the question to allow for additional clarification if necessary. If your work is criticized, avoid becoming defensive and remember that the pushback or criticism is not personal.

After the Meeting

Follow up. If you promised to distribute materials, or provide detailed answers to anyone, provide the promised follow up as soon as possible.

Feedback. Actively solicit feedback about how the meeting went, if possible and appropriate.

Thanks. If anyone helped you get the meeting scheduled, or arrange logistics, be sure to thank them. If the helper was present, ask for feedback; if not, ask whether he or she has heard feedback from other attendees.

Your Selling and Communication Content Toolkit

One of the smartest things to do if you are undertaking a large communications or sales efforts targeted at multiple audiences over an extended period is to create a "content toolkit" that can be used and reused. It is far easier to respond to last minute speaking requests – or step up and ask to appear at an event – if the content you have is essentially complete, and just needs to be assembled. Your content toolkit will evolve over time.

Baseline Ingredients

The baseline ingredients we recommend that your content toolkit have include the following:

- An elevator pitch.
- A generic value prop presentation that you will customize to individual customer needs in multiple lengths (15 minutes, 30 minutes, 45 minutes).
- Supporting quotes from internal and external sources.
- Any relevant metrics or stories, perhaps gathered from surveys that you have conducted.
- Any relevant ROI projections.
- An organizational/alignment chart that calls out who you, and your team members, align with in your work.
- Any success stories.
- Your knowledge-based initiative's timelines, including expansion plans and phases.
- Ready-to-print leave-behinds, such as pamphlets, white papers, studies, etc.
- Ready to burn and/or and distribute multimedia pieces.

On a related note, if your firm does not have a consistent template that is used for all internal communications, develop one yourself. It will save you significant time, especially when people other than you begin developing and sharing presentations. Make sure that your project is called by the same name every time, and if you have access to graphic design talent, consider developing a logo. Make sure it is professional, though; having no logo is better than a poorly done, amateur one.

The Elevator Pitch

Although there are multiple views around what constitutes a successful elevator pitch, one element nobody argues disputes is brevity: an elevator pitch must be shorter than the time it takes– you guessed it – to complete an elevator ride.

An elevator pitch can be anything you want, as long as it is short and effective. Experts advise that you lean heavily on the listener's pain point and *how your solution will address it* during the brief time it takes the elevator to reach its destination. An elevator pitch may be no more than two or three sentences long. Try to limit yourself first to a minute, then to 30 seconds as you develop, and rehearse your elevator pitch.

In essence, the elevator pitch is a boiled-down version of a generic value proposition. Once you become comfortable presenting your generic value proposition in the form of an elevator pitch, shifting its focus slightly to meet the needs of different audiences will become second nature.

The Power of Multimedia

One eye-catching technique that is more do-able than ever before for most people is the incorporation of multimedia into your selling and communication activities. Today's standard for creating interactive web-based pieces is Adobe Flash, but here is the good news: you no longer have to actually learn Flash to be able to create engaging pieces. For example, if technical trainers at your firm use Captivate or a similar product, ask for their assistance in creating a small piece that shows your solution at work, particularly if there is a technical on-screen element. Many people use Swish, a cheaper, easier-to-use tool that renders Flash movies. You should also investigate tools that people in your firm may use to create CBT (computer-based training) or WBT (web-based training). You might be able to engage them to create a piece about your knowledge-based initiative.

Our advice about using multimedia is the same as our advice about developing your own logo: strive for a professional product of the highest quality, or skip the exercise altogether. A poorly done product will do you more harm than not having a product at all.

You are the only person who can evaluate whether your knowledge-based solution lends itself to multimedia presentation, but consider the following possibilities:

- You develop a multimedia piece about knowledge-based initiative that you burn onto CD. Perhaps it shows an animated lifecycle of your work, or the benefits that will be derived from participation. You might use it to illustrate a concept, such as how people look for content in your firm, how data becomes information and then knowledge, or the role of storytelling in a business. You use the CD as a leave-behind at key meetings, give it away at road shows, link to its content from your intranet, and provide it to multiple executives and event coordinators to play in the background during the seating period at large speaking events.
- If your knowledge-based initiative offers clear criteria around who should participate and what they might gain, consider devising a simple survey type test that offers participants feedback at the end. People love to do something

that engages them and tells them how they stack up compared to others, and you get to harvest data, too. You could have a survey like this available to be taken at a road show, or linked from your intranet or other site.

■ You can also offer multimedia pieces to your key customers for their own use. Particularly if they are by-proxy communicating for your knowledge-based initiative, providing them with information they need supports your work.

Charting the Red Carpet at Your Firm

Earlier, we walked you through developing a communication plan with an emphasis on showing you what different groupings and communication elements might look like. Executing a well-formed communications plan is one of the activities that will help you reach, and then remain, on the "red carpet" of your firm.

Some of the communications activities you undertake that will nudge you towards the red carpet are activities you would perform in any event; they are not publicity focused in and of themselves. In addition, you should actively seek opportunities to publicize your work outside of your normal corridors of activity. One way to do that is to "chart the red carpet" at your firm.

One strategy tip: although we recommend that you become as familiar with how the red carpet works at your firm as possible on your own, do not forget that Corporate Communications staff may be able to draw you a diagram! Not only can they identify potential speaking opportunities for you, but they can help get you invited as well.

Speaking Opportunities

Seek out speaking opportunities, using the list below as a guide.

■ What big events happen at your firm? One of the best places to look for pitching opportunities is at any sort of leadership conference or retreat. Unless you are part of the club, you won't get invited to these get-togethers, so you might not know they exist until you ask. You will find that leadership conferences are generally segregated by specialty, which reflects reporting relationships fairly accurately. For example, IT leadership will attend their own conferences; Finance and Legal will attend different ones. You already know who your stakeholders are. Do some snooping, ask your executive sponsor, and build a list of internal meetings that feature your stakeholders or people of influence you need to reach. Then, investigate snagging a speaking or exhibition slot during the conference. Be sure to involve your executive sponsor to help persuade conference organizers of the validity and relevance of your message. In addition, your executive sponsor or manager may have to sign off on any traveling expenses you incur.

- What regular meetings occur from the most granular levels – perhaps a department or a work group in your firm – all the way up? These might be weekly staff meetings, quarterly get-togethers, semi-annual retreats, or annual planning sessions. How often they happen and what they are called will be different from firm to firm. The point is that these pre-scheduled meetings offer you a vehicle to get the word out about your knowledge-based initiative. Leadership that holds mandated meetings – meaning, meetings that happen even if nothing new is going on to discuss – in particular often welcome the chance to have "guest speakers" from outside their work group.
- Think big, and do not overlook national or global gatherings.
- Call on your customers, and investigate speaking opportunities they can refer you into. By sharing news about their success you are strengthening their position as well as yours.
- Keep in mind that executives who offer you significant support will probably welcome the chance to hear from you in a public forum about how things are going.

Road Shows

Your firm may use "road shows" as one way of publicizing a product or message. Road shows often introduce a new framework, initiative, or annual kickoff; senior leadership travels from location to location to speak with their employees. If your knowledge-based initiative has a broad audience, road shows are a great way to reach people you might not be able to speak with in-person otherwise.

The idea is that you either have your own road show, or participate in one that someone else (preferably supporters or customers of your work) is holding. Road shows typically move from location to location. You may participate by presenting at a road show, or setting up a table or booth in the corridors that surround the main event. Keep in mind that even if a road show is making its way around the globe, you might be able to pick up space at the sessions that are held near your location.

What Road Show Participation Means

If you have the chance to participate in a road show, make sure that you understand exactly what is required of you. Logistics are always tricky to manage in new and unfamiliar locations, particularly if Internet or network connectivity is required. Nail down the details before you commit.

- **What will you be doing?** Will you be speaking? Manning a booth?
- **Speaking logistics.** If you are speaking, what is the setup? Will you be using a microphone? How long is your session? How large is the room? Is there a podium provided? Is there a projector for a laptop? Should you bring your own laptop or do you have to use the one they provide? If they provide a laptop, does it have an available USB port? Is Internet connectivity provided or possible?
- **Exhibition logistics.** If you will have booth space, what is the setup? How much room do you have? Do they provide chairs? Can you connect a laptop or other computer, and if so, will you have Internet or network connectivity? What hours are you expected to man the booth? Are there any limitations on what you can provide, or give away? Fun freebies can be a great way to bring people to your booth, but remain sensitive to your firm's general financial atmosphere before you splash out on cool gizmos. You might be better off providing miniature bags of candy. Will your booth be set up for periods outside of the time you are expected to man it? If so, will there be security provided, or do you need to remove valuables (like computer equipment)?

Road Show Expenses

Do not overlook the fact that participating in a road show will probably necessitate spending money. Typical road show expenditures include the following:

- Travel.
- Hotel.
- Meals.
- Materials costs (handouts, banners, give-aways, CDs).

Ensure that whoever approves your expenses agrees that incurring costs related to road shows is valid.

Ensuring Your Continued Success

It can be easy, during the first flush of success that you experience, to not think about what you will have to do to remain successful. Eventually, though, you have to address the issue.

How you will demonstrate the success of your knowledge-based initiative depends heavily on what, exactly, your knowledge-based initiative is designed to do and how it is structured. Unfortunately, we cannot provide the magic recipe that will guarantee your continued success; delivering on what you commit to is squarely in your hands. However, we do have a few general guidelines to help.

Communicate Constantly

Although we advise you to communicate constantly, that does not mean to constantly communicate *the same thing to the same people.* If not done correctly, it is possible to communicate too much. We all know about workplace spam, the emails that while not inappropriate are not wholly necessary either. As knowledge professionals, you also know that communicating in context is the smartest way to ensure that the recipient truly gets what you are trying to say. With that in mind, consider these golden communication rules:

- Communicate for a reason.
- If the reason you are communicating, and the value the communications offers the recipient is not immediately apparent, call it out. If it does not stand up to examination, reconsider.
- Turn even mundane touches (such as a meeting confirmation) into a communications event, and ensure that there is genuinely a reason for communication. It never hurts to slip in a subtle sales message.
- Include celebrations of success in communications.
- Set up passive communications channels, such as religiously keeping your intranet site or blog up to date, and full of interesting content.
- If you distribute newsletters, give people the option to opt out.

Get Organized

Running an organized initiative from start to end – paying attention to the little, irrelevant, no-fun administrative details – is also key to your success. The time saved alone is enough to warrant getting organized administratively. There are other reasons too.

Others will notice. Your organization – or lack of – will be apparent to others that you do business with. Being able to lay your hands on every piece of information at a moment's notice is a huge indicator of competence. It shows that you know what you are doing and are in control.

You will make fewer mistakes. One knowledge practitioner we know of was dismal at budget organization – and did not realize that the lump sum he had been allocated was divided into multiple budget centers. When he queried the single budget center that he thought contained all his funds, he was horrified to see less than half of what he expected – and believed that he was the victim of *someone else's* error. Thankfully, the situation was resolved quickly. Do not become known as the one person who cannot keep his or her act together around the details.

Organization is an indication of leadership skills. Ask any executive, and they will tell you that a baseline level of organization is table stakes. Even if your great organization skills are not overtly noticed, any tendency towards disorganization probably will be.

Develop Your Own Scorecard

We have mentioned that some organizations use scorecarding as a way of ensuring performance relative to alignment. Even if you do not have to scorecard or rate yourself, do. Consult experts at your firm to learn what a scorecard might look like, and how it is used, and evaluate developing one that reflects your knowledge-based initiative's performance. Developing your own metrics and publicizing them may also add to a gentle shift in how your organization perceives ROI. Add your scorecard results to your communications toolkit, and include it in presentations, emails, and on your intranet site. Let people know about your successes.

Network Extensively

Networking inside your firm is obviously key to getting anything done, but we advise that you develop a robust network outside your firm as well. In addition to networking with Knowledge Management people, reach out to people in your firm's area of expertise. Some places to begin building your network include the following:

- Other firms – do not forget competitors.
- Online discussion groups.
- Conferences.
- In-person user groups (which is also a great way to meet your competitors).

Keep a Clipping Folder

As you see things inside and outside your firm that catch your interest, "clip" them (or print them out, which is more likely given the prevalence of online news). In addition, you should keep a clipping folder of all mentions of your work.

Topics to watch out for include the following:

- Internal.
    - ☐ Major changes in organization.
    - ☐ New initiatives that are emerging.
    - ☐ Pain points that arise repeatedly that your knowledge-based initiative could impact.
    - ☐ Announcements of new leaders who have interests that could dovetail with your work.
- External.
    - ☐ How other firms handle issues that you also face, ranging from ROI to getting buy in.
    - ☐ New advances in technology that change how people do anything knowledge-related.
    - ☐ Changes in external forces that could affect how your industry does business.
    - ☐ Knowledge practitioners who seem to have a similar interest or focus as you.

Let Your Story Evolve – and Then Publicize It

Earlier, we spoke about the dangers of an appropriated value proposition, when outside parties take your hard work and ideas and claim them as their own. Although you should guard against appropriation, do not guard against change itself.

Over time, your organization's needs will shift, sometimes subtly, sometimes abruptly. You, and your work, should be ready to shift with it. There is no shame in remaining politically aware of your surroundings, and the types of activities that leadership deems valuable at any given point in time. Being well-aligned with your organization's priorities – even if it is not where you started – does not mean you do not know what you are doing, are a political pawn, or have somehow become dishonest to your higher knowledge-calling. It just means that you recognize you are in a business and need to play by business rules.

15

Selling Knowledge-Based Work in Real Life

Throughout *Managing Knowledge-Based Initiatives*, we have explored the idea that after process, procedure and paperwork are followed and exhausted, the remaining critical element to execution is person-to-person interaction. One facet of that interaction you must become comfortable with is the idea of selling at every appropriate opportunity.

Although it may seem that your objective is to sell your knowledge-based initiative, you are also selling:

- A new way of looking at and valuing knowledge in your organization (even if you are not calling it knowledge or Knowledge Management).
- The hope or belief that a problem or pain point can be solved.
- Your work group or division.
- Yourself.

Selling as an activity can be both formal and informal. Certainly, there will be structured meetings full of slideshows and handouts. You may find, however, that your most important sales interactions happen in casual settings.

Everyone Sells – and That Means You

If you do not believe that selling is part of your job or find the idea distasteful, you may be in for a surprise. Even if you are confident that you will never excel at or enjoy the sales aspect of your job, there is a minimum level of skill you need to develop.

259

Consider this: if you do not sell your work, you will have to find someone to step into that role for you. Whom would you trust to do the following?

- Speak to current, past, and potential customers about your knowledge-based initiative.
- Defend your initiative against finance, reputation, or priority incursions.
- Debate the value of your initiative, particularly when compared to another one.
- Serve as general cheerleader to your team, executive sponsor, and other stakeholders who want to see you succeed.
- Arbitrate disagreements between customers, team members, and governance entities who set priority and funding thresholds.
- Create targeted value propositions for your prime customers and guard them with all possible integrity and vigor.
- Justify your work to skeptics.
- Educate people who do not understand what you are trying to do.
- Smile, even if through clenched teeth, at your competitors.
- Publicize your work using anecdotes and figures.

Upon reflection, you will probably realize that there is no one you can trust with those activities other than yourself.

John Collier, our PMO expert, pointed out a harsh business reality when it comes to competing for funding in a large organization. "They (your competitors for PMO dollars) don't have to be right – *if they sell it better they win.*"

The Executive Point of View

Our panel of experts agrees. Jane Niederberger advocates a realistic point of view about what you are selling and why it matters. "My advice to anyone walking for the first time into the big corporate fray – well, it sounds pat, but it's true – is to really pay attention to how Knowledge Management, and the work you want to do will further the company," Jane explained. "Then, put on a sales hat. You *do* need to sell in corporate America; there's a limited number of dollars in any company. Limited dollars, and limited priority. You have to be able to sell your story, and your personal passion."

Do not overlook that your executive sponsor will play a role in selling your initiative to people at his or her level. Sometimes, their contribution may be getting you in front of the right person. Other times, an executive sponsor may do the higher level selling for you. This is something to negotiate, so make sure you are clear on the details. Joe McGhee perhaps summed it up the best. "Selling," he said, "to me, is solving a customer's problem. Therefore, to some degree, *you're always selling*."

In this section, we share a number of general principles around selling provided by Dave Snowden, a major force behind the movement towards the integration of humanistic approaches to Knowledge Management and sense-making. For a knowledge practitioner who may be new to implementing projects in a large organization, Dave's years of experience in addition to his ability to blend academic and practitioner perspectives is particularly valuable.

We will also learn from Kate Muir, an Australian lecturer at the Canberra Institute of Technology whose students took selling their knowledge-based projects from the classroom into their agencies or companies. Then, we will examine specific strategies for selling your work.

Dave Snowden's Guiding Sales Principles

One way that Dave Snowden, Founder and Chief Scientific Officer of the UK/Singapore-based Cognitive Edge, Pte. Ltd., characterizes his career is that, "I have spent the majority of my life discovering and selling things to skeptical executives." Drawing from his years of experience, Dave has identified a number of principles to keep in mind as you sell your knowledge-based initiative or idea within your firm. The following content has been adapted from Dave's blog, which can be found at http://www.cognitive-edge.com.

Do You Understand and Believe What You are Selling?

"Humans have evolved to sniff out people who are obviously bluffing," Dave said. "You need to understand, at a deep level, the new concept, idea or technology that you are selling, and you have to believe that it will work. If you don't, then no one will believe it is possible."

Throughout *Managing Knowledge-Based Initiatives*, we have emphasized that although you might be able to skate – or bluff – your way around processes and procedures in the short term, in the long term, inattention to those details can shut you down. The same is true about your need to understand every nuance of the work that you are proposing. "Without that deep understanding," Dave pointed out, "even if you get funding, things might not turn out the way that you expected. If you understand your subject, you can always adapt. If not? You're lost."

The One True Path

Even if you believe that your revolutionary, never-before-seen-or-tried solution is the best and only choice, you may want to dial back your positioning. "Don't be an evangelist who rejects all previous approaches and claims to have found the 'stairway to heaven,' " Snowden cautions.

You should also work on curbing your inner zealot. "Don't insist that all others should repent their sins and join you on the path to righteousness," Snowden continued. "Firstly, it will put people off. Secondly, you will be wrong anyway. Most existing things work, they are just limited in their applicability."

If you have followed the exercises in *Managing Knowledge-Based Initiatives*, you have already determined the existence of:

- Tools that may be replaced or phased out due to your work.
- Groups who have a stake in maintaining the *status quo* that you are actively working to change.

In particular, be aware of your tone as you engage parties that will be affected by the items above. This is not to say that having passion about your work is not desirable or necessary in selling your initiative. As Dave pointed out earlier, not only must you believe your solution will work – you have to know everything about it. Find the balance between being authoritatively knowledgeable and engaged and alienating people with your enthusiasm.

Language Matters

Earlier in *Managing Knowledge-Based Initiatives*, we explained that assuming a general proactive stance in launching, growing, and nurturing your knowledge-based initiative helps you to control what is said about your work – and how it is said. Forming, publicizing, and protecting your value proposition, as we discussed in Section V, accomplishes much the same thing.

Snowden believes that differentiating your work via language contributes to creating and maintaining your knowledge-based initiative's unique identity. "Do make sure that you create some new language which differentiates your idea from other approaches. Don't compromise on maintaining that differentiation," he warned. "People will want to pigeonhole you into something familiar. It may be tempting to allow it, but it leads nowhere."

Snowden continued. "For example, the term 'complexity' is often confused with 'systems thinking.' I use the word 'un-order' as a way of distinguishing complexity approaches because it is familiar – but different. It creates a boundary and humans like boundaries. Boundaries let them see that there is something different on the other side."

Engage Interpreters to Enhance Credibility

A common theme throughout *Managing Knowledge-Based Initiatives* has been how your executive sponsor factors into your work. Do not forget that strong executive support can also you sell your work. "Find interpreters," Dave said, "ideally an executive sponsor who can take your ideas and give them credibility and relevance to decision makers. You also need people good at execution who will work with you on the first project. The combination of someone whose knowledge is impressive and has business credibility is a powerful tool for change."

Sell the Journey, Not the Destination

"Don't sell a Utopia," Snowden advises. "You will heighten expectations and then fail to deliver. Utopias are pretty static places anyway – just read Huxley, Orwell or Koestler to see what I mean. Better to sell the possibility of a journey that might solve intractable or difficult problems and engage people in that journey."

Fail-Safe or Safe-Fail?

In Chapter 10, we explored multiple topics around funding and ROI. The link between funding and your ability to sell work cannot be minimized. Take a moment and try to place your work in the categories that Dave describes below. Are you "safe-fail" or "fail-safe"?

"Funding is linked to delivery of projects and projects come into two main categories: safe-fail low cost experiments and fail-safe conventional ones," Snowden said. "A fail-safe project is linked to a specific issue, opportunity, or problem where a new concept can be shown to have a positive impact on a business process or other objective. The impact of that initiative can be measured by positive impact or the cost (opportunity cost or other type of cost) of *not* carrying out the work. ROI, EAV and other accounting measures can work on a fail-safe project. You need to understand those accounting measures and their applications."

On the other hand, Dave explained, "Safe-fail projects are a series of low cost experiments designed to discover what is possible in an uncertain or complex environment in which the probability of failure and the learning that can be achieved from failure is indicated." Because of their nature, safe-fail projects do not lend themselves to traditional measures of impacts. As you position your work, commit only to what is possible; ROI work against a safe-fail project is not.

Basic Sales Skills are Key

Still don't feel like you are up to task of selling your work?

"Book yourself on a basic sales course," Dave advised. "Choose a course that teaches you how to make a cold call, secure an appointment, create pain, and close a sale. There are many skills that you are going to need," he continued. "Silence is one of them!"

Do Not Expect Credit (Even if It is Due)

"Even if, at the end of the day you are proved right, don't expect to be appreciated or get the credit," Dave said. "If you do, it's a bonus."

Selling new ideas should logically become easier with time and experience. However, logic and experience may have little to do with it, according to Snowden. "In over a decade in strategy," Dave continued, "I currently have a near 100% record in calling the new management ideas early. Even my track record doesn't guarantee that my next idea will be treated with less skepticism."

However, the failure to be recognized or being confronted with skepticism does not mean you are doing something wrong. It may mean you are making a huge impact, even if you are causing some discomfort along the way. "People who want to be popular probably don't have the ability to innovate," Snowden concluded.

Selling Knowledge-Based Work in Australia

Kate Muir teaches Information and Knowledge Management (IKM) at the Canberra Institute of Technology. Although previous instructors had focused heavily on technology, Kate redesigned the course to address a broad spectrum of knowledge-related issues. One topic that she included in the reworked course material is how to get management buy in around knowledge-based initiatives. During a typical 18-week semester, Kate's students complete a variety of assignments. The assignments and the order in which they are completed matter, because they follow the same logical order that someone inside an organization would follow to make a change.

"The first assignment," Kate said, "gets students to talk about their organization and its information and/or knowledge issues. This is where students identify pain points in their organization. The second assignment, and their biggest," Muir continued, "is where students identify how they would move their organization forward from that pain point. They build a solution that solves the problem – and get extra marks for how they would 'sell' the idea and implement it."

We spoke to Kate about her students' experiences selling classroom-based KM projects into their organizations, what they learned, what worked well, and what surprised everyone.

Q: *Your students are working professionals with at least some practical experience in their fields. What sort of reaction did they get from their bosses, for example, when they brought ideas back into the workplace?*

A: "Many of my students are doing this course with the active cooperation of their areas at work, and are encouraged to discuss what they are learning," Kate said. "Some aren't, of course, so they have a harder row to hoe."

Q: *What about the students themselves? Did they learn unexpected things, or have a solid idea of what the course would be about?*

A: "None of them, ever, expect the course to be about what it is," Kate said. "Some students have a predetermined idea of what we are going to cover, and some have no idea. One person challenged me last semester and said they thought I was going to 'show them how to get knowledge out of the heads of people retiring and somehow use it.' " Although one of Kate's students did tackle this issue – with much success – the rest addressed many types of knowledge issues in their assignments.

Q: *What surprised your students the most?*

A: "Reviews at the end of the last class are always interesting," Kate said. "Last semester, the discussions seemed to be around how big the subject of Knowledge Management is – much bigger than everyone expected it to be." Because Kate's students had the advantage – and extra work – of learning knowledge fundamentals while holding down full time jobs, they were quick to realize that knowledge-based topics cannot be cordoned off into a segregated business area. "Students noted how pervasive KM is," Kate commented, "and blended through HR, IT, BPR, you name it."

Kate helps her students understand how large the topic is by introducing them to a variety of written topics. "I put together a 'reading brick,' so called because it is so big, and I capture in this a range of articles around archetypes, narrative, ROI, communities of practice, and more," she said.

Q: *How do you balance the theoretical with the practical? KM, as a field, has such a combination of both.*

A: "Because it is the Canberra Institute of Technology, I always start the year by saying what we are going to do is about the practical, not just the theoretical. It is really important for them to get something they can take back to their workplace; they must be able to use their learnings in a practical sense. Of course," Kate explained, "my own practical experience fits into everything I do, so they get lots of stories on the way through."

Q: *Real-life stories from the instructor sound great. Do you have any you can share with us?*

A: "As a long term public servant," Muir said, "I was often moved to problem areas to renovate, renew, or re-engineer processes. This, of course, is how I got interested in KM, as it is so critical to running any major service delivery and IT area."

She continued. "One story I have often shared happened at Centrelink, which is the Australian Social Security Agency. I merged three large Branches, over 300 people, of applications programmers into one Branch. This necessitated a whole new management process, including building a management team, developing a clear vision and goals, and of course, developing work plans. Although my old team had been adept with groupware, these other IT programmers had never used it."

Muir discovered that engaging management and offering a new level of transparency were necessary to transform the use of groupware into a genuine collaborative advantage. "We set up new online collaborative workspaces with all the visions, goals, work plans, and project plans," she said. "Everyone could see everything; it was all transparent. In the course of management presentations, they showed where all the info was stored. We started to get comments in the collaborative spaces, which of course contributed to the review of the final products. This brought the team together as never before because of the transparency of information about who was doing what when."

Public Sector: Pressing on a Pain Point for Results

Q: *Can you share examples of students who took their assignment back to the workplace, and persuaded their management to address a knowledge-based issue or problem?*

A: "One of my students highlighted an issue around incomplete or 'dirty' data that was being used for reporting by her institution. You could even say the data was dodgy, but there was an 'isn't broken, so don't fix it' kind of mentality. She had tried, but couldn't generate any interest in the problem," Muir explained.

"Because the public sector presents an annual report to Parliament, all information has to be the absolute truth. My student was able to prove that her institution was not using good information, and could be viewed as *lying* to the Australian Parliament if it were published. She used a very specific bit of information against a very specific pain point: embarrassment. And, the consequences of not addressing the issue were severe.

This student got her initiative up and running in the workplace."

Private Sector: Enlisting Superiors at Strategic Junctures

Q: *What about in the private sector?*
A: "Another student persuaded her manager to act as her mentor while she was doing the course," Kate said. "On the pretext that she needed her work reviewed, she asked him to read her papers prior to submission."

Muir continued. "The problem she was trying to address is that her organization, a very large Australia-wide firm, wants to be a self-insurer for compensation insurance. To do this, they have to demonstrate that their number of accidents and incidents are well down, managed very seriously, and able to be audited. The organization has no problems with the recording of incidents, but one of the side issues is that there's a bit of a "blame culture" around reporting incidents, finding out if something similar to a given incident has happened before, and being able to track how an incident was managed to completion.

"My student's idea was to set up a community of practice around the issue of workplace occupational health and safety. She hoped that by creating an open environment, people would communicate, which would in turn curb the blame cycle. She proposed a place to post FAQs, and ask online questions of other members. Her plan was to use the community's questions and comments to develop a long-term Occupational Health and Safety framework and strategy. Her boss was hooked after he read her assignment, and wanted it set up immediately. It was up and running before the end of the semester."

Show and Tell in High Tech Defense

Q: *You mentioned another student who worked in the defense industry. This example seems to jibe nicely with other stories we've heard about capturing retiring employees' knowledge. Can you share details?*
A: "This student's concerns were around the very specialized knowledge held by many of the very senior engineers around the high tech gizmos – my word

for things such as specialized radars – who were getting to an age where they began talking about retirement," Kate said.

"In fact," she explained, "this firm had recently sent one of their engineers to Britain at large expense for a number of weeks to be trained on a very specific piece of radar equipment. Unfortunately, this engineer developed the travel bug after he got back and decided to leave; it sent this small company into a bit of a spin."

As we discussed earlier, it is important to have an updated view of your organization's landscape throughout the lifecycle of your knowledge-based initiative. In a situation like this, a number of flags should pop up to a knowledge-practitioner:

- The organization recognizes that it has an issue.
- It has tried to remedy the issue, but wasted time and money.
- The previous attempt at remedying the issue has damaged organizational trust to an extent; leadership anticipated the person they trained would stay some acceptable period of time.

"After thinking about this over the course of the assignments," Kate continued, "my student worked up a solution. She developed her three-minute lift speech, and tried it out on the CEO in the tearoom. Her solution was to film engineers disassembling, and then reassembling various pieces of equipment. She proposed that not only should engineers talk through what they were doing, but also at the same time, another engineer would follow along in the manual that corresponds to the relevant piece of equipment and proof, update or correct it. She was, of course, taking into account Dave Snowden's adage that, 'I know more than I can say, and I can say more than I can write.'"

Kate elaborated on the story. "So they scheduled an hour to try her solution. Several other engineers came into watch the whole process. The CEO came down several times to see how it was going. Here is the interesting bit: the manual said to take the cover off a certain way – this, I might add, was the first step! – but the engineer who took the cover off actually did it differently from the manual. They stopped filming while they worked out what happened. As it turns out, the manual was referring to a slightly different version of the same kit! That was the first finding of value.

"After that, they filmed the engineer as he took apart the machinery, captured his comments throughout the process, the other engineer checked and corrected the manual, and other viewing engineers asked questions on film. The whole thing took not one hour but two and a half hours and the CEO was so impressed that he said every piece of equipment had to go through the process."

This relatively simple exercise produced far more than just a single knowledge artifact. "At the end," Kate said, "this student's project delivered a library of all the manuals, correct and up to date, and a matching video commentary with questions and demonstrations."

Q: *So, how did this all come about? Did students start with the organization's goals and work from there? Or did they see something in their sphere of influence that interested them?*

A: "I don't think anyone thought about goals and visions; my students just found the pain point, or the burning issue and fixed it," Muir said. And, her students functioned in a very grassroots, practical fashion. "It was about bottom-up, rather than an ideological top-down process – it was about what was practical and useful in some way. It just made a difference at the time."

Kate believes it is critical for knowledge-based implementers to be realistic about the difference they can make in organizations, and emphasizes this to her students. "I get them to focus on what they *can* change. Instead of tackling something like, 'Get Docs and Records management working properly,' I steer them towards something that they *can* impact or get working. That is critical because 'winners are grinners' and they feel they have got lots out of the course if they can make a change."

Starting Small Can Increase Sales Leverage

Nearly all our experts advised us to start small and build credibility, which in turn will create the leverage you may need to expand your work or move in different directions. And, let us face it: it is easier to get a small effort funded than a gargantuan one.

Jane Niederberger believes that succeeding on a more conservative scale will help you build the reputation you need to expand. "I do think that you have to start small. You have to build that credibility and relationship with your customers, and your executive sponsor. If you say, 'Give me a little – and I'll show you what I can do with it,' then you have a good start to building that relationship," Jane said. "That's also how good ideas spawn."

Michael Jackman cited huge – and never-ending – deployments as a problem. "At three different places," he said, "I've seen instances where we tried to deploy a very comprehensive CRM system with embedded KM capabilities, and it just didn't happen. I think the solution is to tackle things in small, achievable stages, and not go for the 'total nirvana,' huge projects that take forever and are too complicated."

Jackman believes that simple is often best, even if it means sacrificing optional bells and whistles. "Using CRM as an example," he said, "look at something as simple as salesforce.com. It's easy to implement, and you're quickly online. It can't do everything that Siebel can . . . but it works. Making projects too large, too broad, and too big is where the mistake happens. Small steps where success is achieved and people start using your solution – that's the way to go."

Kate's findings back this up. "In all those cases," she said, "the students were asked if they had any other bright ideas about how to fix other stuff going wrong." Based on their first idea that got attention in their organization, and proved to be relevant, students were actively solicited for additional ideas.

Index

Acme Medical Supplies, case example of
   alignment artifacts, 42
   problems with, 42
administrative minutia, 65
alignment
   alignment artifacts, 57–58
   candidates for alignment with
      knowledge-based initiative, 45–48
   demonstrable alignments, 36
   Google's values and beliefs, 37–41
   mission statement, 36–37
   operating imperatives, goals, and
      activities, 41
   values and beliefs statement, 37
   vision statement, 37
anecdotes, 90, 110
Application Service Providers (ASP), 179
appropriated value proposition, 114–117
areas, of executive sponsorship. *See also*
      executive sponsorship and
      network building
   concept development, 61
   funding, 61
   mentorship, 63
   politics, 61–62
   referrals, 62–63

Audiences, mapping in communications
   plan, 241–243
Australian experience, selling
   knowledge-based initiatives, 264–270

bi-directional mapping, 104–105
bottom-up/top-down approach, to
   organizational alignment, 41–45
brainstorming meeting, with executive
   sponsor, 98–99
budget, 177–180. *See also* funding factors;
   PMOs and its activities, of an
   organization

change control
   as an activity or artifact, 192
   areas of, 193
   as a committee, 130,192
   and end users, 193–195
   violation of, 193
change factors, 19–22
client wish list, 109
collaboration and/or knowledge
   sharing, 45
Collier, John, 139–140, 187
committee, 59
   administrative details about a, 135–137
   defined, 11

333

33333333333

Index

committee (*Continued*)
grouping of, 133–134
meeting schedules of a, 137–138
post-meeting engagements for a, 138
role of a, 124–125
role of legal department in formation of, 125–126
rules for, 124
stakeholders in a, 137
tips for locating key, 126–133
types of change control, 130
communication skills, 76–77, 233–235
communications plan
audiences, identifying, 238–239
details, 240
development of, in phases, 244
element divided by responsible party, 244–245
element grouped by value prop elements, 242
mapping of audiences, 241–243
messages and themes used, 239–240
number of, 241
company evaluation, 22–26
competitive intelligence (CI), 48
competitor perception and IT, 183–184. *See also* technology group, in a firm
concept development, 61
corporate standards, 20–21
cultural landscape analysis and value proposition, 92–93
cultures and subcultures, of organizations, 77–78

data extraction, 180
decision makers, 108
desktop, 179
detractors, 110
diluted value proposition, 112–113
direct constituents, of value proposition, 96
disaster recovery initiatives, 47
dot net, 180

efficiency and knowledge-based solution sets, potential alignment with, 46
encryption methods, 179
engaging first, act of, 7–9
executive sponsorship and network building
approaches for, 69–71, 74–75
cooperative executive vs true sponsor, 55–56
degrees of sponsorship, 57–58
expert opinions, 75–81
facts about executive sponsor, 58–60
and funding, 73–74
meaning of, 71–72
negotiation process for a relationship, 60–63
other supporters, 67–68
questions to sponsor, 66–67
sponsor expectations, 63–66
types of
assigned, 59
day to day operational sponsor, 57
heir apparent, 60
key player, 60
rising star, 60
short timer, 60

factors of understanding, pre-launching, knowledge-based initiatives
change factors, 19–22
company evaluation, 22–26
expert opinion, 22–24
knowledge management in the company, evaluation of, 26–30
misconceptions, 17–19
momentum factor, 19

finance. *See* funding factors
friendly faces
  of constituency group, 97
  defined, 12
funding escalation committees, 131–132.
  See also committee
funding factors, 61
  accountability aspect, 153–154
  administrative aspect, 154–155
  budgeting process, 155–158
  intentional overestimation and
    underestimation, of
    finances, 157–158
  procurement process, 158–163
  project management, of
    knowledge-based initiatives,
    9–10
  ROI factor, 163–170
funding review committee, 131–132

gates and paths, of knowledge-based
    solution
  framing of activities, 4
  role of knowledge practitioners, 5–6
  technology and support frame, 4–5
generic value proposition, 88, 90–91
Goldfedder, Brandon, Q & A with
  communication skills, 207–208
  dealing with IT staff, 201–203
  impact of IT related changes,
    206–207
  IT staff relation with knowledge
    practitioners, 209
  management tips for non-IT
    person, 204–206
  observation on IT groups, 203–204
  organizational knowledge, 208
Google's values and beliefs
  focus on user, 38
  revenue generation, 39–40
  speed, value of, 38–39

team achievements and individual
    accomplishments, 40–41
guiding principles, of finance, 155–156.
    See also funding factors

help desk activities, for knowledge-based
    initiatives
  and knowledge synergies, 217
  organizational landscape of, 213–214
  organizational relationship
    with, 214–217, 227
  services, 211–212
  as support entity, 212–213, 219–227

IM (instant messaging), 92
incorrect value proposition, 111–112
indirect constituents, of value
    proposition, 96–97
influencers, 97
informational events, 245
initiation, of relationships, 58–59
IT security, 128–129

J2EE, 180
Jackman, Michael, 51–52, 72, 75–76, 269

King, Joseph, 171, 178, 179, 180, 181,
    182, 189, 194
knowledge-based initiatives
  act of engaging first, 7–9
  project management, 9–11
  selling. *See* Selling of knowledge-based
    initiative
  as a series of gates and associated
    paths, 3–6
  terms and definitions in, 11–13
knowledge management, 12–13
knowledge management in a company,
    evaluation of, 26–30
Kumar, Santi, 36, 64, 69, 75, 79–81,
    87–88, 92

mapping of audiences, in communication
    plan, 241–243
markup language (HTML), 179
McGhee, Joe, 22–24, 60, 67–68, 71–72,
    76–77, 79, 81
mentorship, 63
metrics, for knowledge-based
    initiatives, 65–66
minimized value proposition, 113–114
mission statement, 36–37
momentum factor, 19
Muir, Kate, selling knowledge-based work
    in defense industry, 267–269
    public sector vs private sector
        attitude, 266–267
    sales leveraging, 269–270
    students' experiences selling KM
        projects, 265–266

negotiation process, 60–63
Niederberger, Jane, 62, 66, 72, 78–79, 87,
    164–165, 269–270

offsite component, of IT, 196
    storage costs, 199
open source, 180
operating imperatives, goals, and
    activities, 41
operating systems, 180–181
organizational design/alignment
        factor, 10–11, 34–35, 90
    alignment artifacts, 35–41
    bottom-up/top-down approach, 41–45
    collaboration and/or knowledge
        sharing, 45
    customers/constituents, identification
        of, 45–48
    disparities with, 51–52
    success evaluation, 48–50

participation, in knowledge-based
    initiative, 20
PMOs and its activities, of an
    organization, 10, 139–140
    accountability and SOX factor, 140–141
    customer experiences, 150–151
    development of business case,
        143–145
    and early bird benefits, 148
    funding factors, 147–148
    history of, 141–142
    information related to, 149–150
    and knowledge-based work, 142
    multiple role of, 145–146
    and relationships, 147–149
    steps in executing a project, 146
    of targeted value proposition, 99–100
    and triple constraint theory, 150
    preferred vendors, 159
procurement process
    areas of influence, 158–162
    concept, 158
    preferred vendors, 159
    purchase order process details,
        162–163
    RFP/RFQ process and
        timelines, 159–160
    single sourcing, 160
    subcontracting relationships, 159
    as a support process, 161
    vendor relations, 161–162
Project Management Professional
    certification, 149
project management, of knowledge-based
    initiatives
    funding factors, 9–10
    organizational design/alignment
        factor, 10–11
    PMO factor, 10
proprietary systems, 130

public resources, for company
information, 25
publicity, 245–246. *See also* red carpet
strategies

query, defined, 181

rebalanced value proposition, 112
rebuked value proposition, 117–118
red carpet strategies
charting of, 252–254
charting success, 254–257
communication plans, 235–245
communication skills, 233–235
role of executives, 247–249
role of publicity, 245–246
selling events, 245
selling ones work, 232–233
toolkits for selling activities and
communications, 249–252
relationships
assigned, 59
and behavior count, 80–81
initiation, 58–59
report, defined, 181
repositioned value proposition, 117
resistance types, to organizational
change, 78–79
RFP/RFQ process and timelines,
159–160
ROI
executive point of views, 164–165
outside assistance with, 169–170
standards, 165–169
Rumizen, Melissie, 13, 76

scheduled/planned events, 245. *See also*
selling events
scope-based entities, 21
secure socket layer (SSL)
technology, 181

selling events
casual events, 245
informational events, 245
scheduled/planned events, 245
Selling of knowledge-based initiative
in Australia, 264–270
minimum skill levels for, 259–261
Snowden's guiding sales
principles, 261–264
server, 181
service level agreements (SLAs)
affecting end users, 191
as a compensation factor, 190–191
impact on knowledge-based
initiatives, 190
violation of, 190
shared responsibility, 21–22
sign-off limits, of executive sponsor, 59
single sourcing, 160
Snowden, Dave's guiding sales
principles, 261–264
SOAP (simple object access
protocol), 181–182
Structured Query Language
(SQL), 181
subcontracting relationships, 159
supporting resources and
knowledge-based initiatives, 127
surplus funds and
consequences, 156–157. *See also*
funding factors

targeted value proposition, development
of. *See also* value proposition
challenges/goals associated with
constituents, 97–98
constituent identification, 96–97
documenting value proposition
components, 100–101
negotiating executive sponsor
relationship, 98–99

targeted value proposition, development
    of (*Continued*)
  PMO artifacts, 99–100
  validation of constituents, 101–102
teacher's pet, 60
technology group, in a firm
  compliance achievements, 195–199
  inputs from, significance of, 174–176
  investigation of, 182–195
  IT language, 177–182
  relation with knowledge
      practitioner, 173–174
  relation with other departments, 176
  role, 171–173
  as a source of information, 176
technology-related committees, 128–130
triple constraint theory, 150

unwritten rules, of finance, 156

value documents, 100–101
value hot buttons, 97–98
value proposition
  areas avoiding, 89
  case example, 102–106
  concept of value in, 89–90
  constituents of, 96–97

and cultural landscape analysis, 92–93
  for customers, 91–92
  definition, 86
  diluted, 112–113
  executive points of view, 86–88
  generic, 90–91
  honoring of, 118–119
  incorrect, 111–112
  interdependencies, 85–86
  leveraging of, 109–110
  lifecycle, 89
  minimized, 13–114
  nurturing of, 109
  protection of, 110–118
  rebalanced value proposition, 112
  rebuked value proposition, 117–118
  repositioned value proposition, 117
  sharing of, 107–109
  targeted, 93–102
  types, 88–89
values and beliefs statement, 37
vendor relations, 161–162
vision statement, 37

web services, 181–182
WIIFM (what is in it for me)
      statement, 86, 88

For Product Safety Concerns and Information please contact our
EU representative GPSR@taylorandfrancis.com Taylor & Francis
Verlag GmbH, Kaufingerstraße 24, 80331 München, Germany